Native Trailblazer

The Glory and Tragedy
of Penobscot Runner
Andrew Sockalexis

Ed Rice

D1264973

Down East Books
Camden, Maine

Down East Books

An imprint of Globe Pequot, the trade division of
The Rowman & Littlefield Publishing Group, Inc.
4501 Forbes Blvd., Ste. 200
Lanham, MD 20706
www.rowman.com

Distributed by NATIONAL BOOK NETWORK

British Library Cataloguing in Publication Information available

Library of Congress Cataloging-in-Publication Data Is Available

ISBN: 978-1-68475-010-8 (pbk. : alk. paper)
ISBN: 978-1-68475-011-5 (electronic)

∞™ The paper used in this publication meets the minimum requirements of
American National Standard for Information Sciences—Permanence of Paper for
Printed Library Materials, ANSI/NISO Z39.48-1992.

Dedicated to

the spirits of Francis and Andrew Sockalexis

and to all those who have followed in their footsteps,

with respect and love for the sport,

on running paths everywhere,

but especially in Maine.

Contents

* * *

Foreword

It truly is an unexpected delight to find myself the bene-
ficiary of a re-issue for my 2008 self-published biography of
Andrew Sockalexis. I am honored to have Down East Books
of Maine acquire the rights to my manuscript, allow me to
freshen it up (particularly with addition of some wonderful
portraits I had no knowledge of originally) and, in so doing,
assist me in my on-going effort to garner respect for this
extraordinary long distance runner, frequently overlooked and
largely forgotten.

My deepest gratitude goes to my Down East Books
publisher, Michael Steere, and to the book-publishing team of
Down East's parent company, Rowman & Littlefield.

On the occasion of my 2003 publication of *Baseball's
First Indian*, a biography of Andrew's cousin, Louis, the
first-known Native American to play professional baseball,
Maine Sunday Telegram book critic William David Barry very
generously wrote: "It always seemed to me that Sockalexis,
the man and the player, was doomed to loom large but indis-
tinctly in the fog of lore. Rice changes all that with a lively,
unpretentious work of historical detection."

If Louis seems fated to hazy literary apparition-status, like Hamlet's father's ghost, then poor Andrew shares a more damning fate, comparable to Godot or The Iceman, the ones that the spotlight never, ever seems to find.

Long, long ago I suspected that if *only* he had won just a single Boston Marathon (instead of finishing a heart-breaking 2nd both in 1912 and again in 1913), and if *only* he had won a gold-silver-or-bronze medal at the 1912 Olympic Games (instead of finishing 4th and outside the storied laurels) that someone would have produced a biography on him years ago, interviewing so many now long-departed souls who had intimate knowledge of him and his story.

As an avid long distance runner, who ran 27 marathons between 1979 and 2001 (including eight Boston Marathons), I had taken quite a bit of teasing from running pals who, with mock hostility, would complain I had written about "the wrong Sockalexis." After completing my manuscript on Louis in the late 1990s, I spent the next decade in a concentrated effort to piece together a solely library-resources-driven profile on Andrew to bookend with the one I'd written on Louis.

All through the early 2000s, I found myself pairing research time on Andrew with seeking a publisher for Louis and confronting the Cleveland professional team with the twofold misguided policies of failing to properly recognize Louis and, of course, continuing the use of an inappropriate nickname and outright racist caricature for a logo/mascot.

I did several library talks in the greater Cleveland area, coupling my historical narrative on Sock's life with a brief, closing message for the team and its supporters to end the practice of embracing "acceptable" institutional racism. I even joined protesters at Cleveland's Progressive Field, for the annual Opening Day exercise-in-futility, that found the good-hearted activists largely subjected to vile verbal abuse and half-filled beer cans thrown their way.

Talk about tilting at windmills.

And so it was, in 2009, I was discussing my frustration with all of this with my good friend, John Bear Mitchell, Penobscot Nation actor, storyteller, and department chairman of the Native American Studies Program at the Orono flagship campus of the University of Maine.

John listened, smiled wanly and commented, simply, "The circle starts in the middle, Ed, not the outside."

Suddenly the road map to constructive activism never seemed so clear. I discovered an absolutely wonderful national web site, created by "iconoclast" Robert Eurich, called American Indian Sports Teams Mascots, devoted to the cause of raising awareness about both public school and professional organizational use of such nicknames and mascots.

Best of all, it offered a map of the United States and provided information state-by-state of the offenders. There were absolutely no states in the entire country free of blemish (except for Hawaii, which never had any in the first place). Some states, like Ohio, had more than 200 offenders.

For Maine, the site identified 34 schools with the nick-name and mascot; however, I immediately noticed that the site hadn't been updated, and I knew a couple of the communities and schools identified had made changes.

Over the course of the next few days, I called each and every school on the list. It was exciting and deeply gratifying to discover that 28 of the schools on the list had changed from an offensive nickname and mascot, or were in the process of so doing! There were really only six offending schools left in the entire state of Maine. (I would enjoy regular communication with Robert over the next decade, updating Maine's list.)

I contacted long-time friend, John Dieffenbacher-Krall, then executive director of the Maine Indian Tribal State Commission (MITSC), discussed my findings, and we enthusiastically agreed to partner and set up a symposium to engage representatives from the six schools outside the fold and raise awareness about the issue. The symposium was held in May of 2010 at the Bangor Public Library, and it included spokespeople from all four Maine tribes, some representatives from schools that had made the change, and just one representative willing to attend from the six schools still clinging to their traditions.

Over the next eight and a half years, several concerted efforts were made to patiently and politely engage the residents of these communities. A number of different eloquent Native American speakers regularly attended school board meetings in four of these communities and attempted to bring a perspective that wasn't always met respectfully or even civilly. Still, in every community, the campaign was also met with equally compassionate and supportive school officials and students, as well as vocal residents. Ultimately, in August of 2019, the last school announced it would make the change.

Today, Maine is the first state in the country to end all public school use of Native American nicknames and mascots.

And, interestingly enough, the Cleveland professional baseball team has announced it will end the use of its nickname and use of Native American imagery for logos and mascots starting with the 2022 season.

For me, the battle remains to encourage Cleveland to properly recognize all of Louis's enduring legacies and for my home state of Maine to find ways to properly acknowledge and recognize both of its "native" Native American sons.

I am deeply indebted to Down East Books of Maine for re-issuing my Louis biography in 2019 and now, in 2021, for re-issuing my Andrew biography so that both of their stories are preserved for posterity.

—Ed Rice

* * *

Preface

Andrew Sockalexis could very well lay claim to the title of "Maine's Greatest Forgotten Athlete."

Sports Illustrated, for instance, has shown tremendous disrespect to the legacies of Penobscot Indian cousins Andrew and Louis Sockalexis, by ignoring their places in history and omitting them completely from its "50 Greatest Athletes from the State of Maine" list in 1999. Andrew Sockalexis finished 2nd in the Boston Marathon in both 1912 and 1913, and was the 4th place finisher in the marathon in the Olympic Games of 1912 in Stockholm.

His second cousin, Louis Sockalexis, inspired the nickname the Cleveland baseball franchise continues to carry when he became the first American Indian to play major league baseball and endured a Jackie Robinson-like experience, too little appreciated to this very day. He paved the way for the next generation of American Indian players, including John Meyers, Baseball Hall of Fame inductee Charlie Bender, and Jim Thorpe, unquestionably the greatest known American

Indian athlete of all time. When the magazine celebrated its 50th year celebration, in 2004, it reprinted the same list, compounding this sorrowful crime *[Author's note: See Appendix for complete list].*

First-ever women's Olympic marathon winner Joan Benoit Samuelson was the obvious first-place choice, but I would argue that either of the Sockalexis cousins rivals any of the choices, certainly from the number two pick right through to the 50th selection. I will not denigrate the lives and careers of any of these choices by focusing on any particular individual by name…but I'll bet anyone who is familiar with Maine sports will be left shaking his or her head when left to compare selection after selection with the feats of the Sockalexis cousins.

In stark contrast, for instance, was the *Bangor Daily News*, celebrating 100 years of history, when it published a special edition looking at all facets of its coverage over the 20th century; it found only three athletes worthy of notation and celebration in that entire time: Benoit Samuelson, Louis Sockalexis and… Andrew Sockalexis. Frankly, if we're looking for athletes from Maine who have made not only a regional name for themselves, but also a national and even an international name, the *Bangor Daily News* probably has it right.

So how does *Sports Illustrated* come to miss the mark so completely?

Is it guilty of racism? It might earnestly seem so to any enlightened Maine sports fans, when this national publication leaves out two great American Indian athletes while mentioning an otherwise nondescript white kid who fired up the luckiest of half-court shots to win a high school state championship game, or elevating the individual who invented waterproof boots to "athlete" status. Or are we just being mocked here in Maine?

I mean how can anyone familiar with the many, many obscure names on this list NOT be familiar with the name "Sockalexis"? This smacks of serious racism to me, unless there is another excuse; one that is equally bad: Ignorance.

In fairness, the list was most certainly compiled by a stringer for *Sports Illustrated* rooted in Maine; to be more specific, this is a correspondent who alerts the national magazine to noteworthy sports personalities or events happening in the state and, occasionally, gets to write on these as well. When I worked for the *Portland Press Herald*, the long-time business writer, the late Frank Sleeper held this post. I have been unable to identify who the person was who compiled this list for the State of Maine but he or she is a complete embarrassment to my home state. While certainly not deserving of being charged guilty of complicity in the omission of the Sockalexis cousins, *Sports Illustrated* is, however, very definitely guilty of negligence and apathy. I have contacted the magazine to demand a public apology, and so too have several school classes and individuals who have heard me speak at various public libraries throughout the state. *Sports Illustrated*, to date, still refuses to even acknowledge concerns about the matter, let alone make a meaningful public apology...

Then there is the case of Andrew Sockalexis and the Maine Sports Hall of Fame, which took until 1984 to elect this 1912 Olympian and highest Maine male finisher ever at the

Boston Marathon...and even then it was something of an after-thought.

For Andrew Sockalexis was elected to accompany Joan Benoit, following her historic victory in the very first marathon for women at the 1984 Olympic Games. With the occasional reference to history in the news – that only Andrew Sockalexis had previously represented Maine in any track event at an Olympic Games – it seemed as much out of embarrassment or to cover up a long-standing oversight that Sockalexis achieved the honor so long, long overdue him. And the honor seems all the more ironic when it is considered that the hall of fame committee waived any rules regarding retire-ment and a completed career of a candidate and elected Benoit Samuelson prematurely...for her career was far, far from over.

The story of Andrew Sockalexis is, apparently, so little known that, even in the Penobscot Indian's home area, a well-regarded former outstanding runner, Dave Mazzeo of Rockland, could make a claim out of ignorance that, when he was named as an alternate to the American marathon squad for an Olympiad in 1948, he was the first Maine athlete so honored. This article appeared in the 1980s at the time when the far more lofty and stellar achievements of Maine natives Benoit Samuelson and Bruce Bickford were garnering atten-tion. And the *Bangor Daily News*, in a not-so-stellar moment, published the claim in a bold headline and story, completely oblivious to the total falsity of Mazzeo's assertion.

Further, an institution called "the American Indian Athletic Hall of Fame," created in the early 1970s, was delin-quent in recognizing the accomplishments of both Andrew and Louis Sockalexis. Indeed, it was this author, working with the Penobscot Nation, who brought the names of both athletes to the attention of the Lawrence, Kansas-based organization in 1999. Both were elected in ceremonies conducted in Tulsa, Oklahoma in 2000.

Even the relatively-new Maine Running Hall of Fame showed a lack of regard for Andrew Sockalexis and his achievements. Created in 1989, the first executive board bypassed Sockalexis as a charter member, bestowing the honor instead on four contemporary figures who largely won their fame in the 1970s and 1980s: Joan Benoit Samuelson of Cape Elizabeth, Bruce Bickford of Benton, Ralph Thomas of Gardiner and Ken Flanders of Portland.

The slight paid to Sockalexis was particularly aggravating to this author: As a member of that first executive board, I presented the nominating papers for Andrew Sockalexis, featuring a history of his achievements, and argued vehemently for his election. I failed, however, to win my case with enough of my colleagues. And I bristled over the fact I could not convince enough of these fellow voters that Sockalexis' achievements, on the national and international scene, easily eclipsed those of two of the proposed candidates, who were solely known on the local and regional New England level.

Andrew Sockalexis was elected to the Maine Running Hall of Fame the following year; however, I will always believe he deserved to be a charter member, selected at the very first opportunity and honored for achievements precious few runners anywhere ever accomplish.

An unusual and very special postscript can now be written to this latest chapter of failed recognition. In 2005 this author was nominated and then elected to a second term on the Maine Running Hall of Fame executive board. At my first meeting, after my introduction to the board, I took the audacious step of proposing an action I'd never heard about any Hall of Fame ever taking: The moving of an inductee into its inaugural, or charter group!

It was agreed all the present members of the board would consider the idea and vote upon it at the next meeting, at a time when we would consider the newest nominees and vote on the 2006 class. Further, the board chairperson, Dr. Peter Millard (himself an inductee of the hall and qualifier for the 1980 U.S. Olympic marathon trials), would survey the members of the inaugural board for their reactions.

At a spring meeting in 2006, by a vote of 6-1, the Maine Running Hall of Fame executive board voted to move Andrew Sockalexis into the hall's 1989 charter class. I will always be grateful to Anne-Marie Davee, Skip Howard, Dale Lincoln, Don Penta and, especially, Dr. Millard, for initiating this bold move and joining me in voting to take this highly unusual step. Dr. Millard noted that all but one of the original board members he spoke to had no objection to the action (the lone dissenter didn't raise any serious objection but merely "didn't see the point") and that Benoit Samuelson, too, agreed with the new proposal.

Helping to gain proper recognition for Andrew Sockalexis, so that "greatest forgotten" tag can be shelved, seems to me to be something like running itself: Put one foot forward, then the other and keep on going.

$* * *$

Chapter 1

Running in his father's footsteps

Very little is known or has been published about the entire life of Andrew Sockalexis, so it's hardly surprising that there are precious few details about his early life.

What is known is this: He was born on January 11, 1892, the son of Francis Sockalexis of Indian Island and the former Sarah LaÇoute, who was originally from St. Stephen, New Brunswick. Most probably the product of a Penobscot father and a Micmac mother, Andrew claimed the Penobscot reservation on Indian Island as his home but, in a *Boston Post* article in 1912, apparently identified himself as a Micmac.[1] He had a sister, Alice, and another sister who died in infancy of tuberculosis. He attended area grade schools and later took a business course in Bangor.[2]

Some sources have claimed Andrew Sockalexis once attended the Carlisle Indian School in Pennsylvania. Carlisle was one of a number of infamous Indian boarding schools in

America, first created in the late 19th century as a nationwide plan to "assimilate" the American Indian into white society. Young American Indians were taken off the reservation and brought to these schools, where they immediately had their hair cut, received suits and dresses to replace their Native garb, and were required to never, ever speak their tribal tongues. As barbaric as the core principles for these schools were, the schools did provide one saving grace: athletics. Carlisle produced outstanding football and baseball teams, helping to catapult wonderful athletes, like Jim Thorpe and Baseball Hall of Fame pitcher Charlie Bender, into national prominence and professional careers in sports. Another of these schools, the Haskell School in Lawrence, Kansas, helped pave the way for a college athletic scholarship for Lakota Sioux runner Billy Mills, who won the Olympic gold medal in the 10,000 meter run at Tokyo in 1964.

So, did Andrew Sockalexis attend Carlisle? The administrative records for the Carlisle School, including student records covering the years between 1879 and 1918, are in the custody of the National Archives and Records Administration in Washington, D.C. In a letter to this author, Mary Frances Morrow, a reference branch librarian who handles old military and civil records, noted that the student folders frequently hold scant information. Some have just an enrollment card, or enrollment application and student record card, or a personal letter. Morrow wrote: "I did not find a card in the index file for Andrew Sockalexis, nor did I find his name listed with the Penobscot students. I checked several different possible spellings."[3] When Sockalexis appeared at the 1912 Olympic

Games, two of the other Native American athletes on the team were Carlisle students, the very famous, double gold medal-winning Thorpe and Lewis Tewanima, who would capture a silver medal in the 10,000 meter run. It's possible some confusion arose later and Sockalexis was mistakenly linked with the other two prominent Olympic Indian athletes as a Carlisle student too. Further, when Andrew Sockalexis returned from the 1912 Olympics and was escorted to a wonderful reception, Fred E. Allen of Old Town noted that the Penobscot athlete had been offered the opportunity to attend the Carlisle school, but had turned it down.

Like many Penobscot Indians of this era, Andrew's father, Francis, worked in the region's prosperous lumbering industry as a river driver. He also carried a much celebrated reputation among his tribesmen as an outstanding runner.

It is highly likely that this interest Francis Sockalexis developed in long distance running evolved from the special place of respect held by the Penobscots, for many, many generations, for a special class of runner, known as the "pure man."[4] Such men of the tribe were legendarily known for their abilities to literally run their prey to death. They would run down deer and moose, in chases that could last for days and days, providing meat that would then be shared with all the members of the tribe. As explained in Frank G. Speck's definitive 1940 book on the tribe, called **Penobscot Man**, such individuals enjoyed an elite, albeit short-lived, status:

> *In each family group were some young men*
> *who acted as runners, to cover large tracts of coun-*

> *try, run down moose, deer and other game, and kill*
> *them in their tracks. These young men, of whom*
> *there might be a small number, two, three or four,*
> *were closely guarded by some old men lest defiling*
> *influences weaken their endurance and fleetness*
> *or cause the game by magic to escape being over-*
> *taken. Such a young man was Kwsiwa'mbe, 'pure*
> *man.' The 'pure men' were chosen for their fleet-*
> *ness of foot. As soon as one of them could be out-*
> *stripped by a younger candidate, the latter would*
> *take his place. To have served as a runner or 'pure*
> *man' was considered a social honor.*[5]

Speck explained Penobscots accorded this honor were "under surveillance all the time." They were not allowed to marry; indeed, they were further forbidden to have any sexual relations whatsoever. They also faced strict dietary guidelines and were only allowed to eat certain foods. Such designated runners were expected to work for the Penobscot "community at large." This meant that when they would run down and kill a moose or a deer, their obligations to their prey was restricted to merely bleeding the carcasses. The runners continued on the hunt, leaving each kill to be found by fellow hunting tribesmen who would follow their tracks and bring the meat back to the village to be shared by all. When one of the youthful runners was beaten by a new challenger in the tribe, he was "released from his ascetic obligations and could then marry and settle down to ordinary life," Speck explained.[6]

According to the Penobscot tribe biographer, the society of selected runners was under the sharp eye of "an old custodian," even when they were unconscious at night, to insure the purity of their fleetness as well as the purity of their souls. The elderly night watchman was expected to see that the runners did not sleep with their legs outstretched, since this was considered a practice that would mar their running abilities. "To make them draw up their knees, the custodian would strike the runners' soles with a stick," Speck noted. Even when awake, the runners were expected to sit with their knees drawn up, to insure their tendons were properly stretched.[7]

Among other health concerns for these youthful runners, Speck noted, was abstinence from the use of chewing spruce gum, which it was thought would "impair their breathing." The gum, it was believed, "originated from scabs from a myth woman's crotch. Should they chew the gum, it would make their testicles clack when they ran, and so forewarn the game."[8]

Well after the early days of the revered "pure man," the tradition of running and earning acclaim for running was an important aspect of Penobscot life.

According to a handful of sources, including then *Old Town Enterprise* newspaper editor John W. Gould and contemporary blood relative Michael Ranco, Francis Sockalexis ran and earned fame in large Penobscot community races. Gould provided this description of Andrew Sockalexis' father:

> *Francis F. Sockalexis, the father is a man about 57 years old and a veteran of the cinder path. He could stay on the path five hours at a time years ago so here is where the son gets his love and stam-*

> *ina for the race. The father looks after the son,*
> *advises and doctors him using only root and herb*
> *remedies for internal and external ailments which*
> *the son says has much to do with his success.*[9]

As a young boy Andrew would watch his father run
in many events, including the Penobscots' popular foot race
challenge – a five-hour race held in the tribal hall on the
island. It's very likely the five-hour training runs "on the path"
were in preparation for these tribal marathons. To prepare the
community building for the marathon, the Penobscots created
a sawdust track, four inches deep and no more than one yard
wide, and laid it around the small hall. Taking up even more
of the valuable hall space were bleachers, to accommodate
supporters and spectators. According to various accounts, the
track was so narrow that, in order to pass a fellow competitor,
a runner would have to wait until he approached the bleachers,
jump up on the first row of the bleachers – deliberately left
vacant for just such a purpose – and then sprint past. Each
contestant had a representative keeping record of total number
of laps. Each lap was counted by placing a wooden bead on a
long peg. It took a plentiful 22 laps to record just one mile on
the short circuit, sawdust track. The runner with the most laps
after five hours was declared the winner.[10]
  Andrew Sockalexis was around 10 years old when
he began running himself. His father built a trail around
their home and encouraged his son to run multiple laps upon
it. On his visit to the Sockalexis home following Andrew's
impressive second place finish in the 1912 Boston Marathon,

Gould reported this "very crude track" encircling the family house required 16 laps to complete just one mile. Gould and companion Kenneth W. Brown accompanied the then "boyish looking Indian of 21 years of age" to his Indian Island home, which the newspaper editor described as "humble." The house, located on Oak Hill about one-half mile from the old ferry docking, long ago burned to the ground. Gould also reported Sockalexis regularly used a three-mile loop around the island, which he was said to "easily" complete in 20 minutes.[11]

However, as Andrew was growing up, he developed a number of routes for training on Indian Island. The late Susie Dana, then 77 years of age when interviewed about Andrew in 1971, told Michael Ranco that she remembered when she and a group of other supportive friends would watch Andrew do his training runs around the island, waiting for him until he finished. Dana recalled he was timed on one occasion of finishing between 13 and 14 minutes for one loop around the island, a distance of 2.7 miles. Andrew, she recalled, was very determined to become a great marathon runner. She related that a confident Andrew once told her: "Some day I will set the world's record by winning the marathon."[12] If, indeed, he said this he very nearly was as good as his proud boast.

For variation in training in winter, Andrew would run on the frozen river. Dana and the late Archie Neptune both poetically related to Ranco, back in 1971, that they could "still hear Andrew's running spikes cutting into the smooth ice." They said they used to watch from the river bank as Andrew came around the bend, following the race track from the landing on Indian Island to Orson Island and back, which was built for car and horse races. The distance around the track was one mile.[13]

An article in the *Boston Sunday Post* on August 11, 1912, offers an intriguing, possible solution to the riddle of why Andrew Sockalexis never appeared in a competitive race until he was 19 years of age. At that time he made what seems to be a rather incredible debut, claiming repeatedly that his very first competition came at the 1911 Boston Marathon.

According to the article, in which the unnamed writer never quotes a single source for his information, it is related matter-of-factly that Andrew's early initiation into the use of tobacco – the claim is that he was only 4 years old when he began smoking cigars! – and prolonged use of same caused him severe health problems during his late adolescence and teen years. Long distance running was, according to the article, strongly suggested to him when he was around 17 years old to help him immediately reverse a path ominously leading to an early death from tuberculosis.[14] Presumably, if all this is accurate, Andrew Sockalexis needed two years to build himself up and then embarked upon his great, albeit short career as a world-class runner.

The *Boston Post* article detailed this rise from the demons of tobacco as follows:

> *...Tobacco, in all its forms, is strictly tabooed by the fleet young Micmac runner and has been for several years. This isn't to say that he is a rabid anti-nicotine specialist without a good, strong rea-*

son. He has a well-developed reason, the same be-
ing that after acquiring the habit about as strongly
as it could be acquired, he discovered that he had
the alternative of leaving tobacco severely alone or
dying at a tender age.[15]

In another eye-popping revelation, if this story is true,
Andrew's very famous cousin, Louis Sockalexis, the former
Holy Cross and major league Cleveland Spider baseball
player, is "credited" with starting Andrew on the road to his
dangerous addiction. The article continues:

> *It can be seen by looking at him (Andrew) in*
> *action that he elected the first alternative, but it*
> *was struggle to overcome the habit which had had*
> *its start when he was 4 years old, the same compris-*
> *ing close to an American record for early use of the*
> *weed. Cousin Louis Sockalexis gets a large portion*
> *of the credit for having initiated the youngster into*
> *the delights of the cigar and pipe. Louis invited*
> *Andrew into a field one fine day and started him*
> *on his career as a smoker of the 33d degree order*
> *without any of the customary preliminaries of the*
> *usual kind.[16]*

The article then notes, rather incredulously, that the
toddler did not begin with any of the "milder" tobacco
products, such as "rattan cigarettes, tea, sweet fern" or any of
the other "mild substitutes common to the novice." Apparently
whoever was providing the information could not provide the
"record as to whether or not he suffered the customary pangs
that overtake the rash beginner in acquaintance with the weed.
That part of the story is not included."[17] This idea sounds very

strange, presuming Sockalexis himself is telling the story and
he seems like the only possible candidate who could know
these kinds of details; perhaps he told the writer he was so
young he just didn't remember his earliest reactions.

The *Boston Post* account then stated that Andrew
Sockalexis "became a veteran tobacco user in very short order
and was able to hold his own with his elders from the time
he was 4 years old, on and up to the time he was forced to
quit. He was 9 years old when he fell in with the old demon,
cigarette, and took to the latter very readily, to his subsequent
sorrow."[18] It then characterized the youthful Sockalexis as
addicted to cigarettes, quaintly referred to as "white coffin
nails," and suffering great consequences immediately:

> *Even for an Indian, out of doors the greater
> part of the time, the white 'coffin nails' showed him
> no consideration. They 'got to him,' and they 'got
> to him' quickly. Athletics were not particularly in
> his mind at this time, naturally, and he did not real-
> ize that the cigarettes were undermining his health
> to a dangerous degree. He started going to school
> when he was 12 and still clung to the cigarette af-
> fectionately.[19]*

This description of Andrew seems in conflict with other
accounts that suggest Andrew began running at around 10
years of age and frequently used the track circling the family
home that his father created for him.

According to this extraordinary tale, the crisis period was
reached at age 17, putting it just two years before Andrew

Sockalexis would stun the American running world with a debut 17th finish at the 1911 Boston Marathon, at only 19 years of age. The account continues:

> *"(Sockalexis) was 17 when his appearance and condition alarmed his parents so much that it was felt necessary to consult a physician. The latter looked Sockalexis over and arrived at the conclusion that he was on the way to consumption unless he left school and followed a course of treatment, the principal of which was living in the open air and the eschewing of cigarettes. As Sockalexis knew that a sister of his had died from consumption, he realized that it was up to him to follow the advice offered.*[20]

The remedy was to send Sockalexis to "the famous camp of Dave Francis," situated in the Maine woods not far from Old Town and Indian Island. After living at the camp for "some time," he returned home "as fit as a fiddle with many extra pounds added to his weight and divorced from the brotherhood of the nicotine habit, the same period marking his introduction into the distance running game, not as a contestant, but merely as something to help him keep in condition."[21] So, if completely true, this is a startling departure from other articles and testimonials that Andrew Sockalexis started running very young, under the guidance of his father, and merely trained for many years before entering race competitions. A very different motivation for starting and a much later initiation, at 17 years of age, is clearly stated here.

Even the running "track," generally credited to Andrew's father as a device to entice the young boy into running at an early age, comes into view with a very different twist. This *Post* account states: "A well-worn trail in the woods still shows where he made his first essay. A box stands on one side of the trail in which he was and still is accustomed to drop a chip to keep track of the number of times he has travelled the course on any occasion."[22] Here, we have the track created not to entice a young boy into following in his father's footsteps as a runner of a note, but created specifically to help him regain his health at 17 years of age.

Finally, the *Post* account discusses an interesting family tradition developed and faithfully followed to help preserve Andrew's health. It states:

> *In connection with his recovery of health the point also arises that the present year marks the seventh and last time of his annual pilgrimage to the shrine of St. Anne de Beaupre in Quebec. He is now 22 years old [Author's note: This is not true... Born in January of 1892, Andrew was only 20 years when this article was written in August of 1912] and it was seven years ago when he was told to make the pilgrimage for seven years in succession at the time when he was badly broken down in health and seemed on the road to consumption. Every year since that time along with his mother and sister he has made the journey to the shrine until he has arrived at the present year, that of his greatest success as an athlete, ready to complete the self-appointed task.[23]*

Ironically and quite tragically, the trips to the shrine may have coincided with seven years free of the threat of consumption, but consumption would very shortly derail his promising running career and ultimately take his life at only 27 years of age.

This *Boston Post* article seems to dampen the charming notion that Andrew was influenced to run by his father at an early age and ran frequently with him, under his guidance, hoping to follow in his footsteps as a legendary Penobscot runner.

Yet, in a curious reversal of roles, it was the elderly father who wished to run in his then world-famous son's footsteps in 1914 when Francis Sockalexis, at nearly the age of 60, expressed a desire to run in the Boston Marathon and filed an entry.[24] In those days the members of the Boston Athletic Association reserved the right to reject any potential marathon entrant, frequently barring anyone it deemed as outright lacking any chance of winning or turning down anyone who might be creating a health risk to himself as a result of running. Apparently Francis Sockalexis was rejected simply based on his age.

Son Andrew, who recorded back-to-back second place finishes in the 1912 and 1913 Boston races and whose absence would confound for decades those casually interested in learning why he did not attempt to win the great race in 1914 *[Author's note: The answer is revealed in Chapter 13]*, complained about this treatment of his father to a Boston reporter. He noted, with great pride, that his father could and did frequently keep pace with him on many of his longer runs. He felt his father was still capable of matching steps with many of those registered and accepted for the Boston Marathon of 1914.[25]

Tuberculosis, or "consumption" as it was commonly called in those days, was on the horizon for destroying the running career of Andrew Sockalexis and, ultimately, it killed him in 1919. Still, Francis Sockalexis not only inspired his son to pursue the great feats he would achieve but apparently enjoyed sharing running with him for as long as his son was able to, literally, follow in his footsteps on the running "path."

And one can only imagine the sadness the elder Sockalexis felt in the years after his son's passing, himself crippled in a logging accident and confined to a wheelchair, living out his remaining days as a shut-in, surrounded by silence and his son's running trophies.[26]

* * *

Chapter 2

Auspicious debut at Boston

In 1911, Andrew Sockalexis began his short but illustrious career in long distance running. He would tell newspaper reporters on several occasions that his racing debut came in the 1911 Boston Marathon.[1] Despite Sockalexis' matter-of-fact responses to such inquiries, the Boston Marathon, quite simply, was the most prestigious race of Sockalexis' day and the foot race that to this day unquestionably remains the most prestigious one in the world. Only 19 years of age, Sockalexis recorded a 2-hour, 43-minute, 45-second run over the celebrated Boston course to finish in an admirable 17th place as a complete unknown.

If this was, indeed, his first official race ever, it was a remarkable one. By today's standards for developing as a national- or world-class runner, it would be unheard of for anyone to *start* with the 26.2-mile marathon distance (or even the nearly 25-mile distance the Boston course was in its earliest days) without having first developed training and competitive techniques over the shorter distances. Every year at the Boston Marathon it seems an unheralded runner finishes surprisingly high in the standings, but upon further inspection that runner will be discovered to have outstanding high school or college credentials, or to have developed remarkably quickly through amateur competitions or regional town races.

However, Andrew Sockalexis' record offered no evidence of any such previous experience. He'd quite literally and figuratively run in his father's footsteps, training alone and diligently under the watchful eyes of Francis Sockalexis. And in his first race, with many of America's and Canada's most celebrated distance runners present, he'd proved his skill and would be listed among the favorites in every race that would follow. It truly was an astounding "before" and "after" transformation – from complete unknown to contender – Andrew Sockalexis made in this race, although none of the Boston journalists or those writing in Maine ever really put his career into this perspective at any time.

There was very little written about Andrew Sockalexis just prior to the 1911 Boston Marathon and his "unknown" status seems to be the obvious reason why. *Boston Post* newspaper columnist Arthur Duffey, after noting that a Boston Athletic Association race "would not be complete without an Indian entry," cited the presence of Mike Thomas, a Lenox Indian from Prince Edward Island, and Sockalexis. Duffey praised Thomas as a contender to win the race, but curtly dismissed the Penobscot: "Sockalexis has shown nothing."[2] Whether Duffey had come away unimpressed with a prior viewing of Sockalexis or was merely alluding to the Penobscot's unproven record was not made clear. However, another unnamed columnist from the *Post* reported there were actually four Indians registered to run: "Besides Padden and Thomas, there is Andrew Sockalexis of Oldtown [sic], Me., and Charles Honyoust, a full-blooded Oneida. They all look good."[3]

In the official entries list published by the *Post*, Sockalexis was listed as Number 24 from "Oldtown," Maine, a spelling mistake that many of the newspapers "from away" would make over the next few years.

The 1911 race is filled with interesting elements, linking Andrew Sockalexis' name with two of the greatest names in running history, two names that would arise again at significant turning points in the Penobscot Indian's life. The names were those of Clarence DeMar, the all-time champion of the Boston Marathon with seven victories, and the legendary Indian runner Tom Longboat from Canada. For at the 1911 race, the 23-year-old DeMar from nearby Melrose, Mass., a printer in a newspaper office, captured his very first Boston title with a record-breaking performance. And the record DeMar broke was Longboat's, set in 1907 and thought at that time to be invincible.

The Boston Marathon popped into existence in the spring of 1897 after members of the Boston Athletic Association traveled to Greece to witness the running of the Olympic marathon of 1896. From 1897 until 1924 the marathon was run over a route of only 24 and 1/2 miles. Originally the route began in Ashland, but in 1907 BAA officials moved the start to its present site, Hopkinton. Like Sockalexis, Tom Longboat was only 19 years old when he ran his first Boston Marathon in

1907, in one of the most memorable races of Boston's earliest days. An Onondaga Indian from Hamilton, Ontario, Longboat joined Bostonian James Lee in a red-hot early pace that proved fortuitous; for Lee, Longboat and seven others managed to get across the railroad crossing in South Framingham – just before a long freight train roared into view! The rest of the field was resigned to waiting for the train to pass by, waiting perhaps as long as two full minutes. Among those waiting was Johnny Hayes, the American winner of the 1908 Olympic marathon. After holding back for a time, in sixth place, Longboat "began to shoot down the palefaces," according to the account by *Boston Globe* editor Jerry Nason, long-time chronicler of the marathon.[4] By Wellesley, Longboat was in second place and he took over the lead in Auburndale. At the Exeter Street finish line, Longboat was all alone, establishing a new record of 2 hours, 24 minutes, 24 seconds. None of the previous Boston Marathons had been run within five minutes of Longboat's new winning time. More than 40 years later Nason quoted this DeMar assessment of the legendary Indian: "If Longboat had today's race conditions – macadam roads and no accompanying cars – he might have set a 2:06 record for the old 24 1/2-mile course."[5] The often murky or muddy dirt roads and the terrible exhaust fumes released into the faces of the runners by passing cars were tormenting obstacles to be dealt with by competitors in the early years of the marathon.

In the 1911 race, DeMar joined Longboat in the marathon's truly select circle of exceptional winners. He smashed the Indian's previous course record with a time of 2 hours, 21 minutes, 39 seconds. DeMar, second place finisher in the race the year before, hadn't begun running until he attended the University of Vermont and was in his third year. Though he distinguished himself in cross country running he hardly gave evidence of becoming an international great and, ultimately, the one time-honored name synonymous with Boston Marathon greatness. In his book **Marathon**, on the eve of his first Boston triumph, DeMar claimed he "distinctly" dreamed about winning the big race. However, he almost didn't get to depart from the starting line on April 19, 1911 (for much of its history the Boston Marathon was run on Patriots Day, specifically April 19, and not the Monday closest to that date, as is currently the case). DeMar explained that, as was the custom, a staff of doctors examined all the contestants, advising one or two of them not to participate. They listened for quite some time to the beating of DeMar's heart, ultimately deciding that the runner should make this event his last marathon run...or drop out of it altogether "if I got tired." The doctors told him he had heart murmurs. DeMar caustically responded to their advice this way: "I do not know whether it is possible to run a marathon in competition and not get tired, but at any rate I've never done it. At the finish one doctor expressed much surprise at how well I had run. He didn't ask whether I had become fatigued or not."[6]

Clarence DeMar actually dropped out of marathon running after the 1912 Olympic marathon for about five years. Although the "frequent warnings" from both doctors and friends about the dangers of marathon running on the heart "had left their impression," DeMar also cited religious reasons: "I took my religion somewhat seriously...I had a suspicion that the whole game of running was a selfish vain-glorious search for praise and honor." There were also his work and educational concerns. He cited his "reasonably hard job," standing for long hours and setting hot type as a printer in a stifling back room newspaper office, plus the university extension courses he took in his spare time at Harvard and Boston University.[7]

During his 1911 victory, DeMar began conservatively, running in 15th place through the first two check points on the course. Ultimately, 82 of the 127 starters finished the race, with only the first 38 having their positions and times officially recorded. Though Andrew Sockalexis' individual recorded times for the check points were not recorded, his placements were. Clearly, he ran a very strong second half of the race. At the five official check points Sockalexis was recorded in the following places: South Framingham, 41st place; Natick, 42nd place; Wellesley, 36th place; Boulevard, 23rd place; and Coolidge Corner, 16th place.

An unnamed writer devoted a special paragraph to Sockalexis in his post-race account:

> *Andy Sokalexis [sic], the Oldtown [sic] Indian,*
> *was one of the greatest surprises of the redskin en-*
> *try list. Before the race the Maine Indian was not*
> *considered along with Mike Thomas, the Lenox*
> *grinder, but Sokalexis showed he was one of the*
> *fastest Indians that ever competed in the contest. If*
> *the Oldtown brave had trained more and had more*

experience, he would have proved one of the hardest to beat in the race. As it was he finished among the leaders and will be one of the runners to note in next year's race. [8]

One can only wonder whether Sockalexis bristled at the notion that he hadn't trained hard enough or was flattered merely to be considered a contender and mentioned at all. Still, the unnamed writer misspelled his name and his home town, and then questioned the teen-ager for his lack of experience, which hardly seems fair, and for his training, without ever demonstrating any knowledge of knowing how Sockalexis trained for his first marathon. Just how much any of the so-called "sports writers" know about long distance running in this era continuously raises concerns.

On September 7, 1911 Andrew Sockalexis ran a 15-mile race in Nashua, New Hampshire, taking fourth place. That race apparently proved a good tune-up for the popular Brockton (Massachusetts) Marathon, held in October in conjunction with the Brockton Fair, where Sockalexis finished third in a time of 2 hours and 31 minutes.

Sockalexis rounded out his first year of racing with an impressive victory back in Maine. "**SOCKALEXIS WINS**" shouted out the first deck of *Bangor Daily Commercial* headline on December 1, 1911, and the subsequent account noted the youth's triumph in the Bangor YMCA 5-mile Thanksgiving Day race.

The opening paragraph read:

> *Speeding along the hard frozen road like a dusty phantom, Andrew Sockalexis, a Penobscot Indian from Old Town, won the Y.M.C.A. Marathon [Author's note: The term "marathon" is frequently misused, even today, to refer to a variety of long distance running events. A marathon actually refers to the distance of a 26.2-mile race] run Thanksgiving forenoon, defeating Harold Barton, the nimble legged High school football player... The route was from the Y.M.C.A. building across Franklin and up Harlow streets, along Valley avenue to Bulls-Eye bridge and back Ohio and Court streets to the building again. The Indian covered it in 30 minutes and 37 seconds and was far from being exhausted at the finish."* [9]

Barton was second, in 32 minutes, 14 seconds.

There were only eight runners in the race and they drew lots for positions on the starting line, with Sockalexis drawing the eighth and final spot. However, starting places in a 5-mile race really are of little consequence. According to the *Commercial* account the runners kept well together for the first half mile, with Sockalexis taking the lead at Prospect Street and Barton only a short distance behind. Sockalexis had "little difficulty" in maintaining his lead on the long stretch up Valley Avenue to the turn at Bull's Eye Bridge. On the steep hill beyond the bridge he increased his lead "appreciably." [10]

The *Bangor Daily News* account of the race concurred, noting the race had not been in progress long before it was "clearly evident" that Barton posed the only threat to Sockalexis, "but when the red-hued flyer had passed the steep hill beyond Bull's Eye bridge his gain was of such size that

Barton was found to be no longer in the running as far as the premier position was concerned." After noting the starting gun worked better than it did the year before, the *News* stated Sockalexis, in his black and orange stocking cap, took the lead just after passing Prospect Street "and he was not led thereafter..."[11]

The *Commercial* account concluded: "...when the Indian turned into Court Street it was evident that the race was his by a good margin." It reported a "good-sized crowd" awaited the runners at the YMCA building and gave Sockalexis a cheer as he broke the finish line tape.[12] The *News* summary commented that some of the spectators were "admiring friends" of the victor from Old Town and Sockalexis "smilingly" broke the tape.[13] Both publications reported that Sockalexis claimed he could have run a few more miles without difficulty. *[Author's note: Many, many years later, in the 1980s and 1990s, the Bangor YMCA and Grant's Dairy used essentially the same course for a popular 5-mile run held during the summer.]* Sockalexis' prize for winning was a sweater. Both newspaper accounts, quoting Sockalexis' trainer Thomas Daley, reported the runner planned to train all winter for the 1912 Boston Marathon, with a second goal of making the American Olympic team. Accompanying the runners on the route was an automobile, containing Daley, Andrew's father, and the two newspaper reporters.

During Andrew's teenage years, he received coaching assistance from Thomas Daley of Bangor. But following his success at the 1911 Boston Marathon, and with an ambitious eye towards winning the 1912 Boston Marathon and qualifying

for the 1912 U.S. Olympic marathoning team, Andrew
Sockalexis moved under the coaching tutelage of Arthur Smith
of Orono, then the track coach at the University of Maine and
regarded as one of the best trainer-coaches of his time.

* * *

Chapter 3

Titanic mud-slinger at 1912 Boston Marathon

An account of Andrew Sockalexis's preparation for
the 1912 Boston Marathon was related in a *Bangor Daily
News* article under the headline: "**Sockalexis Doing/Hard
Training**."[1] The newspaper reported several of "the stunts"
the athlete was doing in training, including a 25-mile trek over
muddy roads in 2 hours, 52 minutes, 10 seconds. He also told
the newspaper he'd completed a 5-mile run in 26 minutes,
54 seconds and a 10-mile run in 1 hour, 4 minutes. For these
runs, conducted without a pacing partner, Sockalexis stated his
training garb included two sweaters, heavy pants and shoes.
Clearly attempting to promote more public interest in his
running goals, Sockalexis said he was passing up representing
his running club, the prestigious North Dorchester (Mass.)
Athletic Association, in a race that very Saturday in favor of
a local training run. He announced he would be doing a run
that afternoon from the Bangor City Hall to the Old Town City
Hall, beginning at 2 o'clock. Then, following this last training

effort, he would leave by boat Monday for Boston to run in the marathon on Friday, April 19. There were two specific goals he had in mind: to win the first place cup at Boston and be selected to represent the United States at the Olympic Games, scheduled for that summer in Sweden.

The *Old Town Enterprise* was the only newspaper in the area to carry coverage of the Sockalexis training run. The editor's column for the issue of the week ending April 20 reported Sockalexis ran the 13-mile workout from Bangor to Old Town in 1 hour, 17 minutes, and enthused about how "fresh" he looked completing the task. His ease indicated "great stamina and health and that the Indian still retains them both in spite of the temptations of our present civilization."[2] The runner's weight was reported at 128 pounds, the weight at which he desired to compete.

That Monday, April 15, a report from Boston appeared in the *Bangor Daily News* announcing Andrew Sockalexis was set to race with 150 others in Friday's Boston Marathon. The article explained how the Boston Marathon would serve as the first of the official trials to determine the members of America's marathon team for the Olympic Games that summer. Because of his record-breaking performance the year before, and because of the caution he had received from physicians concerning a heart murmur, Clarence DeMar was named to the U.S. team and allowed to forgo competing at Boston. Festus J. Madden, a club mate of DeMar's from the North Dorchester A.A. and one of the big favorites to win the 1912 Boston Marathon, would not be allowed to represent the United States at the Olympics. It was reported that Madden lacked, by several months, the required amount of time of residency to secure his United States citizenship. With DeMar out of the competition, more than 20 runners in the listed 150-member field were given a chance to win. Mention of Sockalexis was made, noting his credible 17th place finish "as a novice."[3] Other Native American entrants included four runners enrolled at the Carlisle Indian School, including Louis Tewanima and Mitchell Arquette.

On Tuesday, April 16, another article about the marathon appeared, proclaiming that "more high class runners" would be competing in this year's event than had ever done so before.[4] But, apparently, these contenders brought with them a not-so-desirable element – runners who were not contenders. The unnamed writer moaned: "Every year a large number of runners have entered who have not had the slightest chance of getting inside the prize list."[5] The Boston Athletic Association was praised for its "remarkable work" in handling ever-growing fields of runners, and "drawing the restrictions tighter, cutting out undeveloped boys and older men who are not deemed physically fit for the severe test."[6] Every runner granted admission into the event was still required to undergo a physical examination before participating.

Looking over the contenders, the writer singled out Andrew Sockalexis as being "among the local runners who are expected to cut a prominent figure in the big race."[7] An aside to the pre-race analysis was the speculation that Colonel Theodore Roosevelt might attend the marathon, with the former President stating he hoped to be present if his schedule permitted. In another sports page headline a white challenger

offered to fight the highly controversial black heavyweight
boxing champion Jack Johnson for nothing.

But the real headline for Tuesday, April 16, 1912 came on
the front page of the *Bangor Daily News* with the following
staggering news: "**THE TITANIC SINKS; HUNDREDS
ARE LOST**" in huge, bold capital letters followed by the sub-
heading, "**Great White Star Liner Plunges Into The/Deep
After Colliding With Huge Iceberg/Messages Account For
Only 675/Out of 2200 Souls on Board.**"[8] The Titanic was the
largest, most celebrated vessel ever constructed, and had left
Southampton, England on her maiden voyage for New York on
April 10. The Titanic was 46,328 tons and 882 feet long. Just
before midnight on Sunday, April 14 it struck an iceberg and
during the early morning hours of Monday, April 15 it sank.
The rescue vessel, the Carpathia, reached the luxury liner's
position at dawn Monday morning to pick up the survivors
in their lifeboats. In the days that followed a steady, somber
processional of trains, making their way to Boston and New
York, came through Bangor carrying the bodies of the Titanic
dead, including the famous businessman of wealth and power,
John Jacob Astor.

Attention on the marathon in Boston found well-known
Boston Post columnist Arthur Duffey predicting a Festus
Madden victory; however, he listed Sockalexis as a favorite as
well. A prevailing attitude at the time, among many observers
of the sport, held that runners could not repeat as victors
at Boston. The obvious exception to the rule was Canadian
champion John Caffery of Hamilton, Ontario, who won in
1900 and 1901, but after Caffery there would be no repeat

winners until DeMar began his reign of domination in the 1920s. Runners were thought to be "used up" by their training and the effort it took to win "the great race" once. Adhering to that philosophy, Duffey seemed confident that it was time for popular local runner Festus Madden, a member of the local North Dorchester club, to break through and capture his long-awaited Boston title. Finishing second the year before, as Madden had during DeMar's record-breaking 1911 victory, often made that "bride's maid" the writers' choice as odds-on favorite for the following year. Writing in the *Post*'s all-purpose sports feature entitled "**Arthur Duffey's Column**," the columnist wrote: "In particular Sockalexis and Hackett *[Author's note: A runner who never figured at all in the actual race]* are liked. Both of these champions showed to advantage in the race last year and both appear to be fit for the race this year."[9]

On April 19, 1912, in only his third marathon, Andrew Sockalexis ran a truly remarkable race – the fastest he would ever run – and just missed equaling DeMar's course record by only 14 seconds. Unfortunately, his superb effort wasn't good enough to capture the race, as he finished just 34 seconds behind winner Mike Ryan.

Ryan's time was 2 hours, 21 minutes, 18 and 1/5 seconds, with Sockalexis timed in 2 hours, 21 minutes, 52 and 3/5 seconds. Sockalexis and Ryan both ran what appear to be very evenly paced races, holding back and waiting for what they believed was the right time to seize the lead and try for the victory. Ryan was in 9th place at South Framingham, 7th at Natick, 8th at Wellesley, 9th at the Boulevard, 6th at

Lake Street, and 4th at Coolidge Corner. At the same check points, Sockalexis was 11th at South Framingham, 10th at Natick, 13th at Wellesley, 5th at the Boulevard, 4th at Lake Street and took over 1st place at Coolidge Corner.

This author had the opportunity to look at different accounts from two unnamed wire service correspondents, published in the *Bangor Daily News* and the *Bangor Daily Commercial*, plus an account from Harry B. Center, writing for the *Boston Post*. These three all-but-forgotten eyewitness accounts, all commending Sockalexis for an extraordinary effort, are in sharp contrast to the succinct and very critically damning appraisal of Sockalexis' alleged "too fast-too soon" effort, as characterized by long-time *Boston Globe* editor Jerry Nason, which is the account most often cited by Boston Marathon chroniclers. Nason's terse and very possibly most unfair assessment will then follow.

The unnamed writer of the marathon account that appeared in the *Bangor Daily News* on Saturday, April 20, stated: "Over an unusually sticky course, Mike Ryan wearing the colors of the Irish-American A.C. of New York won the Boston Athletic Association's 16th Marathon race...against a field that included western athletes, Carlisle Indians and the fastest and sturdiest long distance men in the east..."[10]

The *Bangor Daily News* account noted the race was "run in a drizzling rain which turned the surface of the road into a slime and it was only by taking to the sidewalks at intervals that the runners were able to make time."[11] The writer of this wire service account claimed Ryan ran a "well-judged race." He let the three Carlisle Indians, Arquette, Hermequatewa and

Telyumptewa and Gallagher of Yale set the pace for him for a great part of the distance. But after he reached the Chestnut Hill reservoir and "the dome of the state house loomed up ahead, five miles away," Ryan made his move. According to this reporter, Ryan "tore through the field until Sockalexis was the only rival left. The Irishman outran the Indian in the last two miles and had not the last half mile been ankle deep in mud the record would have suffered a much greater slump."[12]

The finishing order, after Ryan and Sockalexis, included: Madden (Duffey's pre-race favorite and North Dorchester A.A. member who was destined never to win the Boston Marathon), Lilley, Carlson, Jensen, Piggott and Fabre. In all, the first 13 runners crossed the finish line in under 2 hours and 30 minutes.

Harry B. Center, writing the marathon account for the *Boston Post*, called Ryan "king of the mudlarks...wallowing through mud over ankle deep a good part of the way." Center noted that Ryan ran the "fastest 25 miles ever timed over this or any other course" and added, "Ryan had to break the record to win the race."[13]

The reason, Center asserted, was Sockalexis, who "had run a truly remarkable race, was always in the fight and steadily improved his position until, at Coolidge Corner, he led the procession." Center continued: "Ryan won the race in the last two miles and broke the record in doing it. He had a merry fight to pass the fleet Indian but, at the corner of Keswick and Beacon streets, he nosed into the lead...yet the Oldtown *[sic]* brave, not even if he had been passed, pressed every stride."

Center concluded his description of the climactic moments of
the race by noting that Ryan, with a "dazzling burst of speed,"
increased his "winning advantage to 300 yards" that he
retained to the finish line tape.[14]

Center wrote that Sockalexis' and Ryan's "desperate
battle...was all fought and settled in that final, desperate two
miles—two long miles that came at the end of one of the
hardest, most grueling and most bitterly contested races ever
run over any marathon course."[15]

Focusing specifically on the Penobscot Indian, Center
commented:

> *Andrew Sockalexis lived up to the old tradi-*
> *tion of the Red man by the speed and endurance he*
> *showed in finishing second to Ryan. If it had not*
> *been for such a competitor as Sockalexis, along*
> *with Festus Madden of North Dorchester AA and*
> *Gallagher of Yale, Ryan would never have made*
> *his record-breaking run. The Redskin, however,*
> *appeared to have shot his bolt on the last stretch*
> *and it was here that the New Yorker's experience*
> *and head work stood him in good stead. The Indian*
> *has now come to the front as one of the coming*
> *marathoners. Last year he made a most credible*
> *showing in the run and after yesterday's showing*
> *should be favored to win next season.[16]*

Another unnamed wire service writer also offered a
compelling first-hand account of the race, published in
the *Bangor Daily Commercial*. According to this writer,
Sockalexis, wearing Number 22, was clearly biding his time,

as was Ryan, hanging well back from the leaders Israel Saklad and Gallagher, but running alongside the veteran Madden.[17]

The writer noted that just outside of Framingham, Ryan was running eighth and "taking his own time about it." Close behind was Fritz Carlson *[Author's note: Carlson, who defeated Sockalexis in the 1913 Boston Marathon, is incorrectly identified as "Corlson"]* of Minneapolis, who had "worked up from far in the rear," and next to him was Andrew Sockalexis, "now beginning to look decidedly dangerous. His clean cut running and evident splendid condition was noted by many along the route."[18] At Natick, the second official timing station, a tired Israel Saklad dropped from the front as pacemaker. Gallagher seized the position and was never headed until he was passed by Sockalexis, near Keswick Road in Brookline.

The unnamed wire service correspondent stated: "It was near Keswick road in Brookline, when despite his attempt to hit up a faster pace and put Madden and Sockalexis farther in the rear, Gallagher was not only unable to do so, but found himself being forced from the lead. His bolt was shot and he could do no more. Amid the cheers of the crowd, Madden and Sockalexis passed him, the Indian taking the lead with the white brother but a foot behind him." And so it remained until, with two miles left to go, Ryan put on his heroic charge down Beacon Street.[19]

Though Ryan's name wasn't mentioned in the pre-race publicity as a possible winner or dark horse contender for any previous Boston Marathon titles, he had apparently hoped to win a number of times earlier.

According to this wire service newspaper account Ryan, a veteran of six Boston Marathons, stated before the race that it would be his last if he did not win. "He (Ryan) has tried time and time again, always figuring well up, but never been able to get first place." Reportedly Jim Sullivan, a former president of the Amateur Athletic Union, was a spectator at the race and told Ryan before the starting gun was fired: "Mike, I want to take you to Stockholm [for the 1912 Olympic Games], so go and do some business today."[20]

Sockalexis, too, was known to want to go to Stockholm as a result of Boston and "had centered his entire efforts on this race. He, too, followed predictions by winning second place."[21] These three eyewitness accounts all seem unanimous in praising Andrew Sockalexis for a superlative effort and a nearly perfectly judged race that fell just short in the face of a record-breaking performance by Mike Ryan.

Yet it is Jerry Nason's handful of summary sentences that has, it seems, forever left Sockalexis to be criticized for misjudging a victory that might have been his.

Boston Globe sports editor Jerry Nason, long recognized as the great historian for the Boston Marathon, never published a book on the race but did write a lengthy "booklet" which carried capsules of each race from 1897 to 1966. And it's clearly his description, repeated by a number of Boston Marathon race historians (including Joe Falls and Tom Derderian), which damns Sockalexis forever as having "gone out too fast" in the 1912 race when the actual race accounts themselves suggest that this isn't necessarily the story at all.

For starters, Nason doesn't take into account Sockalexis'
youthfulness – he's only 20 years old at the time – and
lack of experience (it's only his third marathon and just his
fifth official race ever). Secondly, and even worse, Nason's
characterization of Sockalexis' alleged "early speed" in the
1912 race doesn't match the eyewitness descriptions of writers
and those who registered places at the various check posts
who all claimed Sockalexis and Ryan both held back, while
Gallagher and Saklad pressed the pace for most of the
race.

Nason began his 1913 account with this assessment of
Andrew Sockalexis' back-to-back second place performances
at the Boston Marathon:

> *Of this race the Old Guard insists, 'Carlson*
> *didn't win it; Andrew Sockalexis lost it.' This con-*
> *tention is based on the fact that the Indian, who'd*
> *paid the penalty for his early speed in 1912, this*
> *time ran so cautiously to the halfway point (five*
> *minute arrears) that his tremendous spurt in the*
> *final nine miles fell 1 minute 58 seconds short of*
> *victory.*[22]

Nason's crisp, five-paragraph description of the 1912 race
noted that DeMar's "rousing record" lasted just one year, shot
down by the 23-year-old Ryan and his "long determined chase
of the Penobscot Indian, Andrew Sockalexis, in the mud and
slush of a Winter's day." Nason noted that the "unbridled early
pace by Johnny Gallagher, a Yale freshman, made a shambles
of the favorites' race plans." And he astutely assessed that

Gallagher's "brash bid between the sixth and 21st miles" was reminiscent of Fred Cameron's "steal" of the 1910 race "with similar tactics." However, Nason claimed Gallagher's "rivals were forced to accelerate with him."[23] In truth, only Saklad and, perhaps, Madden spent themselves prematurely.

Nason maintained: "The foremost contenders at the campus boy's heels were little Andrew Sockalexis, the Indian boy from Old Town, Me. and Festus Madden, the County Galway-born veteran from South Boston. Madden clung stubbornly to the redskin's shoulder in a 12-mile pursuit of Gallagher."[24]

But just a quick glance at the recorded finishes at the checkpoints shows something different. For instance, at the 10-mile mark in Natick, Ryan was actually in 7th place while Sockalexis was in 10th. At the 13-mile mark in Wellesley, Ryan was 8th, while Sockalexis was 13th. Inside the last 10 miles, Sockalexis was 5th at the Boulevard and 4th at Lake Street, while Ryan was close by, in 9th and 6th places, respectively.

Nason wrote of the climactic moments:

> *The collegian [Gallagher] finally 'burned out' near Cleveland Circle, 21 miles, and Sockalexis shot into the lead, with Madden next. After a fast flight over the hills, red-headed Mike Ryan was closing fast on them. Ryan's great run the length of Beacon St. quickly subdued Madden, and brought him past the Indian leader at the Boston Brookline line, two miles from the tape. Sockalexis fought bravely, but his stamina was spent. Ryan's record run beat him by 34 seconds.[25]*

Misjudging a victory, if indeed it can be called that, by a margin of 34 seconds when the victor broke the existing course record by 21 seconds, hardly seems deserving of such harsh criticism.

Nason's time-honored assessment of a Sockalexis miscalculation stemmed, perhaps, from a column in the *Boston Post* where the writer was both effusive in his praise and damning in his criticism of the Penobscot Indian's effort. Those editorial comments found their way into an account, which peripherally announced that Sockalexis had been named to the U.S. Olympic team, published a few days after the marathon.

In the April 22, 1912 issue of the *Bangor Daily News* an article carried the following headline: **"Old Town Indian Will Run/in the Olympic Marathon—Andrew Sockalexis Earns a Place on American Team in/Greatest World Athletic Event in Sweden—Real/Hero of the B.A.A. Marathon."**[26]

Sockalexis was praised for his "plucky performance" and then immediately second guessed: "All accounts agree that with a little judicious handling he might have won."[27] Clearly, this writer and others like him don't have the same lack of faith and regard for the bicycle-pedaling trainers that great runners like Clarence DeMar had. DeMar and others – especially all the members of the 1924 American Olympic marathon team who voted unanimously against having an Olympic marathon trainer – saw the trainers as meddling nuisances harmfully interfering with their individual preparations.

The account then quoted the remarks of an unnamed writer, who could have been Arthur Duffey, Harry B. Center or someone else, in the *Boston Post* who stated: "To my mind Andrew Sockalexis, the sturdy little Old Town, Me. redskin is just as big a hero as the stalwart Ryan of the Irish-American A.C. of New York. He deserves just as much credit as the winner of the contest."[28]

The writer began with a rather blatant racist appraisal of Sockalexis' ability, noting the Indian "started in the athletic game because it is a part of his nature." There followed two sentences in direct opposition to one another. Sockalexis was said to be "fond of athletics, principally running, and has kept plugging at the long distance game hitherto attracting a great deal of attention." But the writer, in the very next sentence, then immediately acknowledged: "Last year was the first time his running came to be noticed and though he finished around 16th *[Author's note: it was 17th]* in the Boston Marathon of that year, many favorable predictions were made concerning him."[29]

The writer readily acknowledged Sockalexis was considered a favorite for the 1912 Boston Marathon victory, with the rather understated comment that he "surely was watched." He quickly added, "Before the race started many fancied the Maine representative to win the contest." Speaking before the run about this front-runner status, the quiet youth was quoted as saying, simply, "I will do my best." The writer added, "That the Indian did his best we all know now."[30]

The writer then offered this characterization of Sockalexis' race: "Starting at Ashland last Friday noon with the greatest

Marathoners in the game by his side, he ran the first part of
the race like a seasoned champion."[31] This hardly sounds like
Sockalexis started too fast or made any mistake of any sort at
the outset.

Now the writer stated: "Coming into South Framingham
he was in 11th position. Although well back this position did
not seem to feaze [sic] him in the least."[32] Here, the writer
seemed more concerned with what number in the pack
Sockalexis was, rather than how many minutes or seconds
behind he was, which would be the more significant factor
to offer if it were significant. There's a suggestion this
writer believes the winner should be at the front the entire way.

Then he wrote: "At Natick, encouraged by his trainer
*[Author's note: Is this Arthur Smith? There has been no
mention anywhere else of a trainer following Sockalexis along
on the course or observing him at various junctures]* the
Indian moved up to the 10th position. For a time it then looked
as if he had shot his bolt, and as he passed into Wellesley he
fell back into 13th position."[33] Of course, none of this matters
one bit, unless he had fallen many minutes off the pace.
Clearly Sockalexis had not. But those with limited knowledge
apparently expect 'a winner' to lead all the way and look
great doing it. Perhaps Sockalexis and the other contenders
believed Gallagher's early frantic pace was suicidal and he and
the others were merely biding their times, knowing there's no
reason to be concerned about not leading at the halfway mark
of a 24.5-mile race.

The writer continued: "At the boulevard, where so many runners come to grief, (Sockalexis) quickened his gait and found his second wind. Johnny Gallagher, the Yale champion, up to this point proved a great pacer for him."[34] This hardly seems likely at all. From all of the above accounts, Gallagher was of no "pacing" value to anyone. He was running too fast, trying to blow away the whole field. He was clearly of no use to Sockalexis and the rest of the top runners. Gallagher only provided anxiety, causing all the contenders behind him to worry whether he had enough to beat them all with his crazy pace and "steal" the race a la Fred Cameron in 1910.

Now, entering the later stages of the race, the writer wrote: "At Lake Street Sockalexis kept up his splendid stride and there were only three runners in front of him."[35] It's hard to know how much of this is Gallagher, Saklad and Madden coming back to him or Sockalexis really stepping up his stride. It's probably both elements. But two things should be clear: It's now close to that time he should make a move if he wants to be in contention to win the race. And the man who actually won the race was still behind him...and moving hard as well.

Then the writer unleashed the words that may have forever unfairly damned Sockalexis: "Encouraged by being so near the lead he let out a few kinks, and at Coolidge Corner was leading the long list of runners. It was at this point that Sockalexis appeared to make a fatal mistake. He came into the lead too soon." [36]

Sockalexis took the lead at Mile 23 of a 24.5-Mile race and attempted to win the world's most prestigious foot race. Earlier this writer criticized him for being too far back, off the pace. Now the writer is criticizing him for going for the win, with the same momentum he has employed to break the spirits of hometown favorites Madden and Saklad plus Gallagher, the man who has led the way for 12 miles, in the closing stages of just his fourth official race and just his third marathon. To this point, Ryan has not even been a factor in the race.

However, the writer doesn't actually blame Sockalexis for the "fatal mistake": "But when one comes to look into the case it was no more than to be expected. Sockalexis was running the race on his own hook. He had no real advisers to tell him what to do."[37] Just a few paragraphs earlier, the writer said his trainer offered advice in Natick earlier. So Sockalexis did seem to have a trainer present. But that aside, what would have a trainer told him to do at that point? Sockalexis had passed a fading Saklad, then a fading Gallagher and was outdistancing a tiring Madden. Ryan was not a factor until he challenged Sockalexis for the lead and Sockalexis responded with all he had and came up just short.

The writer believed victory or defeat depended on a trainer, not the athlete:

> *It was only his [Sockalexis'] grit that kept him on the move. There was no Lawson Robertson, McCaffrey, and a dozen other trainers to advise him just what to do, as was the case with Mike Ryan. If the redskin had either of these advisers there is no knowing who would have won the race and what the record performance would have been.[38]*

Only if trainers could somehow intuitively look inside each runner and assess energy expended and energy and desire left to succeed, would they truly serve some value. History records, ironically enough, that it was trainers who "killed" the chances of the United States 1912 Olympic marathon team and may well have cost Andrew Sockalexis, the fourth place finisher, an Olympic medal. Great runners have no need of follow-along trainers and that is the reason that such trainers have been an extinct breed for many, many years.

Concluded the writer:

> *Mike Ryan's name will always be associated with the great Boston Marathon of 1912, but among those athletic followers of the grind who followed the whole race, many will acclaim Sockalexis as the real champion. To this affect [sic] many predict that he will show his real class in the Olympic Marathon at Sweden.*[39]

The *Boston Post* writer offered a very telling remark from Ryan, the winner, who reportedly offered this fine tribute to the Penobscot Indian. Ryan said:

> *That I succeeded is due in large measure to Sockalexis' great gameness. He certainly pulled me out a fast mile when I tried to get him, and he did not stop either, when I went by, so that I had to keep up a fast clip to keep my lead over the little Indian. He is a wonder, and when he gains a little more experience he will be a tough one to beat.*[40]

After Sockalexis returned to Indian Island after the marathon he was interviewed by *Old Town Enterprise* editor John W. Gould, who wrote: "Under the most crude conditions for training, he *[Sockalexis]* made himself fit for the great Marathon race at Boston last Friday, Patriot's day, and came within 34 seconds of winning the coveted prize. By doing this turn Sockalexis has not only made himself but Old Town famous."[41]

Gould reported from the Sockalexis home one week after the race, where he found the runner's father and mother and another visitor looking at his runner-up trophy from the marathon. For the 1912 marathon, Sockalexis told Gould he began training on February 1, running on the frozen Penobscot River, running at the University of Maine gymnasium and taking longer training runs to Olaman and back.

The *Enterprise* editor offered the following description of the runner:

> *To look at Sockalexis one wonders where he gets all the stamina or power of endurance but an examination of his chest shows a lung expansion of a man of 200 pounds rather than a lad of 128 pounds when down to weight. His leg muscles though small are well developed and look as if they would stand him as long as needed. His feet never blistered except this time, which was on account of the wet roads. His feet were wet the entire distance on account of so much mud and water in the road. Neither he nor his father believe in stimulants; he does not even use alcohol to bath in, keeping close to mother nature.*[42]

Gould commented that Sockalexis "went into the race with the idea of winning and breaking the record and would have done so if he had had the same care and training the other runners had and the roads had been dry." He said he "was not tired nor winded" when he came in but "could have gone five miles more."[43]

Gould stated from his interview:

> *Ryan was all in at the end while Sockalexis was as fresh as a daisy. He had had a lunch rubdown and was presented to the crowd before Ryan had recovered. If there was any bad part it was the first four or five mile [sic] after which he never worried as he had a feeling of safety as to the result and his confidence was well borne out. He had his course well laid out and held to it never slowing up at all for the entire course. He said if they had had another quarter of a mile he would have won as Ryan was fast tiring.[44]*

Here, again, is another apparent paradox: Supposedly Andrew Sockalexis went out too fast, too soon and was passed in the very last crucial stages by the more experienced Ryan who smashed the course record with a well-planned sprint at the finish. Now Andrew Sockalexis is telling the press, or perhaps a writer is projecting the idea from his post-race comments, that he was still fresh and could have run further. Well, Andrew Sockalexis is only 20 years old, clearly ran a well-paced race until the last stages and then, just as clearly, recovered after the race as such a young, vital athlete might well be expected to do. Ryan, the veteran who had been disappointed in the past many times at Boston, was clearly at the end of his career, making one last great attempt to win. Once he took the lead in the last two miles of the race, and Sockalexis mounted his challenge, Ryan gave everything he had to the effort to hold off the younger man and measured those last steps to the finish line and the last of his energy perfectly. That the aging marathoner needed more time to recover after his record-breaking run shouldn't surprise anyone.

Concluded Gould: "Andrew Sockalexis is a first *[Author's note: Actually, they're second cousins]* cousin to Louis Sockalexis, the well known ball player; he is a total abstainer and intends to stay so. If he had had a quarter of the attention some of the other runners had he would have won out. The worst shock he had was when he was told on his 21st mile that he was a minute ahead of the best time *[Author's note: DeMar's record time from the previous year to that point]*."[45]

Gould concluded his interview, noting that Andrew Sockalexis had "some strong friends in the young ladies from the island" who raised money for the runner's expenses through a benefit dance on the island and by seeking donations. A couple of them attended the race and followed the race in the automobile of the *Herald*, one of the newspapers covering the event.

* * *

Chapter 4

Controversy over selection to Olympic team

The original men selected for the U.S. team to compete in
the marathon at the 1912 Olympic Games included: Clarence
DeMar, Thomas Lilley and Andrew Sockalexis, representing
the North Dorchester A.A. of Boston; Dick Piggott of
Medford, Mass; Mike Ryan, Irish-American Athletic Club, and
Harry Jensen, Pastime Athletic Club, both of New York; John
J. Gallagher of Philadelphia and Yale; Lewis Tewanima, who
would also be running the 10,000-meter race, of the Carlisle
Indian School; Sidney Hatch and L. Pillivant, both of Chicago;
and Fritz Carlson, of Cook's Gymnasium, Minneapolis.

Because of their outstanding performances in the 1912
Boston Marathon, winner Ryan, second place finisher
Sockalexis and fourth place finisher Lilley had firmly
cemented their spots. Third place finisher Festus Madden
had already been eliminated from contention for the Olympic
team before the race because the Irish native had not gotten
his citizenship papers in proper order. Fifth place finisher Fritz

Carlson of Minneapolis, too, had recently immigrated from
Sweden, but his U.S. citizenship had officially been approved.
However Carlson, after paying his own way and traveling
apart from the team earlier over to his native country to visit
relatives, would encounter a heart-breaking decision rendered
by American officials that kept him from participating.
Carlson departed for Sweden, still believing he was an official
U.S. entrant in the Olympic marathon at Stockholm, only
to learn just a short time before the event that he had been
dropped from the roster. Also from the 1912 Boston Marathon,
the sixth place runner, Jensen from New York, and the
veteran Piggott, who was seventh in the race, were originally
selected.

Shortly after the Boston Marathon, the selected runners
participated in a 10-mile "exhibition" run at Harvard to
secure their positions on the team. In his book *Marathon*,
1911 Boston Marathon winner Clarence DeMar, who had
been granted a waiver from participating in that spring's
Boston Marathon because of a heart murmur, wrote that he
participated in that trial "to satisfy Mr. Babb of the Olympic
committee."[1] After the trials, several of the names changed.
DeMar and 11 others were then officially informed that they
had been selected to the Olympic team. DeMar, Sockalexis,
Lilley, Piggott, Tewanima, Gallagher, Hatch and Ryan were
eight carryovers from the first list. Jensen was no longer on
the list but two other runners from New York were – Harry
Smith and John Reynolds. Chicago entrant Pillivant was
dropped from the team but 1908 Olympic third-place finisher
Joe Forshaw and Joseph Erxleben, both of St. Louis, were now

on it. Hatch was a last minute dropout. According to DeMar, Hatch "had some work he thought more important" and at the last moment gave up his position on the team.[2] The 12th and last position on the U.S. marathon team was filled by Gaston Strobino, who had apparently done well in a large 12-mile race in New York to warrant the consideration.

Significantly, Strobino was not added to the team until it had departed, by vessel, for Sweden. This allowed Strobino to run on his own, apart from the rigid training regimen established for the marathon contingent; this freedom would be specifically credited for his ultimate surprising finish in the actual Olympic event.

The highly regarded track coach, Mike Murphy of Pennsylvania was the overall coach for the American Olympic team, with Mike Ryan, the new record holder for the Boston Marathon course, running at the head of the marathon squad, setting the pace and establishing the daily training regimen. Johnny Hayes, the winner of the marathon at the previous Olympic Games in London, served the marathon squad as a special trainer.

How the best marathoners in the United States were selected for the Olympic team turns out to be no less controversial back in the early years of the 20th century than it remains to this day. Today, many observers and participants are concerned that one major competition held only three to four months before the actual Olympic run doesn't necessarily ferret out America's top three marathon runners. And, perhaps, it seriously damages the chances those select three might have had at the Olympics by forcing them to put forth a major effort in a rigorous race much too close to an Olympiad.

Back in 1912, the selection process came under fire – even though the United States could send 12 competitors for the marathon run. In an article published just prior to the 1912 Boston Marathon, a *Bangor Daily News* headline announced that: "**Twelve Americans Sure to Start/at Big Stockholm Marathon Race.**" The unnamed writer of the piece noted that it was "certain" that America would choose to send "the full entry of twelve." The writer went on to add that it was "an open secret" how the selection committee favored this "safe" policy, allowing as many participants as possible in an event "where there is so much chance for men to go wrong."[3]

The 1908 marathon is cited, by the unnamed writer, as a "good precedent to go by...when the men who earned their right to represent America in the tryouts failed to figure in the case at all." The writer explained that: "Then, as now, the Boston Marathon, on Patriots Day, was the real tryout for the purpose of finding who was really the best American at the game..." He noted that a runner named Thomas P. Morrissey of Yonkers had won the Boston Marathon but faltered badly at the Olympic marathon in London and another of the selections, Joe Forshaw, had finished third. It was Johnny Hayes, who was not an official selection but was "sent by his club to take a trial and see what luck had in store for him," who came up as the winner.[4]

Actually, the 1908 marathon was a particularly historic one. The official distance of 26 miles, 385 yards for a marathon was set, when the royal family requested that the marathon course go by their dwellings during the London Olympiad. Further, the ending to this marathon was particularly controversial, stirringly poignant. The Italian Dorando Pietri staggered into the stadium and shakily made his way to the finish line. But just yards short of the finish line, he collapsed and was clearly unable to go any further under his own power. Compassionate officials helped him up and literally carried him across the finish line. Ultimately this aiding of a runner was protested and the American Johnny Hayes, who finished second, was awarded the top spot. It was declared, for future marathon competitions, that no competitor could be aided in any way or that competitor would be disqualified. In the 1984 Olympics, the nearly sickening sight of a woman, suffering from apparent heat stroke and staggering to the finish, caused a lot of viewers concern and then created an enormous dilemma for watching officials, officials who wanted to help but knew that her entire effort would be lost to the Olympic record book if they so much as touched her. The Swiss woman barely finished under her own power.

Back in 1912, Olympic rules allowed entry of up to 12 competitors for the marathon per country. That Pietri faltered, that Hayes was an apparent afterthought and ultimately won, seemed to suggest that the American Olympic selection committee send as many candidates as possible.

How would that be done?

A selection committee was created and the members were to consider the performances from the Boston Marathon on April 19, as well as later marathon runs at Chicago and St. Louis and a fourth one on the Pacific Coast. It was noted that "men who have tried over the distance and who have demonstrated that they can stay will be considered – that is, if they have stayed in training and are ambitious for glory at Stockholm."[5]

It had already been determined that two men had been selected without having to try out. One was Clarence DeMar, sitting out the Boston Marathon allegedly "on account of his weak heart." Another was Lewis Tewanima, the Carlisle Indian, said to be "one of the grittiest little fellows that ever donned a running shoe, and who can be depended on to put up a game fight over the full distance and to be there at the finish." Two others, Joe Forshaw and Sidney Hatch, were being "regarded in the same light" and they, too, ultimately were named to the team.[6]

The controversy concerning the selection process involved how many runners should come from the various trials around the country. At the outset, some members of the selection committee favored the idea of taking three men from Boston, three men from Chicago, three men from the Pacific Coast, and then, in order to make up a dozen competitors, three others would be "selected at large." An opposition arose, offering the sentiment that three should not be selected from the Pacific district as "they might be lacking in class." It was pointed out that marathoning had "not been very rampant of late around the Golden Gate, a fact which means there has been little or no development." It was stated there had not been a big marathon race since the fall of 1909, "a state of affairs which would seem to indicate that the devotees of the long grind are all out of training."[7]

Though an uncontested pick for the U.S. Olympic marathon team through two selection processes, Andrew Sockalexis would himself become a surprising candidate to be dropped from the team before the ship departed for Europe.

* * *

Chapter 5

Amateur status questioned

The spring of 1912 offered momentous times, momentous people. There was, of course, the tragedy of the Titanic. That was followed by Amundsen, the Norwegian, dueling Scott, the Englishman, in a race to be the first to the South Pole. Admiral Peary, the first to the North Pole (supported in this effort by Donald MacMillan and his strong link to Maine's Bowdoin College), speculated that both courageous adventurers had been successful in their quests, and would later be proved correct. When Scott's vessel, the Terra Nova, returned without him an ominous mystery puzzled the world for several days before the news was learned that not only had he failed to beat Amundsen to the goal but the effort had cost him and his crew their lives.

Just a week before the Boston Marathon, Red Cross founder Clara Barton died. In early May Bangor residents would somberly observe the passing through of a train bound for Boston and New York, bearing recovered bodies from the Titanic disaster.

But the news wasn't all morbid. There was the incomparable Teddy Roosevelt, the fiery William Jennings Bryan, the robust William Taft. The sports world regularly carried the feats of legendary figures in the making – Christy Mathewson, Smoky Joe Wood and Shoeless Joe Jackson in baseball, and the first black, heavyweight boxing champion, Jack Johnson.

In one article in the spring of 1912, Johnson was quoted as saying: "I'm like Alexander the Great – I'm too good. There isn't anyone else to lick that is worth a whoop. After July 4 I expect to meet red, white, blue or black hopes, one a week. That means Sam Langford too but Sam will have to put a side bet. I don't like that man and I want his money."[1] Clearly, Cassius Clay/Muhammad Ali didn't think up something new, bragging and stirring emotions of fight fans, smartly building up the box office gate through arrogance and even playing upon racism. Jack Johnson was using all these ploys more than 50 years before him.

After Andrew Sockalexis' near record-breaking, near victorious run at the 1912 Boston Marathon he became news locally on a weekly basis. And interest in him remained high as he prepared for the upcoming Olympic Games, to be held in July in Stockholm, Sweden.

The 1912 Boston Marathon had been held on Patriot's Day, April 19, which was a Friday. Sockalexis returned home immediately, arriving by train in Old Town Saturday afternoon. According to a blurb in the town news column **"Up in Old Town,"** from the *Bangor Daily Commercial* for Monday, he arrived without a bit of fanfare. The paper reported: "There was no brass band at the station to meet him, in fact nobody knew that he was coming." Word on the island had it that he would not be returning before Monday. He was accompanied by three girls from the Penobscot tribe, who had attended the race and cheered him on. As they walked up from the station, two of the girls were "swinging the handsome cup by two of its handles as they walked, that its beauties might be manifest to all on the street at the time." The cup was a "very handsome object, silver and with gold lining."[2]

A couple days later the Penobscot tribe held a special reception, featuring a concert and dance and a "hearty" supper at the intermission, in honor of the runner's outstanding effort. The reception was held in the hall on Indian Island. The evening began with a concert, featuring several vocal and musical instrument presentations. Among those tribe members performing a solo at the concert was Andrew's cousin, Louis Sockalexis, still a most revered athletic hero on the island. Misidentified as "Lewis" by the *Bangor Daily Commercial* correspondent writing this "**Up in Old Town**" column, Louis Sockalexis sang a number entitled "Everybody Has Their Eyes on Me." The unnamed correspondent noted that "the feature of the evening" was the formal presenting to the assembly of around 150 people of runner Andrew Sockalexis by "Lewis Sockalexis, the old Cleveland baseball star." It is the only published account this author found of the two athletic heroes appearing at a public event together. The correspondent wrote: "...there was a universal feeling of satisfaction in this, as one of the most satisfactory social events held on the island in a long time." After being introduced, Andrew Sockalexis spoke briefly, stating that he "would return the high honor conferred upon him, by doing his utmost to win the Olympic Marathon, for which he is already in training."[3]

By the end of the week the local newspapers began showing recognition of Andrew Sockalexis as both a national and international hero in the making. The Old Town newspaper, the *Enterprise*, went so far as to brashly dub him as the next "champion Marathon runner of the world." In the editor's column, a mishmash of random notes on the community, the following was written: "The citizens of this city have in their midst one who is to be, according to all probabilities, the champion Marathon runner of the world." The newspaper cited this assessment as "the consensus opinion of all the best sportsmen of New England at least and all his work so far justifies the prediction." Noting that "if any other city or town had such a personage in their midst, especially where he is such a good citizen as Andrew Sockalexis," the editor bluntly declared, "he would receive more than scant courtesey [sic] we are giving him." The editor urged that something should be done on his behalf and in his honor before he left for Stockholm in June and that, his "superior ability" should be "fittingly recognized" in the future as well.

A week later the same unnamed editor again urged community support for Andrew. Ironically, the editor suggested a field day. Though there would be no field day in Sockalexis' honor in 1912, there would be one, sadly, in 1914 to support the diminutive runner in facing the illness, tuberculosis, which would ultimately kill him in 1919. In this second column, the editor acknowledged the efforts and influence of his father, Francis:

> *Andrew Sockalexis wants to take his father with him to Stockholm in June because his father has directed his training ever since he took to the cinder path and has done it most successfully as results show. We wonder if there is enough local pride in our city, in a Marathon runner who promises to be the champion of the world, for us to get enough money together to send his father along with him to train him?*[4]

The editor suggested contacting the University of Maine for the use of one of its athletic fields for a field day or possibly arranging for the use of city hall for a concert or dance for Sockalexis' benefit. The editor noted ominously that time was short and "whatever is done must be done quickly."

Exactly one week after Sockalexis' outstanding effort at Boston, this startling headline greeted area readers of the *Bangor Daily News*: "**SOCKALEXIS IS/PURE AMATEUR/ Positively Denies Report That He/ Ever Raced St. Yves, the French/ Professional.**"[5]

The first part of the account, taken directly from one of the Boston newspapers, stated in its opening paragraph:

> *The Boston Post says: An attempt is afoot to pull Andrew Sockalexis from the American Marathon team that is to represent the United States in the Swedish Olympics, according to reports received in this city yesterday. It is charged that the Indian has*

> *forfeited his amateur standing by competing in a*
> *race against a professional.*[6]

The professional athlete mentioned was Henri St. Yves, a
famous French runner. Absent from the account was a "when"
and "where," citing the circumstances under which St. Yves
and Sockalexis allegedly raced together, nor was "the person
who started the report" identified. Unnamed Boston sources
immediately said they suspected members of the New York
athletic club of starting the rumor in order "to push another
New Yorker, one of those who competed in the recent B.A.A.
marathon, to the front, thus giving the Big Town three men
instead of two as at present, Ryan and Jensen."[7]

The *Boston Post* quickly noted that while the rumor
had "thrown some scares" into Olympic officials and the
local running community, "those who are acquainted with
Sockalexis are placing little stock in it and are certain that
the Indian will go with the team to Sweden." Two sources
who were quoted in the article, E.E. Babb of the Olympic
committee and Herbert S. Coles of the North Dorchester
Athletic Association, the prestigious Boston-area track club for
whom Sockalexis ran on April 19, said they were certain the
charge was untrue.[8]

Again, it was noted that the 20-year-old runner had only
competed in four official races to that date: "According to
all information at hand Sockalexis has competed only in the
B.A.A. and Brockton Marathon in 1911, in a race in Bangor
that same year *[Author's note: This would be the YMCA 5-miler
on Thanksgiving Day]* and the recent Patriots' Day event." The

Boston people then issued a "Show me" challenge to the charge made against Sockalexis: "If he had taken part in any other races of moment or ever competed against St. Yves athletic followers in Boston are Missourians for the next few days."[9]

An unnamed writer in that same *Bangor Daily News* article then noted that "Sockalexis, when interviewed last night in Old Town, was very indignant at the report." He told the reporter "he had never raced St. Yves or even seen him; that the only races he was ever in was [sic] the four mentioned above."[10]

From the above turmoil it's amusing to see that, quite apparently, the spirited city athletic rivalry between Boston and New York has roots and antagonisms that are older and go deeper than the Red Sox-Yankees, Red Sox-Mets, Celtics-Knicks, etc.

Quite obviously no proof of Sockalexis competing against a professional runner was forthcoming; the whole matter quickly vanished from the sports pages and Sockalexis continued training for the Olympic Games.

However, a new far-less-serious controversy concerning him just as quickly arose, this time focused on the running apparel Sockalexis would wear to compete at the Olympic Games in Stockholm.

Following only three official races and just prior to the 1912 Boston Marathon Sockalexis had been invited to join the elite North Dorchester Athletic Association, and he wore the club's racing jersey as he captured second place in his epic struggle with Ryan at the 1912 race. The union between the two was clearly mutually beneficial: The track club gained

another New England-based member who had a distinct
chance of bringing honor to the association, not only at future
Boston Marathons but also the upcoming Olympic Games;
Sockalexis gained vital sponsorship and financial backing
without which he might not be able to travel and compete
on a regular basis. But the idea that Sockalexis would not be
"wearing the colors" of a track club in Maine, that he would be
competing at the Olympic Games wearing a competition jersey
proclaiming "North Dorchester Athletic Association" provoked
the following very editorial-style "news article" in the *Bangor
Commercial.* This headline read: "**SPORTS ARE
AROUSED/ Believe Bangor People Should/ Have Helped
Sockalexis/ FOR B.A.A. MARATHON/ Should Have
Represented Local Organization and Brought Credit/
Nearer Home.**"[11]

The article, sympathetic to Sockalexis, was critical of
local sports followers for not offering the Indian runner even
meager subsidizing, thus insuring that he would represent
the State of Maine when he appeared at the Olympic
Games.

The article stated:

> *There seems to be considerable feeling among
> the local sports that some arrangement could have
> been made whereby Andrew Sockalexis ... could
> have run under the name of some local organiza-
> tion and thus brought some of the credit of his good
> work a little nearer home. Had this been done there
> is little doubt but that he would have carried this
> representation to the Swedish Olympics.*

> *It seems that several weeks before the B.A.A.*
> *race, an effort was made to solicit small subscrip-*
> *tions from local merchants and others to defray*
> *Sockalexis' expenses and thus make it possible*
> *for him to enter the contest. Only a small amount*
> *was secured and later an offer from the North*
> *Dorchester A.A. to run under its name, was ac-*
> *cepted by Sockalexis and consequently about*
> *all the attendant credit of his fine showing*
> *has gone to that club and furthermore he will prob-*
> *ably be compelled to join the Olympic team as a*
> *member of the North Dorchester A.A. since it was*
> *under it that he won the right to a place on the*
> *team.*[12]

It was suggested that had Sockalexis represented a local organization it would most likely have been the Bangor Y.M.C.A., to which both he and his manager, Thomas Daley, were members. The article closed with this prophecy: "A member of the Olympic team, which will probably be the greatest in the history of athletics, hailing from Bangor would be a good thing for the city and it is not improbable that the fleet Indian will distinguish himself abroad as he did in the Boston Marathon."[13]

Runners and other athletes from less popular sports than football, basketball and baseball might smile, shake their heads and ponder the idea that things were not too much different in earlier days than in contemporary times. Only for a brief moment, during the running boom of the mid-1970s and 1980s, did outstanding runners find financial support for their activities. And only those who found the elite spotlight, like

Maine Olympians Joan Benoit Samuelson of Cape Elizabeth
and Bruce Bickford of Benton, need apply.

Clearly, from the starkly blunt language of the newspaper
account, hardly any of the local influential business and city
leaders cared anything about Sockalexis or his running. But
now the opportunity was ripe to climb upon the bandwagon
and affix the community's name to an international winner's
for a relative few dollars. A good point to make here as well is
that Sockalexis was probably finding it increasingly difficult
to travel and compete. Though he listed his occupation
as "athlete" on his marriage certificate, when he married
in November of 1913, he could have hardly survived and
supported a wife in this manner. Previously, he'd identified
himself as "a maker of fancy baskets." As an amateur athlete
for most of these years, he could only accept "expense money."
As Clarence DeMar would make clear in his book, this money
was strictly for travel and room and board. Athletes received
trophies and gifts, like watches and clothing, for winning
performances. There was an extremely rigid code of conduct
for receiving money and its use, as Jim Thorpe would shortly
discover when he was stripped of his Olympic gold medals for
having received money for playing minor league
baseball.

In mid-May a training run by Sockalexis made news. He
was reported to have taken "a practice spin" from Bangor to
Old Town, on Saturday, May 11. He departed from Sweet's
corner clothing store and ran to F.E. Allan & Company's
clothing store in 1 hour, 16 minutes, 57 seconds. Because the
roads were reported as "heavy," he only bettered his time of

three weeks ago by three seconds. It was stated he expected
to run the same route again on Memorial Day and predicted
that, if good conditions existed, he expected to cut about five
minutes off his best previous time for the distance.[14]

A couple of weeks later, a further updating of Sockalexis'
training appeared. This report about his "road work to keep
in condition," noted that he recently ran from the ferry to
Costigan and back. The item ended: "He is receiving much
attention and everyone is interested in him and wants him well
looked after when he goes abroad."[15]

Considering the earlier furor raised questioning
Sockalexis' amateur standing and the significance of his
selection to go to the Olympic Games, it was a very strange
item which appeared in the Saturday, mid-May issue of the
Bangor Daily News under the headline: "**A Challenge/ to
Sockalexis**." [16]

It stated that James Scott, identified as an Old Town
runner, had come into the newspaper office and issued a race
challenge to Sockalexis, daring the much-celebrated athlete to
race him from Old Town to Bangor for a prize of $50. Scott,
out of ignorance or arrogance, was incredibly neglectful of
the huge cost – to Sockalexis and his amateur standing – that
a wagered race would mean. Doing such a race would get
him kicked off the U.S. Olympic team and deny him any
further chance of competing in the Boston Marathon. Scott
even acknowledged that, "of course this isn't big money, but it
shows I mean business, and I want people around here to know
that I'm as good as Sockalexis ever dared to be. I've beaten
him in trial runs, and he knows it."[17]

A reply came quickly to Scott but, even more oddly enough, it didn't come from Sockalexis. In the following Monday's issue of the *Bangor Daily News* came this reply, headlined: **"Scott's Chance,/ if He Really/ Wants to Run."**[18]

Writer Frank Miller explained the obvious: why Sockalexis certainly wouldn't want anything to do with a challenge involving money, whether Scott was formidable or not. There also came the question of how good a runner Scott was, as Miller, a seemingly well-known runner in the area, appeared to be unfamiliar with Scott's name. Miller, of Bangor, said, "if Scott's challenge goes for everyone, and is not confined exclusively to Sockalexis," Miller was ready to race him – from Old Town to Bangor or over any other "reasonable" course. Miller upped the ante: "I am willing to put up $50 a side, and wouldn't mind making it $100." Miller testily commented: "Of course Sockalexis couldn't accept Scott's challenge without forfeiting his amateur standing; and it seems to me Scott had better get a reputation before challenging the leaders, any way. If he really wants a run I'm willing to give him one, and I'm not afraid of the result."

The Bangor newspaper characterized Miller as being "well known for his knowledge of the game as well as for his ability as a runner, in this locality." And, as if entering into the promotional business, without any apparent knowledge of Scott's ability offered, the newspaper editorialized, "if a match is arranged it ought to be a good one. Meantime, Sockalexis has ignored the original challenge."[19]

None of the local newspapers carried any further word about a Scott-Miller match race in the next few days that followed.

Whether or not to provide community financial funding for Sockalexis apparently became a controversial local issue. In an article offered as a news item, but heavily tinged with emotional editorializing, the May 31 issue of the *Bangor Daily News* noted that interest in Maine's first Olympian was heating up and that a committee of prominent local citizens was hurriedly at work trying to raise enough money to allow A. N. Smith, the athletic coach at the University of Maine, and Thomas Daley of Bangor, Sockalexis's original manager, to accompany Sockalexis as coach and as manager/handler, respectively. The action was urged:

> *...because, for the first time in history, the State of Maine has produced an athlete fully qualified to compete against the world...it seems most fitting and proper that Maine's representative should go to Stockholm with an adequate equipment of preliminary training and with skilled coaching and handling.*

> *It should be a matter of local pride that a native son of Maine should be as fit and ready as ample funds can make him, when he toes the mark with the flower of the British, Germans, Italians, Greeks, Canadians, French, Scandinavians from almost all the countries of the world. And it would surely be a reflection upon Maine spirit and loyalty if he should fail for lack of such.*

> *At the B.A.A. meet in Boston, a few weeks*
> *ago, without a trainer, handler, timer or anything*
> *or anybody to gauge his speed, he finished second,*
> *being beaten only at the finish because he had but*
> *little idea of time or distance. He finished strong*
> *and all agree that he could have won at a mile more*
> *to go, or had started his final dash with proper*
> *judgment.*[20]

Continuing to build on the theme of showing support for
Sockalexis, the Indian was described as "a natural running
machine of excellent habits, cool, confident and plucky. His
training up to this time has been running over rough roads
and often without a rub-down. There is no doubt that the boy
is worth giving a show; no reason why he has not a chance to
send the Stars and Stripes to the mast-head when the Marathon
race is over and be in line when the king passes around the
laurel wreaths. Anyway, as they say up in Old Town, 'They'll
have to go some to beat our Injun.'"[21] One seriously doubts, of
course, that was the phrase used on the island or to Sockalexis'
face.

So the problem came down to this: Only the expenses of
the members of the Olympic team were paid – no allowances
were made for trainers and handlers. The article pleaded:
"Unless he has help, Sockalexis will have to go to Sweden
alone and rely on his own resources. What would happen to
him under such conditions can easily be imagined. At least he
would get scant attention."

Apparently a movement had been initiated to raise funds
for the purpose of sending Smith and Daly along and, it was

noted, "decided impetus" had been given to this goal through
"the enlarging of the committee and the assurance that if
$1000 can be raised" both would go. Smith was cited as "one
of the best athletic coaches in the country." It was said that
he had been to England twice and served the American team
at the 1908 Olympic Games "as assistant to the famous Mike
Murphy."[22]

The committee consisted of: Mayor C.W. Mullen, Harry
A. Chapman and Hosea B. Buck, all of Bangor; the Hon.
Herbert Gray, George H. Richardson and O.B. Fernandez, all
of Old Town; and Alden Webster of Orono. Finally, the article
stressed urgency in the matter of raising the funds for Smith
and Daley, since the boat trip for Stockholm was about 10 days
off. It was noted that Smith was already "taking charge" of
Sockalexis' training by having him work out at the University
of Maine.[23]

On June 5 the *Bangor Daily News* carried two very
large, stiffly formal portraits of Sockalexis and Smith, both
ostensively preparing for the upcoming Olympic Games.[24]
The barrel-chested, diminutive Andrew stood solemnly facing
the camera, clad in a white, short sleeve jersey and white
running shorts, plus running shoes. The other portrait was of
a rigidly erect A.N. Smith, his hands behind his back, wearing
turtleneck shirt and blazer, slacks and a beret.

Two days later, the *Bangor Daily News* carried the
following headline: "**SOCKALEXIS WILL/ SHOW
HIS GATE/ Olympic Runner To Try For New Record,
Bangor to Old Town This Afternoon**." The story stated that
Sockalexis would leave the West Market Square in Bangor at

3 o'clock in the afternoon and run to Old Town, hoping to beat
his previous record for the distance which was 1 hour,
16 minutes and 57 seconds. The account proudly boasted: "As
the running time of the electrics [the train] is one hour and ten
minutes for this distance, some idea may be gained of the way
the Indian can cover the ground."[25]

Following the run, that night, Sockalexis and trainer A.N.
Smith were to leave for Boston. After observing Olympic tryouts
in track and field, the pair would then depart for New York.

The entire American team was scheduled to embark
upon the voyage to Sweden on Friday. The article continued:
"Sockalexis is in fine trim and with the sole care and attention
of an experienced trainer like Smith, ought to be in shape
to run well in the great Olympic Marathon. Mr. Smith has
received a letter from Mike Murphy, the famous trainer,
expressing gratification that the Indian is to be handled by
Smith." It added that while the fundraising to send Smith had
"insured" the trainer's presence, the amount was still short of
"being fully adequate to meet the demands of the trip" and
that more money was needed.

In the last paragraph the editorializing went even further:
"In Sockalexis the State has a very promising representative
for the greatest honors of the Olympiad and he should be
amply equipped with funds to enable him to compete with the
world to the best advantage. He will run under the colors of the
United States, only, and if he wins, the State of Maine will get
the full credit."[26]

The results of Andrew's publicized training run appeared
in the following day's *Bangor Daily News*, with a headline

which declared that his "farewell run" had been completed in "record-breaking time."[27]

According to the account, Sockalexis, joined by "a large crowd at Sweet's drug-store," set off for Old Town right at the stroke of 3 p.m. Old Town's Main Street was said to be "lined with people when the Indian crossed the mark in front of F.E. Allen's clothing store, just 13 miles and 300 yards from the start, accompanied by automobiles and cheered all the way." Andrew's time was "snapped" at 1 hour, 14 minutes and 49 seconds, beating his previous best by better than two minutes. It was further noted that the run was made "not under the best conditions, a heavy cross-wind prevailing over much of the course and the footing none too good." Sockalexis told those gathered that he felt "fresh" and could have turned around and run back to Bangor. The article reported, too, that Sockalexis and Smith had, indeed, departed on the midnight train for Boston and were expected to leave for Stockholm the following Friday on the steamer Finland.[28]

Sockalexis was now almost daily news. A short item, headlined "**Quick Glance**" in the June 11 edition of the *Bangor Daily News*, simply noted that Sockalexis and trainer Smith were residing at the Copley Square Hotel in Boston and working out at Revere Beach. The pair was scheduled to leave Wednesday night for New York, with the ship leaving that Friday at 9 a.m. for the long voyage to Sweden.[29]

While Sockalexis was en route to Sweden, the Bangor "Marathon" was held as part of Bangor's carnival week. It was a scheduled 10-mile run, from Monument Square in Orono to Bangor's Maplewood Park *[Author's note: Maplewood Park is now known as Bass Park].* Registered for the event were runners from the University of Maine, Bates, Bowdoin and Colby, as well as two Penobscots from Indian Island, Arthur Neptune and John Lewis. The boastful Mr. Scott, by the way, isn't listed among the entries but there is an F.R. Miller, who very well could be Frank Miller.

On June 25, there was a lengthy analysis of the Olympic marathon in an article, featuring an unnamed "expert," in the *Bangor Daily News*. The headline blared out: "**PICK SOCKALEXIS OLYMPIC FAVORITE/ His Chances in Swedish Marathon/ Better Than Those of Ryan or/ DeMar Says Expert.**"[30]

The story, as it becomes abundantly clear in the first sentence, was written shortly after the Boston Marathon, by a writer for the *Boston Post*. The Bangor newspaper apparently saved it for use much closer to the actual Olympic event itself. The article opened: "With the muddy track not yet dry over which Mike Ryan ran his record-breaking Marathon to victory last Friday already speculation is rife as to the chances of the American 25-milers on July 14 after they leave the tape on the long grind in the Swedish Olympics in Stockholm, says the *Boston Post*."[31]

The article featured a bit of patriotic bravado, claiming an American victory was all but assured: "Of course, no one will admit anything but an American victory in the Olympic Marathon, which point is conceded by many foreign authorities on sport, who can see no place for England, one of our greatest rivals, in this branch of the game." However, picking the actual winner, it was conceded, was much tougher, especially since the condition of the great Clarence DeMar was in question: "But as to probable winner of the Olympic event, there is much division among the local track sharps, more than perhaps would have occurred had Clarence DeMar, the victor in the classic last year, run over the course on April 19, instead of covering it in an automobile. Consequently, DeMar, while a known quantity a year ago, and the same may be said for 1910, is somewhat of a stumbling block when it comes to the fine figuring on a winner at Stockholm."[32]

From any runner's perspective, this thinking, concerning DeMar, is quite arguable. If DeMar had no need to run a grueling marathon on April 19th to qualify to run what would certainly be a hot, summer marathon just three months later, he was truly taking the most prudent steps in terms of being best properly prepared for the Olympic running test. Later, in this same article, the writer would completely contradict himself on this same issue.

This article seems especially important because it sized up the chances of the large American contingent—12 American runners were selected and participated—and narrowed the field down to Andrew Sockalexis as the United States runner with the best chance of winning.

The unnamed writer continued:

> *Naturally, just now Mike Ryan is the centre of all eyes and the New Yorkers can see nothing but the Irish-American A.C. star as the eventual win-*

ner in the Olympic Marathon. Farther away from New York, while Ryan deservedly has admirers by the score, he is forced to split the honors with Andrew Sockalexis, the Old Town Indian, who, under the colors of the North Dorchester A.A. came in second in the recent B.A.A. event. For while the Indian did not win the classic, by many of those who watched him along the course as well as those who saw him finish he is considered the most dangerous rival and well worthy of a place with DeMar and Ryan as a trio of the foremost long distance men that have ever been assembled to represent America abroad. All three are record breakers, all have the grit, endurance and plugging ability needed in the Marathon game, and while there may be other favorites in the list picked for the American team, and perhaps a dark horse hidden in the bunch, the three runners named will stand, for the present at least, a head above their mates.[33]

Here, the writer seems to contradict his earlier remark, that because DeMar hadn't run a marathon recently his status should be considered questionable: "As to which of the three will win final honors abroad that is a difficult matter to say, but the writer is inclined to favor the man who has run the least Marathons. This is based in the theory, perhaps a personal one, that a runner can only make good just so many times in a Marathon; that is, every 25-miler grind takes just so much out of him and lessens his chances of winning on some future occasion."[34]

Exactly. Especially, if that marathon is coming up just three months later. Yes, the writer is really talking about total marathons run in a career, but this is also the precise reason DeMar was wise for not running Boston in mid-April, if he hoped to have his best chance at winning the Olympic marathon in mid-July. With the exception of J.J. Caffery, it had been the history of the B.A.A. run up to 1912 that a one-time winner of the event never repeated. The writer's theory about a marathoner "making good" only so many times would require far more history for the event to be thoroughly destroyed. DeMar, after taking more than a decade off from competitive running, would return to score six more Boston triumphs, including his last one at the remarkable age of 41. Henri Cote and Bill Rodgers would win four times at Boston, and the list goes on and on of marathoners performing capably and victoriously over extended careers.

The writer conjectured: "The runner reaches one supreme moment in his career, grasps the standard of victory, but rarely again crosses the tape with the first few leaders."[35]

It's this kind of thinking and writing which should make any reader skeptical of the kind of journalistic expertise appearing in the newspapers of this era. These writers are far too concerned with how a runner "looks" as he finishes, so they never would have regarded a great runner who does not look particularly good as a contender; one immediately thinks of performers like the legendary Czech runner Emil Zatopek, who won the 5,000 meter race, 10,000 meter race and the marathon, all in the 1952 Olympic Games, yet was always described as appearing in terrible shape from the earliest stages of any of his races. Further, these writers are too concerned with how a runner is handled and trained; yet, it will be quickly discovered how coaches destroyed American chances at the 1912 marathon with too much strenuous training beforehand, too many group dynamics for a very singular sport (forcing all the runners to conform to one training regimen), and too much strategizing before the run. Indeed, it will be the "outsider," the American runner named to the team at the last moment, who turned out to be the only one to earn a medal (the late arrival Strobino who replaced Hatch). It isn't hard for a knowledgeable runner to quickly form disparaging thoughts about these so-called "experts." They often appear to be heavy smokers, heavy drinkers with little understanding of running (one possible exception might be Arthur Duffey, who was a champion sprinter but seemed largely ignorant of long distance running) who do little personal research and largely editorialize.

Interestingly enough, the unnamed writer came to a solid assessment almost in spite of himself: "To the mind of the writer, if this holds good, the chances of Sockalexis, who has yet to arrive at the supreme station of victor, are better than those of either Ryan or DeMar in the Olympic race."[36]

Yes, the writer wound up right on target. Neither Ryan, who dropped out, nor DeMar, who struggled to a 12th place finish, were factors, while Sockalexis came on strong to finish fourth. Yet, DeMar had victories in his future that make his name synonymous with the greatest runners who have ever lived. And the writer's thinking does not allow at all for what makes marathoning, and most individual athletic events for that matter, truly exciting: The possibility that someone will have that spectacular break-through to the next level of ability or just have the one sensational moment, the perfect race which may never happen again but happened in the one race the athlete most would like.

The writer went on to characterize Sockalexis this way:

A year ago, in the B.A.A. Marathon, Sockalexis, a fairly green runner, finished far behind the leaders. In the fall, in the Brockton race, the Indian finished third. As everyone knows, on April 19 he finished second, mind you, in the fastest time that a Marathon has yet been run. DeMar's time for the B.A.A. in 1911 was 2:21:39 3-5 seconds and later at Brockton, in covering a distance of 23 1/2 miles, it took him 2 hours, 29 minutes, 55 4-5 seconds, more time than he used up in the mile and a half longer event. In the recent B.A.A. run the Indian, second man, came in 2:21:52 3-5 seconds, or within a few seconds of the time made by DeMar, the winner a year before, and certainly finished in fine condition. On actual figures, the Indian in the two years has shown decided improvement, while as for DeMar, there certainly was a slow down last year, and at the present distance we do not know just what he could do the distance in. And what has been said of DeMar in comparison to Sockalexis also applies to Ryan, for he has been at the game for more years than the Indian and last week attained the zenith of his ambitions.

Consequently, having won the B.A.A. Marathon, the question arises, has he another victory tucked away? The experience of the past would say that he has not.

> *Of the three favorites, Sockalexis, DeMar and Ryan, another question arises: Which will resist the climactic effects of Sweden the best? Will it be the Indian, fitted by nature to stand many of the vicissitudes of wind and weather, or the white man, brought up under American conditions? It is history that climate was a big figure in the Marathon at the last Olympic held outside of London, and the change was sufficient to wreck Thomas P. Morrissey of Yonkers, winner here in 1903, while the best showing was made by the team selected on this side was by Joe Forshaw, who finished third in the London race. J.J. Hayes, the victor in the last Olympic run, was not an official selection. While it is possible that the Swedish climate may not affect the runners from this side, on the point that it probably will, it would seem that of the trio under discussion the chances of Sockalexis coming through it the least scathed are the best.*[37]

Outrageous racism aside, the writer, ironically enough, was more on target than he could have ever imagined on this point.

Running a marathon in mid afternoon in the middle of July, the middle of summer, at Stockholm would prove incredibly dangerous. It would result in the first fatality in Olympic history, and the only death as a result of actual competition in Olympic history to date, when a Portuguese runner collapsed and later died as a result of the heat and humidity. The near 2 o'clock start would be changed for the next Olympiad and for every Olympic Games since.

It's also interesting that the writer raised the specter of an unknown winning, citing the 1908 marathon, yet didn't offer any suggestion that it could happen again, as it would with two completely unheralded South African runners and one last-minute replacement runner from the United States taking the first three places and the medals at the 1912 Olympic marathon.

Because wire service reports did not come as rapidly as they do today, news about the American athletes came in brief, and not always correct, blurbs. The Wednesday, June 26 *Bangor Daily News* reported, in a crisp note, that Mike Ryan had sprained his ankle while training on board the ship bound for Sweden.[38] But just two days later, the June 28 issue of the *Bangor Daily News*, in an equally succinct note, quoted Mike Ryan as refuting the injury rumor.[39]

Chapter 6

Sockalexis widely regarded as Olympic race favorite

Just a week prior to the Boston Marathon newspaper headlines rang out with the concern that nationally-renowned trainer Mike Murphy might be too ill to lead the U.S. Olympic team into the competition at Stockholm. According to the report from Philadelphia, which did not identify his malady, Murphy was "on his legs...but far from being a well man." The task, it was said, of being responsible for nearly 100 men while making such an arduous journey would surely be too much for him. "To prepare the Pennsylvania team for the Intercollegiate meet is as much as Mike will be able to endure, and he will need a long rest after the affair is over," the report stated. Several trainers, including one from the East and one from the West, were suggested replacements. So who would replace Murphy? James E. Sullivan, secretary of the Olympic committee, was quoted as saying, "I do not know. Every man is at liberty to apply. We are not worrying about the trainer just now. So far Mike Murphy is the official coach and until we are sure that he is not well enough to take the job the Olympic committee will take no action."[1]

The reports of Murphy's demise proved, ultimately, premature. He did accompany the team to Stockholm as the overall coach.

On July 4, 1912, F.E. Allen of Old Town shared a letter he'd received from Andrew Sockalexis with the *Bangor Daily News*. Sockalexis was quoted, from his letter, as being "in magnificent condition" and feeling as though there was "no question" that he would be the winner of the marathon if he were in the same condition on the day of the race as he was now. He also reported that on June 25th he ran 16 miles in 1 hour and 30 minutes, breaking all his previous Bangor records for that distance. Finally, he noted that he found the ocean trip to be "very pleasant" and was pleased with his European surroundings.[2]

Two days later, on July 6, the *Bangor Daily News* carried an account from Stockholm, by an unnamed correspondent, which pronounced in bold headlines: "**PREDICT AMERICANS/ WILL SWEEP THE FIELD**." Noting that on the eve of the Olympic Games, the American team members were all in "fine condition," the second sentence of the lead paragraph brashly proclaimed: "It is so fully recognized by all the competitors that the Americans will sweep the field that the others have largely lost interest."

Large crowds of all nationalities were said to be watching the Americans train. Ralph Rose, a San Francisco weight thrower, was reported to have put the shot 7 inches further than the world's record for the event. The marathon runners, reportedly, "jogged over the whole course and seemed to be in fine form." Whether they actually ran all 26 miles or were just running sections of it wasn't made clear. The last sentence of the report noted that the Americans "were put to sleep on the Finland at 9 o'clock tonight"; so, apparently, at least previous to the start of the games, the team members were still living on the ship they'd traveled upon to Sweden.[3]

On that same July 6 date, the weekly *Old Town Enterprise* offered at the very top of its Saturday edition front page, centered between two ads, the actual post card sent to its editor by Sockalexis, under the headline: "**ANDREW SOCKALEXIS ARRIVES/AT ANTWERP.**"[4]

It read:

Dear Mr. Brown:—

Arrived here to - day after ten days on the ocean. Sea did not affect me a bit. Am even stronger. We trained on board coming over. We have a dandy place now to train. Having a grand time and am seeing many beautiful and curious sights. We shall be at Sweden June 29th. and I run July 14th. Will leave for home July 20th. Am in great form and hope to make good.

A. Sockalexis[5]

Brown, in a short note following the post card, noted that the citizens of Old Town "will be pleased with the optimistic

spirit in which it is written and we all hope he will be able
to bring the much coveted trophy home. It will be glory
and honor enough for him as an individual and add no little
notoriety to us as a city."[6]

A story published on July 8 in the *Bangor Daily News*
was headlined: "**Marathon a Puzzle/Says Mike Murphy.**"[7]
Writing from Stockholm on July 5, Murphy, who most
definitely went with the team after all, offered the following
brief insights into the team's chances of a marathon victory.
He was clearly impressed with Sockalexis in spite of his brief
acquaintanceship with him. Murphy said he felt the 1912
marathon run would surely prove to be "as much of a puzzle
to us" as it was to the U.S. team in 1908. He said the team
was presently at 11 men *[Author's note: Strobino, the 12th
member, was en route on his own]* and that only the race itself
would prove who the best of the Americans, and even then
"our best may even then be poorer than the best from England
and Sweden." There were just three veterans returning from
the 1908 team. They included: Forshaw, who finished third in
that year; Tewanima, who was 12th; and the unlucky Ryan,
who did not finish that year...and was destined to not finish
an Olympic marathon again. The new eight members had
not worked out enough, Murphy said, for him to determine
who the best prospects were. But he did offer the following
appraisals: "DeMar of Boston looks very good, as do
Sockalexis, an Indian, and Lilley of Boston. However,
this is such an uncertain event that I would not dare to
predict what the men will do or, who is the best of the
lot..."[8]

On the actual day of the Olympic marathon, July 14, 1912, taking place half a world away, another short analysis of America's prospects in the marathon was offered in "**Arthur Duffey's Column**" in the *Boston Post*.[9] Duffey began with an unabashedly bold remark that the marathon "promises to be more sensational than any of the other events yet held." Certainly today, drawing close to 100 years later, the 1912 Olympics are remembered for just one athlete and two events – Jim Thorpe and his unequaled "double" of winning both the pentathlon and the decathlon. In fairness to Duffey, the first day of the decathlon was held just the day before, and the grueling 10-category event would conclude almost simultaneously with the afternoon's running of the marathon. Duffey, however, made it abundantly clear he, a former celebrated sprinter, had more admiration for the marathoners than any of the other Olympic performers. He wrote:

> *Incidentally if I were a contender, I would rather win the Marathon than all the other contests put together. It takes a real champion to win such a contest. A runner who can win the race today and especially against such a field of runners is indeed the greatest champion of all. Of course everybody is trying to pick the winner of the race. Many of the critics have burned the midnight oil trying to dope out the possible victor. But all the dope counts for naught. If there is one contest in which past performances count for little, it is a Marathon race. In nearly every Olympic Marathon race that has been held, it has generally been the runner who has not been given the slightest lookin [sic] that has run away with the prize. Today it looks to be the same old story.*[10]

Duffey made quick mention of Sockalexis, DeMar, Ryan and Lilley as being among the American threats, but then commented that "the foreigners, however, appear more formidable" than at any previous time in Olympic history. After noting that "I wouldn't be surprised if one of the foreign champions ran away with the honors," Duffey cited Finland and Sweden runners for their long distance prowess, citing Finlander Kohlemainen for his victories in the 5000 and 10,000 meter runs at Stockholm. Frenchman Jean Bouin was acknowledged, for his strong second place finish in the 5000, and Englishman A. Jackson, for his win in the 200 meter run. Duffey, being ever diplomatic, then returned to supporting the U.S. contingent: "The Americans, however, will strongly look to Andrew Sockalexis or Mike Ryan to hold the American end up, and if they can find their American form they should win."[11]

The *Boston Sunday Post*, carrying its "Price Five Cents" notification in the upper left hand corner, had the following front page headline on July 14, 1912: "**ALL EYES ON/ THE MARATHON/ America's Hopes on Sockalexis/ in the Great Olympic Race at Stockholm Today**." One section of information on the Olympics carried the schedule that the 400 meter relay race trials, the hammer throw, and the second day of the decathlon joined the marathon as events for the day. Another section contained the results of competition from the previous day, including notification that one "James Thorpe, Carlisle Indian School" had accumulated the most points on the first day of competition in the decathlon. Following these entries came the following sub-heading: "**FULL**

MARATHON RACE/ IN TOMORROW'S POST." It was stated that a complete account of Sunday's marathon would appear in the Monday morning edition, sent by cable by the *Post*'s "special commissioner to the games," Howard G. Reynolds. Reynolds's succinct impressions about the outcome of the marathon also appeared on the front page.[12]

Reynolds proved to be just as great a fan of the marathon as Duffey. He began: "With the great Olympic Marathon, the real climax of the meet, on the eve of decision, interest in everything else is overshadowed. Nothing else is discussed." That seems hard to believe, considering Thorpe's extraordinary performances and the respect they earned around the world and even from the king of Sweden. Reynolds added, "Interest in the class long distance run is at fever heat and discussions pro and con regarding its outcome gain in warmth, to continue until the immense field of representatives from almost every country in the world started over the dusty roads of Stockholm."[13] Reynolds' truly ironic choice of words, "fever heat," would not only prove metaphorically apt but perfectly appropriate to describe the actual climate the runners faced that day.

Reynolds, too, acknowledged that picking a favorite was next to impossible, noting that "more than at any time in the history of the Olympics is the outcome in doubt." The first name Reynolds felt "takes precedence in the argument" was "the sturdy, strong" Kohlemainen from Finland. "Then in turn," Reynolds stated, "come the names of Andrew Sockalexis, the American Indian; James Corkery of Canada and McArthur of South Africa." Reynolds proved a knowledgeable and accurate judge of marathon running talent, picking the ultimate winner, McArthur, and the fourth place finisher, Sockalexis, and then allowed himself a little latitude, noting there was "shift after shift in favoritism, while interspersed with the chances pro and con of these four is an echo of 'dark horses.'" The Finns, Reynolds stated, boasted Kohlemainen would "outdistance his rivals as no Marathoner has ever done before."[14] On marathon day, alas, Kohlemainen would prove to be another casualty of the heat and drop out.

In the same issue of the *Boston Post*, another writer appraised the chances of the Americans and reached the same conclusion Duffey and Reynolds had – Andrew Sockalexis had the best chance to win of any runner in the select field. Taking "a second look at the American contenders and their prospects" was Robert A. Fowler, "the famous American marathoner." In a promotional note on the front page of the *Boston Post*, leading the reader to the sports pages for Fowler's analysis, was the remark that Fowler had "selected his favorite for the race and goes deeply into his reasons for pinning his hopes on the athlete he expects will win the race for America."[15] And that athlete was Andrew Sockalexis. Ironically, it was Fowler who would serve as Sockalexis' bicycle-riding trainer at the 1913 Boston Marathon and both would receive criticism when Sockalexis narrowly failed to capture victory.

The Page 16 story carried the following headline: **"KOHLEMAINEN AND/ CORKERY STAR MEN/ Will Give Indian Battle for First Place in Long Olympic/ Grind."**[16] Following several paragraphs that were celebratory in nature, concerning the big event finally being at hand,

Fowler discussed his own credentials for understanding the marathon in another few paragraphs and then he went into specific analysis of 11 of the 12 Americans who'd made the trip to Stockholm for the marathon. The runner Fowler overlooked was Lewis Tewanima, who was also running the 10,000 meter race.

Ryan, the most recent winner of the Boston Marathon, was dismissed for several reasons; the New Yorker is "heavily built...thrives on cool weather and the midsummer heat will prove fatal to him." That Ryan was inclined towards having "accidents" (injuries) and "naturally inclined to put on flesh" also troubled Fowler.[17] The writer couldn't have been more accurate in his projection: The heat proved "fatal" to Ryan and he dropped out of his second straight Olympic race.

The popular man from Yale who led so much of the 1912 Boston Marathon, John Gallagher, also did not figure to succeed, according to Fowler. Gallagher was "too fast naturally to be a real marathoner of a winning type," suggested Fowler, who further predicted – very wrongly – that Gallagher wouldn't finish the marathon.[18]

The perplexing specter of DeMar, the 1911 champion who had not competed at Boston in 1912, left Fowler believing that there were several "ironclad facts" which "militate against him." The foremost of these, Fowler asserted, was that DeMar was not "physically endowed for the hard strain of the marathon."

While acknowledging that DeMar, indeed, had already run and won a great many long distance races, Fowler felt DeMar was "not the kind to thrive on repeated marathons." Finally, Fowler believed the layoff was good for DeMar but bemoaned the fact that he hadn't been able to add any weight to "his skinny frame" during the time away.[19] Fowler might have appeared very accurate about DeMar's performance at the 1912 Olympics...but he couldn't have been more wrong than he was about the future of one of history's greatest marathoners.

Two runners Fowler felt weren't capable of winning but might place high in the standings were Dick Piggott and Sidney Hatch. "I look for him (Piggott) to make an excellent showing," wrote Fowler. He then added that Piggott was only "an average performer" but one who could "plug away" over the dusty Swedish roads under a "scorching sun" and is "well endowed for the struggle." Hatch, from Chicago, was seen as a proven commodity for "placing well" up in the field.[20] Fowler's prophecy for Piggott was very accurate as the veteran finished ninth; however, Hatch was the man who left the team at the 12th hour, allowing Strobino the special opportunity of which he would make the best.

Former Olympian Forshaw, from St. Louis, simply "has reached the end of his tether as a marathoner," declared Fowler, feeling that the veteran was no longer capable of competing with younger, stronger athletes.[21]

Erxleben of St. Louis and Harry Smith of New York "do not rate as formidable contenders," Fowler stated. Smith was said to be a good 15-mile runner, "but has not shown any particular ability to continue on..."[22]

Tom Lilley, a teammate of Sockalexis' from the North Dorchester A.A., was dismissed by Fowler with the curt remark that: "I have my doubts that he (Lilley) can improve on his good work at the last Boston."[23]

Fowler misjudged what Forshaw (10th place) had left in his tank and what Erxleben could do among the world's best (8th place), but neither Smith nor Lilley were able to crack the top 12 finishers.

That left Andrew Sockalexis, Fowler's pick as the best American in the field, and the best marathoner in the world. Fowler offered this reasoning:

> *Now I come to the American contender, upon whom I am certain the United States can pin its hopes to a strong certainty. If there is any man of the American team to win, Andrew Sockalexis, the Oldtown [sic], Me., Indian of the North Dorchester A.A., I am certain will prove to be the one. He is by all odds one of the greatest Marathoners I have ever seen and every element of distance running enters in to back up this estimate of him and his abilities.*
>
> *To begin with he is a great runner, naturally, the only drawback to his arrival at the heights as a champion being his lack of experience to date. Indians seem to take to distance running like a duck to water and Sockalexis comes naturally by his inclination toward the sport. His father was a great runner and young Sockalexis is following in his footsteps. Where Sockalexis differs from the average Indian athlete is in his superior mental equipment. A quiet, stoical athlete, he absorbs more from comment with his white rivals than appears on the surface. Since making the trip to Sweden he has picked up a fund of running knowledge that will add completely to his better than bright chances previous to the departure to Sweden.[24]*

Leaving aside his troubling racist remarks, particularly about the average Indian's "mental equipment," Fowler, finally, represented a writer who cited Sockalexis' youthfulness and obvious inexperience and did not condemn him unfairly.

Fowler continued:

> *Just at present he is at the zenith of his powers as an athlete, his arrival having been slow but steady. Speed of just the proper degree joined to unlimited endurance are the two big factors that make him as prime a favorite as the American team can muster, while the climatic conditions should hardly cause any apprehension so far as he is concerned.*[25]

This remark, again, seems racist and extremely unfair. Having lived his whole life in Maine, Sockalexis is not going to find a very hot day comfortable simply because he is Native American.

Fowler then characterized Sockalexis this way:

> *What impresses me most about him is his spirit of enthusiasm and ambition, a larger point of consideration than might appear at first sight. There is that about the Marathon when it is a novelty that puts spurs to the spirit of a genuine racer and I have never seen the point so exemplified as in the case of the Indian. No defeat has cast him down or discouraged him from the idea that he will ultimately be the champion of champions, and with this idea firmly settled in his mind, it augurs well for his mental attitude and its effect in today's great test.*

> *Those who have competed in Marathons re-*
> *alize what this can mean. After the race has lost*
> *its variety and appeal, the fact has an effect on a*
> *competitor more than can be realized. It becomes*
> *a grind, which it has not yet become to Sockalexis.*

> *I was particularly struck with the little Indian's*
> *attitude toward the race in the last BAA Marathon*
> *in which he ran a splendid race, finishing only*
> *27 seconds [sic...Author's note: it was actually 34*
> *seconds] behind the winner, Ryan. In my estima-*
> *tion, a victory for the Indian was lacking only in his*
> *failure to use judgment, which is no criticism, as it*
> *could hardly be expected that he, with his lack of ad-*
> *visers and experience, would be able to make a per-*
> *fect plan of campaign. Pure running ability brought*
> *him to his high position, and judgment would have*
> *undoubtedly captured the high honor of winner.*[26]

So Fowler, too, belongs to the legion believing in the
value of bike-riding advisers, but at least he did not condemn
Sockalexis for completely throwing away the 1912 Boston race.
Added Fowler about Sockalexis' earlier races:

> *Physically he was stronger than any man I ever*
> *saw finishing the Marathon over the B.A.A. course,*
> *his condition being a repetition of that shown in*
> *his race in the Brockton Marathon of 1911, one of*
> *his very first races, in which it first impressed me*
> *that here was the coming champion. On this occa-*
> *sion lack of judgment caused him to lose out after*
> *leading Clarence De Mar by three minutes at the*
> *10-mile mark...He can run his races alone and un-*
> *aided, and this alone will stand out as a possible*
> *heavy factor for his good in his race today.*

> *Another point in his favor is that for the first time in his career he has been able to enjoy the benefits of perfect training at Stockholm. It goes without saying that a victory by the Indian would be a very popular one among the Americans. His personality is of the best and it only remains for him to accomplish the victory to insure him a standing in the athletic world, which I believe he deserves.* [27]

Just how "perfect" that training was is particularly suspect. DeMar, Sockalexis and others bitterly complained that the marathon runners were over trained and forced to break from their personal training habits to conform to a daily group program. That the latecomer, the unheralded Strobino – the only American athlete not subjected to this training regimen – was the only United States athlete to finish in the top three and receive a medal seems stark proof the criticism is just.

Fowler then devoted a few paragraphs to the top foreign competition in the race. He cited the Finn, Kohlemainen, and the veteran runner "with savy *[sic]*," Tornos of Sweden. He devoted a couple of sentences to James Corkery of Canada, noting that the Canadian ace had a good record on hot days. Of Corkery, he concluded: "Grit and stamina are the long suits of the Canadian in addition to his physical qualities. He and Sockalexis are worthy and well-matched rivals, equally deserving of winning on account of their personal as well as athletic qualities..."[28] The irony of Fowler's last predictions, concerning Kohlemainen and especially Corkery and his "good record on hot days," is that both would drop out of the race on the blistering hot day at Stockholm.

* * *

Chapter 7

Sockalexis runs courageous fourth in Olympic Marathon

SOUTH AFRICAN
WINS MARATHON

**McArthur Defeats Pick of World's Runners —
Gertshaw, Another South African, Is Second,
Strobino of America Third — Winner's
Time Was 2 Hours 36 Minutes**

**Sockalexis, Picked as
the Winner, Finishes
in Fourth Place**

POOR JUDGMENT LOST
THE RACE FOR AMERICA

**7 Americans in First
12—De Mar Was
12th Man**

FINISH OF LEADERS
IN BIG MARATHON

Winner—K.K. McArthur of South Africa. Time: 2h 36m
Second—W. Gertshaw of South Africa. Time: 2h 37m 52s
Third—Gaston Strobino of Paterson, N.J. Time: 2h 38m 42s
 4—Andrew Sockalexis, Old Town, Me [Author's note –
  Time: 2h 42m 07s]
 5—J. Duffy, Canada [Author's note – Time: 2h 42m 18s]
 6—S. Jacobsson, Sweden
 7—John J. Gallagher, Yale University
 8—Joseph Erxleben, Missouri A.C., St. Louis
 9—Richard Piggott, North Dorchester A.A.
 10—Joseph Forshaw, Jr., Missouri A.C.
 11—E. Fabre, Canada
 12—Clarence H. De Mar, North Dorchester A.A.

The multiple lines, multiple deck format for headlines in print journalism's earlier days practically provided the whole story without need to read the text. The first two decks ("SOUTH AFRICAN..." and "McArthur Defeats...") covered three columns of the *Boston Post* and then the newspaper placed the rest of the headline decks and copy from the story into one column. Here, in arguably Sockalexis' most important race and his one and only truly international race, there are several different accounts. They are varied and detailed. For the most part, they offer criticism of Sockalexis and of the American strategy, of "holding back" too long and allowing the two South Africans to run off with the victory.[1]

Harold Reynolds' account in the *Boston Post* is reverently respectful of Kenneth K. McArthur's effort, but he is blunt in his assessment that Sockalexis, by virtue of his very strong finish, held back too long and should have been the Olympic champion. He blamed the American strategy – though he did not condemn marathon coach/runner Mike Ryan by name. And he was not all that respectful of Strobino's third place finish. DeMar stated, in his book *Marathon*, that because Strobino was the only one spared the uniform, regimented training schedule imposed by Ryan, he was the only American rested and properly trained enough to capture a medal.[2] Sockalexis, at a special ceremony to honor him in Old Town upon his return from the Olympics, also very bluntly said that he felt Strobino had profited from being spared from training with the team and was not a deserving medal winner.[3]

For his part, *Boston Post* columnist Arthur Duffey was not nearly so harsh; however, he was not in Stockholm and, presumably, was writing his column from the results and special correspondent Reynolds' dispatches. Duffey merely condemned the heat as having, once again, derailed American hopes.

Duffey congratulated South Africa for furnishing "the surprise" in the Marathon at Stockholm just as the American Johnny Hayes had done in the London Olympic Games of 1908. He asked: "What happened to the American Marathoners?" After claiming the United States "was never represented by such a formidable list of pluggers in the games as this year," citing Sockalexis and Mike Ryan by name as well as "the rest of the string from the North Dorchester A.A.," Duffey stated:

> *Apparently it was the same old story: climactic conditions were too much for them. Under the circumstances the victories of McArthur and his teammate were all the greater. From all account Sockalexis, the Oldtown [sic] Indian, was a great favorite before the grind by the American contingent, but there was a hunch going the rounds that McArthur, the South African, would be the runner to cop the prize.[4]*

Reynolds, however, was not nearly so sympathetic about the climactic considerations. He very clearly thought terrible strategy cost the Americans the overall victory.

Reynolds' opening sentence in his *Post* account read: "K.K. McArthur, a strong-hearted, tireless son of South Africa, placed his name high in the annals of international athletics today when the crowning event of the Olympics, the Marathon, brought him the full meed of glory as victor."[5] Characterizing McArthur as "weary and dust-begrimed" at the finish, Reynolds gave the victor's official finishing time as a generally-speaking unimpressive 2 hours, 36 minutes. The *Post* correspondent's second paragraph gave praise to South Africa and Chris Gertshaw for capturing second.

Incidentally, for the journalists of the time, spelling, particularly correct spelling of proper names, rarely seemed to be of much concern. Some accounts referred to the second-place South African as "Gitshaw" or "Gitsham" rather than "Gertshaw." Kohlemainen's name, too, found a variety of spellings, including "Kolehmainen" and "Kolemainen." *[Author's note: The preferred spelling for this manuscript*

will be "Gertshaw" and "Kohlemainen," using the spellings
offered by Reynolds, who was actually present and his writing,
while very opinionated, shows a conciseness that led this
author to trust him over others.]

It is in Reynolds' third paragraph that he blasted the effort of the Americans: "Baffled and with a plan of campaign well thought out but poorly accomplished, the Americans upon whom fell the bulk of reliance abandoned the certain favors of fortune for the bare rewards of extreme caution."[6]

Reynolds then credited Strobino for his surprising effort: "But one man, Gaston Strobino of Paterson, N.J., a supplementary member of the American team, made his race with the correct balance of judgment. His reward, unexpected in the extreme, came with the not despised laurels of third place."[7]

Then came the remarks for Sockalexis, to be repeated in other newspaper accounts in the days to follow, that have damned him forever with the idea that he should have been the Olympic champion: "Fresh and strong, running like a champion, but too late to be the real champion that he should have been, followed Andrew Sockalexis, America's sturdiest hope, fourth, when he might have been acclaimed as the uncrowned peer of all the world."[8]

Reynolds briefly returned to his tribute to McArthur, the "genuine champion," noting that he deserved all the applause, all the acclamation because his victory was "set in the hard bedrock of fact." Concerning McArthur, Reynolds concluded: "He won and won gloriously, cleanly and by displaying his powers of running and without stint."[9]

But by his fifth paragraph the newspaper columnist returned with renewed ardor to his full scale condemnation of America's failed "policies" in approaching a marathon victory. Following up his sincere respect for McArthur's "unstinting" attempt to win at all costs, Reynolds wrote: "There was the rub when the long details of factors that held America from victory paraded into view. In the final analysis the American stars were niggardly with their great reservoirs of running ability but the blame rests less with any one of them as with a plan of campaign that petered out when excessive conscientiousness replaced all disposition to take the initiative and run the race undaunted by conditions."[10]

So, Reynolds made it clear he was not at all upset with the individual athletes, but his virulent attack seems strange in that he did not condemn the coaching by name. Here's Reynolds' rather theatrical version of how America's fatal strategy was set before the U.S. marathoners:

Caution was the watchword given the American contenders and caution held full sway until it was too late despite heroic efforts to overcome the tremendous handicap. Wisdom lay in the instructions given the hopes of the United States. 'Go slowly in the first part of the race and the hot sun will have cooked off the impetuous, speeding foreign leaders by the time the grinding test of the final stages arrives. Then go out and win.' To better than the letter the instructions were followed out. Far back in the ruck the Americans, all but one [Strobino], jogged along serenely confident that when the broiling sun had got in its work, the leaders would fall back, but they waited in vain and postponed their plans to start in and make their advance to the front until the proper moment had vanished. Then, when the climb, to the heights of a vanished goal had begun in earnest, the running of the Americans showed, in spite of its futility, that the United States has its distance runners of heart and stamina.[11]

Here, Reynolds gave an extremely poignant, vivid description of Sockalexis' attempt to overcome the failed strategy, and his writer's passion and compassion were glaringly evident.

Reynolds wrote:

Sockalexis and Gallagher stood out in bold relief as the great battle to recover lost ground began. Speed is Gallagher's middle name and he had long chafed under the necessity of holding back, something that he has never done in any race. He darted away in the long stern chase, eating up the miles like a machine, while Sockalexis, with oceans of running in his wiry body, took up his task with determination marked on his dark Indian face. This was at eight miles from the finish and the Americans sped along with untiring strides, hoping every minute to have the welcome sight of the leaders greet their eyes. They went on and on, untiring and willing, but their efforts had been started far too late and as man after man was passed in the search for the leaders and yet no sign of the advance athletes came, the hopelessness of the task was evident. Neither gave up his work but stout-heartedly kept on, hoping against hope...[12]

Reynolds followed this description with another reworded vilification of the American strategy, condemning it for killing American chances for victory. In so doing, the reporter was outright cruel to Strobino, dismissing him as "an ordinary performer at best" and crediting his third place effort as merely an aberration that grew out of a terrible strategy which stripped others who were better prepared of a fair chance. DeMar had a little different opinion, suggesting Strobino was successful because he was better rested and had not been forced to conform to group training methods.[13] Still, from all accounts, Strobino clearly gave his all and ran a race worthy of far more praise than he got.

Reynolds wrote:

> *To summarize America's part in the race it can be said that either Gallagher or Sockalexis would have stood the strongest chances of winning but for the too strict interpretation of their orders. Strobino, rated as an ordinary performer at best, went his own way, unmindful of the heat and its possible effect. With but a small fraction of the judgment employed by the Paterson athlete, the pair of fast American contestants either one would have by all means been well qualified to wrest the laurels of winner from the representative of any other country.[14]*

Wow! Reynolds has left Sockalexis, and Gallagher too, with a damning epitaph to their Olympic careers. Did Sockalexis get "cheated" out of his chance by too conservative coaching? How poignant if this is true! And did Sockalexis need someone to tell him to turn it on a little sooner than eight miles out, or was it his own "inexperience" again? What about Kohlemainen, Ryan and Corkery...who all apparently self-destructed in the heat, with all three highly regarded marathon runners actually dropping out? Also, the highly thought of Swedes, too, ran well off the pace on their own home turf. Many, many runners failed to achieve their dreams that day and the heat was a very serious, deciding factor.

Without knowledge of the runners' split times – each runner's time at various checkpoints (5 miles, 10 miles, half way, etc.) – and without knowledge of where Sockalexis was, time-wise and not just place-wise, it's really impossible to know whether Sockalexis badly miscalculated, or was induced to miscalculate based on poor advice, or was conservative because of the heat. Would Sockalexis have had to drop out, like many of the leaders, or, even most tragically of all, suffer the same fate as the poor Portuguese runner who died, if he had attempted to force the pace?

Reynolds summarized that the "only honor positions" for the United States went to Strobino and Sockalexis, for third and fourth places, and noted that DeMar was able "to get no better than 12th place, a very creditable performance when his far from ideal condition is taken into consideration."[15] This went unexplained. Was Reynolds talking about DeMar's heart murmur, for his emaciated look, or something else?

What an incredible irony of sorts concerning Sockalexis and his place in history. Consider that in the 1984 Olympics, in the women's first ever marathon, when Maine's Joan Benoit took a quick lead on an early but hot L.A. morning, she gambled on passing the first water stop (she felt she'd had plenty just before the start) to make a break from the field. Grete Waitz (the "Andrew Sockalexis" figure here), Norway's great champion, the greatest name in women's running in her era, and the most feared of the three favorites (along with Benoit and Ingrid Kristensen), decided to hold back, thinking the charge needed to be made later, not so early. Later, when Waitz made her move, she did pick up 10-to-12 seconds per mile but Benoit was entering the stadium. It was too late. Yet, no one remembers Waitz as "a loser" or suggests she made some horrible miscalculation she never should have. Benoit seized an opportunity and made it stick, but that doesn't mean Andrew Sockalexis choked because he may have followed the same type of thinking Waitz did or, worse, followed a strategy demanded of him.

Reynolds' Monday morning account appeared in the *Bangor Daily Commercial* under the headline: "**OLYMPIC MARATHON WON BY A SOUTH AFRICAN/ McArthur A Tall Transvaal Policeman Takes/First Honors in Premier Event—Sockalexis the Old Town Indian Ran Fourth.**"[16]

The *Bangor Daily News*, however, had a different account. Datelined Stockholm, it carried no correspondent's name but some far more colorful writing, particularly of the top competitors' finishes, including that of Sockalexis. A problem, however, with this unnamed writer is credibility, particularly with spellings of many key figures' names and omissions and contradictions in reporting. For instance, in this writer's second paragraph he alludes to the "great pain" third place finisher Strobino was suffering at the finish, yet a few paragraphs later refers to the "fine condition" all the Americans were in for their final stretch lap around the stadium track.[17]

The newspaper used the large portrait of Andrew Sockalexis taken before he left and offered the following headline for its Monday, July 15 edition: "**SOUTH AFRICAN/ WINS MARATHON/ K. K. McArthur Captures the Big Event of the Olympic Games—Andrew Sockalexis of Old Town Finishes Fourth in the Great Race.**"[18]

The lead sentence, by this unnamed reporter, opened rather strangely, focusing on the nation rather than the individual:

> *South Africa, which heretofore played rather a modest part in this Olympic drama, came to the center of the stage at the moment of its culmination today, winning the Marathon race the most important number on the Olympic program. This might have been honor enough for a small nation, but South Africa also won second place by a secure lead, which was piling up the glory.*[19]

It is interesting, as we fast approach 100 years later, to witness the importance of the marathon, over the decathlon and all other events. That is rather startling, considering it is Thorpe and the dual pentathlon/decathlon victories which have been remembered. Just how important the marathon is is shown, perhaps, by the capitalizing of the "M" on the word "marathon." The second paragraph provided not only the winner's name, but different spellings of both the second-

and third-place finishers' names. Also, the writer alluded
to McArthur's unblemished record as a marathoner, which,
certainly, most Americans would not know about; yet the
writer never provided any evidence of that record:

> *The winner of the classical Marathon was
> K.K. McArthur, a tall Transvaal policeman, who
> has never yet been headed in a similar event. His
> compatriot, C.W. Gitshaw, came second into the
> stadium several hundred yards behind, and third to
> appear was the American Gasten [sic] Strobino of
> the South Paterson A.C., who put up a braver fight
> than most of the runners for his feet were skinned
> and bleeding and he was suffering great pain.*[20]

The writer, in his second paragraph, gave the finishing
times for the first three runners and had them just the same
as those accompanying the Reynolds' account: McArthur,
2 hours and 36 minutes flat; "Gitshaw," 2 hours, 37 minutes,
52 seconds; and Strobino, 2 hours, 38 minutes,
42 3/5 seconds.

This writer's assessment showed no concern for a failed
strategy whatsoever. Did he know about it? Was he just
a superficial observer, or was he just not so critical of the
Americans on a very hot day, a day on which 30,000 spectators
(the writer was the only one to give an attendance figure) were
"grilled" on their seats, to use his colorful description?

Here is how this writer characterized the U.S. team
overall:

> *The Americans certainly gave a death blow*
> *to the theory that the athletes of the United States*
> *are better on contests which require quickness and*
> *agility than in tests of endurance. While 30,000*
> *spectators who were grilled on the stadium seats,*
> *strained their eyes toward the archway from un-*
> *der which runners emerged they saw the American*
> *shield on the breasts of six of the first ten men who*
> *entered.*[21]

This writer's approach was to look at the individuals' efforts, by teams. The second team to be scrutinized was the home country, Sweden. The Swedes, he noted, like the Americans, had also put the allowed, full complement of 12 competitors on the starting line, and "if their strength had been equal to their ambition they would have had a different tale to tell. They started at a great pace, the cheers of their countrymen inspiring them to extort *[sic]* themselves to the limit. During the first few miles they put forward all their strength and had nothing to draw on when the final test came."[22] Except for the sixth place finisher, Jacobsson, that is.

"Canada," the unnamed writer stated, "had no reason to be ashamed for two of her representatives [Duffy and Forsythe]... finished fifth and 16th respectively." There was a huge, obvious omission here in reporting. What about the Canadian Fabre, who was a factor in the race throughout and finished 11th? But it was this unnamed writer who came up with the poignant information that the American Ryan joined the Canadian Corkery in bowing out of the competition together, apparently at around Mile 19; for an earlier report mentioned only that it was Ryan who dropped out at this juncture. The writer noted: "Canada's great hope, Corkery, ran with Ryan for several miles and they gave it up together."[23] This sad, sad circumstance just screams out for further description but, alas, none is forthcoming.

The unknown correspondent went on to mention the Finn star, the front-running Kohlemainen, but did not provide why he dropped out or where: "The tall Finn, Kohlemainen, another favorite, was outclassed. He took the lead at the beginning, but Gitshaw caught him at five miles and ran at his heels, with McArthur and F. Lord of Great Britain, for ten miles more; then robbed him of the leadership."[24]

What this correspondent did provide was a very colorful description of the individual finishes of the top five runners, starting, of course, with McArthur:

> *Two miles and a half from the goal McArthur went to the front and held the lead to the end. He had completed the circuit of the arena before Gitshaw was observed running under the archway and he fell to the ground exhausted. The spectators cheered him lustily and as he lay panting Crown Prince Gustave Adolph shook him by the hand and patted him on the back. A small party of South Africa enthusiasts had an enormous laurel wreath ready in anticipation of victory of which they were confident from the first. They lifted the two green jerseyed athletes on their shoulders and slung the laurel over McArthur, carrying the pair across the field. Half an hour later after champagne had been opened in the dressing room the African delegation again brought out the victors and bore them around the track, the band playing frantically.[25]*

Strobino's courageous run received far better treatment at the hands of this unknown writer than the New Jersey runner received from Reynolds, although the writer had a miserable time getting the spellings right of his greatest rivals in the race. It is unfortunate it was not recorded just how far behind Strobino was, in terms of minutes and seconds, when he was in 15th place at the turnaround. But, clearly, he ran his heart out and deserved a lot of credit for giving everything he had to reach the finish line without falling prey to the heat like so many of his more celebrated rivals.

It was written: "Strobino was 15th at the turning around the quaint Sollentuna church, which the runners rounded to retrace their tracks. Two Americans were ahead of him at that time and he ran seven miles with Tewanima; then joined Kolehmainen until the Finn dropped far back in the rear. He finished well up with the two leaders and seemed to be in much better shape than either of them for he stopped to shake hands with a few friends and then walked briskly from the track."[26] This description of Strobino's finish certainly contrasts starkly with his earlier description that the New Jersey runner was "suffering great pain" and had "skinned and bleeding feet" from the earlier paragraph.

Then, this unnamed writer provided the only description from a Boston or local Maine newspaper of the race of Sockalexis. It began:

> *It was a long wait after Strobino finished before another runner appeared. Then a second shield appeared with the American device.*

> *It was the Indian Sockalexis. Fifty yards behind him came the Canadian, Duffy, who strove hard to overcome the lead of the American. He succeeded in some degree, but the Indian crossed the line twenty yards in front. Both were in fine condition. While Gitshaw arrived a little less than two minutes behind McArthur and Strobino fifty seconds later, a period of more than three minutes elopsed [sic] before Sockalexis and Duffy came through.*[27]

The writer remarked that about a dozen more runners followed in fairly quick succession after that, adding each American got a "rousing cheer" when passing by the American stand. "Everyone *[sic]* of the American runners came in strongly," the writer added, noting that Forshaw seemed to be running as easily at the end as he had been in the beginning and even waved his hand in response to the American cheering.[28]

Next, McArthur received a short but compelling tribute. "I went out to win or die," McArthur reportedly said after the race. "I am proud to win for Africa and myself." McArthur was described as anything but small and thin – a "Hayes-Dorando-Tewanima type" of runner. He was listed as 29 years of age, 6 feet tall and 174 pounds. The writer added that McArthur's career had "suffered from bad luck. He went to Greece for a Marathon which was postponed on account of political troubles, and afterwards went to England to take part in one which was postponed on account of the death of King Edward."[29]

Then, in what almost seems like an afterthought paragraph, the writer, representing an unknown publication or wire service, discussed the heat factor and then provided the key moment when McArthur seized the race from Gertshaw.

The writer stated: "The American contestants hardly came up to the expectation of Hayes who has had them under his care *[Author's note: 1908 Olympic marathon champion Johnny Hayes was one of three coach-trainers for the American marathon running team]*. He attributed this largely to the extreme heat. Most of the American marathons have been run in winter or spring and many of the men today were compelled to slow up at times to take refreshments. The South African Gitshaw stopped two miles and a half from the end to drink water and it was here that McArthur forged into the lead."[30]

Finally, the unknown writer offered two condemnations of how the marathon was run:

The crowds massed in the road increased the heat as they formed a barrier against the slightest breeze. This marathon was not really a marathon, according to the view of those who have seen the real thing. When the start and the finish are at the same place and the runners double around the same road, coming and going half the tension and excitement and waiting for the first man, which made the London marathon dramatic—almost tragical—is lost. Spectators and runners agree that they find it less inspiring for it becomes merely a long distance road race.[31]

Interesting. Today the argument continues – only going the other way. Many running authorities want the Boston Marathon bounced from consideration for Olympic considerations, or even for world record considerations, because it goes point-to-point, and certainly violates the modern concept for determining marathon records that a marathon should not "venture beyond 8 miles from the start at any point" on the course.

This unknown writer seems to make a huge misstatement in his last paragraph before going into the same lengthy checkpoint by checkpoint summary of the run: "The great marathon day at the Olympic games was ushered in with a blasting sun and a high temperature which meant much suffering for the runners, particularly those from countries like the United Kingdom, where such weather is practically unknown. On the other hand the long distance runners belonging to the United States team felt quite at home and regarded the burning rays as a good augury for them."[32] Strange remark, considering the American strategy in the race and results. This statement also seems flat out false, since almost all of the American runners were from or lived in northern climates.

His next series of paragraphs, the summary part, are almost word-for-word like that offered by Reynolds. So who really wrote this? That too goes unanswered. Though missing the very relevant split times for each check point, which would significantly support or defeat Reynolds' contentions, here are the scant details of the marathon as it actually took place, provided by Reynolds and the unnamed writer.

It was reported that 68 athletes started the race, including 12 Americans, that covered 40,200 meters, or about 25 miles. The course was characterized as "rambling...abounding in hills and dales, over a combination of rough and smooth, hard and soft surfaces."[33] Sockalexis would later claim there were "54 hills" on the course!

A large crowd greeted the appearance of the runners, with the hometown Swedes receiving, of course, the largest cheers. The South Africans were said to be "conspicuous" in their green silk running outfits and, reportedly, were the only athletes on the field "to brave the sun's heat by competing without covering on their heads." Several of the English runners wore wide-brimmed canvas hats. Many of the runners had handkerchiefs bound around their heads "for the sun's rays poured down with great intensity."[34] U.S. team members were among the last to appear. Lewis Tewanima, the Carlisle Indian who had already captured the silver medal in the 10,000 meter run, reportedly came on the field first and the rest of the Americans followed him, clumped in a group.

The men lined up on the starting line in rows, seven per row, and no American took a place with those in the first rank. DeMar noted this was the only marathon he ever ran where, at the start, the officials "plotted and drew for each position" on the starting line, arranging the runners in "sort of a military squad instead of a huddle." It was noted that several of the Americans were wearing wrist watches. The runners had begun appearing in the great stadium arena "soon after 1 o'clock." The crowd resounded with yells and cries in many languages as national favorites were sighted and recognized.

At exactly 10 minutes to 2 the runners received the starting signal.[35]

Wrote Reynolds: "To spectators who had witnessed the theatrical scene at the start of the Marathon race in 1908, with the towers of old Windsor castle for a background and the massive century-old oaks of Windsor forest overhead, this year's start seemed a comparatively tame spectacle."[36]

Immediately after the starting pistol, the whole pack "spread out like a flock of frightened geese." They went nearly one full circle around the stadium track before starting out into the countryside. The Swedes, "always ambitious starters," had five runners among the first 10 who disappeared through the exit under the stadium archway. The "different policies," or strategies of the runners became apparent almost at once: Before the entire pack had left the stadium, the runner "who brought up the rear was quite 150 yards behind the leader."[37]

Clearly, the heat was going to be a serious factor in the race. Just how serious – indeed, how fatal – a factor it would be would not be learned until after it was completed. A great cheer followed the marathoners, characterized as "one of pity rather than of enthusiasm" by one observer, and the throng then turned its attention to the big men throwing the hammer and the running of the 400-meter heats for the decathlon.[38]

The first major checkpoint in the race was reached at the town of Stocksund, three miles from the start. The Finn hero, Kohlemainen was the leader, followed by A. Ahlgren of Sweden, G.S. Peroni of Italy and K.K. McArthur. The next four runners were Swedes: H. Dahlberg, S. Jacobsson, C. Anderson and G. Tornros.

Reynolds then snidely noted: "The Americans, all excepting Strobino, legged along in leisurely fashion well to the rear." No times are listed, nor the distances between the runners. Whether they were packed together, or widely spaced is lost to history. Reynolds does state that at this early juncture: "In spite of the intense heat all the leading runners were traveling a fast pace seemingly untroubled by the deep dust that blew in clouds as it was shuffled up by the hurrying feet of the athletes or by the terrific heat which beat down steadily from a clear sky."[39]

At the 6-mile checkpoint, Reynolds reported that the leaders held the "same positions"; however, Mike Ryan had moved up to become the first of the Americans. Was "coach" Mike Ryan using "runner" Mike Ryan to control the American contingent's pace? Ryan was reported as being the 14th man to reach this second checkpoint station. From the accounts available there is no way to know how far back he was; however, Reynolds noted that at this point in the race: "...well within striking distance of the leaders were the Americans, destined to play a big part in the scramble for second honors after South Africa."[40] This hardly matched his vilifying remarks about the Americans "leisurely" running and allowing themselves to fall completely out of the competition. And the approach to hold back a bit and let others set the pace has always seemed the appropriate strategy for running on a very hot day.

Reynolds reported that at the 9.3-mile (15 kilometers), the third checkpoint area, Kohlemainen still led, with the South Africans McArthur and Gertshaw close behind. Lord, of England, had moved up to join the Swedes, the Italian Peroni and a Frenchman, Boisiere. Ryan remained the first American. There was no mention of Sockalexis to this point, in either of these sections featuring the checkpoint-by-checkpoint summary of the run.

Sockalexis' name first surfaced at Sollentuna, the halfway distance and the turn-around point in the race. Gertshaw had taken the lead, with Kohlemainen reported as being "15 seconds down" and McArthur, third, "another 20 seconds down." This was one of the rare instances where distance intervals between the runners was provided in terms of specific times. Lord was in fourth place. Then came the first mention of some of the significant Americans and the Canadian star Corkery. Corkery was in ninth, followed by these Americans: Harry Smith in 10th, Ryan in 11th, Tewanima in 12th, Sockalexis in 13th place, and Erxleben, in 14th place. Just how far behind they are, in specific and meaningful minutes and seconds, is not reported.

The next to last reported checkpoint, a little over 5 miles from the finish on the journey back to the stadium, still found Gertshaw leading the field. Then came, in order, Kohlemainen, McArthur, Peroni, an unnamed Swede, Lord, Piggott, Tewanima, and, now in ninth place, Strobino. Sockalexis, still in 13th place overall, had Smith, Boisiere and an unnamed runner also ahead of him, and Corkery, in 14th place, immediately behind him. Though no time intervals between the respective runners were given, it clearly was a "tightly packed" field for the runners in the vicinity where Sockalexis was; for example, Gallagher, who would shortly begin his charge accompanied by Sockalexis, was reported in "around 20th place" at this checkpoint, according to Reynolds.[41]

The last checkpoint came "seven furlongs from Stocksund." One furlong is 1/8th of a mile, or 220 yards; Stocksund was said to be about 3 miles from the start/finish line – so the total means a little under 4 miles to go. The standings at that time had: Gertshaw in the lead, followed by countryman McArthur and, now, Strobino in third place. Swede Sigge Jacobsson was in fourth place. The Canadian Duffy was fifth, followed by two Americans, Harry Smith and Tewanima. Sockalexis was in the midst of his great spurt, and he was in eighth place at the checkpoint. Immediately behind him were four Americans, including Erxleben, Gallagher, Lilley and Piggott. DeMar was never even mentioned. And, at this point, Kohlemainen, Corkery, Ryan, Lord, Peroni and Boisiere had completely disappeared from the front runners, and so would Tewanima and Smith before the brutally hot run ended.

McArthur was said to have overtaken Gertshaw when the leader stopped for a drink. Strobino had no battle for third. Sockalexis overtook Duffy and then held on for fourth place. The only Swede to hold on after their group fast start was Jacobsson. Seventh place through tenth went to Americans, in the following order: Gallagher, Erxleben, Piggott and Forshaw. The second Canadian, Fabre took 11th, with DeMar, 12th.

The next grouping went as follows: Boisiere, 13th; H. Green (England), 14th; Smith, 15th; Forsythe (Canada), 16th; Tewanima, 17th; and Lilley, 18th. Lord fell off to 21st and a large Swedish contingent finished after him. Kohlemainen appears to have continued further than Ryan and Corkery but dropped out between the last checkpoint and the finish line. According to one report Ryan and Corkery dropped at around 19 miles, although DeMar, who made no secret of his disdain for Ryan, reported Ryan "quit the race" not long after reaching the half-way point. The 12th and final American, John Reynolds of the New York-based, Irish-American A.A., reportedly dropped out very early in the contest. It was actually John Reynolds, not Strobino, who turned out to be the team's so-called "afterthought." Reynolds was never a factor, and was not ever mentioned.

Harold Reynolds reported that the "first nine of the U.S. team who appeared in the stadium all finished strong and ran briskly around the track."[42]

In spite of the writers' lofty sentiments about the importance of the marathon and the marathoners and their place in history, if anything at all is remembered about the 1912 Olympic Games of Stockholm, as noted earlier, it is Jim Thorpe and his decathlon/pentathlon "double." And, tragically, the marathon of that Olympiad is certainly not remembered for McArthur, Gertshaw, Strobino and Sockalexis but, largely, for an unnamed Portuguese runner not even mentioned in any account of the race itself.

The *Bangor Daily Commercial*, carrying a July 15, Stockholm dateline, told the tragic story in its third and fourth headline decks: "**LAST DAY OF THE/ OLYMPIC GAMES/ United States Will Receive First Honors at Awarding/ of the Trophies/ PORTUGUESE RUNNER/ DIES AFTER MARATHON/ Suffered Sunstroke in Sun-/day's Race and Was Taken/ to Hospital in Delirium.**"

The lead sentence read: "Gloom was cast over the spectators and participants in the Olympic games Monday when it became known that the only Portuguese runner in Sunday's historic marathon race, F. *[Author's note: Francisco]* Lazaro, had died in the hospital Monday morning. He suffered from sunstroke during Sunday's race and fell out after running 19 miles."[43]

There was no further mention of the unfortunate runner until the final section of the story. The second paragraph offered the news that the death had caused "great distress" to the king, crown prince and other royal family figures of Sweden.

Then, even more incongruously, the unnamed correspondent used the next four paragraphs to recount the color, pageantry and athletic competitions in a cursory review of the last day of the Olympics. The writer noted, for instance, "only a few scattered hundreds of spectators occupied the benches" at the stadium on Monday for the final day of competition. It was stated: "The pole vaulting event in the decathlon was the only attraction and that proceeded very slowly." So, where were so many of the spectators who had come to see the Olympic Games on that final day? Why had they passed up the chance to see Jim Thorpe write his name (at least temporarily) into the annals of Olympic history? The correspondent reported: "Most of the people preferred to visit the neighboring athletic grounds, where mixed teams of American and Swedish athletes gave an exhibition of baseball for the benefit of those foreigners who had never seen a game."[44]

There was, however, "an enormous crowd" present Monday afternoon when all the prizes were presented to the winners. So, it would come later in Olympic history before the practice of presenting medals and playing national anthems would be conducted while the various competitions continued. In addition to the final events of the decathlon, swimming and "military riding" competitions were also in progress throughout the final day of the 1912 Olympics.

At last, the writer returned to the topic of the first death (and the only death to this day as a result of actual competition) at an Olympic Games:

> *The tragic sequel to Sunday's marathon, in the death of the young Portuguese runner is the subject of conversation everywhere here Monday. Lazaro died at half past six Monday morning in the hospital to which he was taken from the course, suffering from the almost superhuman effort under the blazing sun to which all the runners were subjected. The doctors declare sunstroke to have been the direct cause of his death.*

> *Lazaro fell after covering 19 miles in the marathon at about where Kolehemainen, the Finn, Michael J. Ryan, I.A.A.C., and J. Corkerry [sic], Canada, dropped out. A squad of boy scouts who*

> *were patrolling the course to help any runners in*
> *distress, picked up the Portuguese and telephoned*
> *for an ambulance. In the meantime Lazaro was*
> *taken unconscious to a medical station, several of*
> *which had been erected along the course. From*
> *there an ambulance transported him to Stockholm.*
> *Lazaro never recovered consciousness. He was de-*
> *lirious throughout the night and imagined he was*
> *still running the race.*[45]

It was also noted that a Bohemian runner, named F. Slavik, also required hospitalization, but that his condition was not considered serious.

The real lesson learned, under the most unfortunate of circumstances, concerned the starting time. Beginning a marathon at 1:50 p.m. on a mid-July day is as horrifying a thought today as it should have been back then. Wrote the correspondent:

> *Every one [sic] concerned now realizes that it*
> *was a great mistake to start the race at 2 o'clock*
> *on one of the hottest days of the year...members of*
> *the United States team who are more accustomed*
> *to the sun than most of the competitors were dis-*
> *tressed by Sunday's heat while the English runners*
> *entirely wilted and were unable to approach their*
> *ordinary record. The tragedy of this year's mara-*
> *thon, coming after that of the painful exhibition*
> *of Dornado's finish in 1908 is likely to lead to a*
> *change of rules or the abandonment in the future*
> *of this feature of the meetings.*[46]

And, yes, the death led to an immediate change in the starting time, to either early morning or late afternoon, of the Olympic marathon. The correspondent, in the closing paragraph, noted that it could not "be learned whether Lazaro was properly trained. The majority of the runners of Sunday are in good condition Monday."[47] In fairness to the 21-year-old Lazaro, he was no novice; indeed, he was a three-time national champion at the marathon distance in Portugal.

Thus, a day after the event, all the runners were accounted for – except for one. According to Tom Ecker, in his book **Olympic Facts and Fables**, the mysterious disappearance of a Japanese runner in the marathon would not be resolved for 50 years! After the marathon was completed, Ecker related, Olympic officials attempted to account for all 34 runners who had not completed the course, quite obviously because of the extreme heat. The only one they could not account for was Siso Kanakuri of Japan. Even the Swedish police could not locate him. He was labeled "disappeared," and, as the years passed, the legend grew. There were all-in-good-fun "Kanakuri sightings": some said he was in the company of two Swedish girls, with no desire to return home; others said he was still running local, wayward streets, trying to find his way back to the Olympic stadium.[48]

On the 50th anniversary of the race, in 1962, a Stockholm newspaper reporter was dispatched to Japan to see if he could find Kanakuri. Ecker relates that, without much difficulty at all, the journalist found Kanakuri, who was a public school instructor, teaching geography. The explanation was simple and obvious: Kanakuri explained that he had completed half the marathon when the heat overcame him. He staggered into the yard of a Swedish family, who took him in, gave him drinks and provided a bed for a long nap. When he awoke, they assisted him to the train station and provided him a ride back into Stockholm. Embarrassed that he had not finished the race, he quietly left the country, taking a boat back to Japan. He was completely unaware that, for 50 years, he had been "the Japanese who disappeared" and a playful Swedish legend.[49]

According to Ecker, in 1967, at the age of 76, Siso Kanakuri was flown back to Stockholm to participate in the opening of a new department store in Rotebro, the community where he had disappeared from the marathon course. Then he was taken to the Olympic stadium, where he ran across the finish line, to the delight of a large, assembled crowd familiar with the tale. "Kanakuri's 55-year marathon was finally over," Ecker quipped.[50]

In a one-paragraph account published in the *Bangor Daily News* on July 15, humbly headlined "STROBINO A MACHINIST," unexpected third-place finisher Gaston Strobino received all-too-brief praise for his achievement. The account noted that Strobino, a runner for three years, was 21 years old and an employee of a big machine shop. He was born in Switzerland, of French parents, and was brought to America when he was 8 years old. It took "a public benefit and subscription, organized by Mayor McBride and other prominent citizens," to fund Strobino's trip to Sweden. Plans were already under way "for celebrating his return with a holiday."[51]

131

It was good that Strobino was at least appreciated and receiving recognition in his own home area. For elsewhere, alas, more condemnation for the American team and its strategy, and the heat of that Sunday marathon, were somehow turning Strobino's accomplishment into an outright miscarriage of justice, an aberration painful to contemplate and bear.

Even in a story about the greatest heroes at the games, published in the *Bangor Daily News* the week after the Olympics concluded, the controversy over the marathon still provoked the sharpest retorts and the nastiest of second-guess quibbling. The article tried to pinpoint the most outstanding performer at the just-concluded Olympiad. Modern readers will probably be very surprised to learn that Jim Thorpe, in spite of winning both the pentathlon and decathlon, was not selected hands-down victor. Thorpe's name is, to this very day, synonymous with the 1912 Olympics – thanks to his remarkable double victory, thanks to the now legendary award ceremony with the Swedish King saying to him: "You, sir, are the greatest athlete in the world," and thanks to the controversy concerning the stripping of his amateur status and his medals (later-to-be restored years after his death). Apparently it was not immediately grasped by the writers of his day that his achievement was all that wonderful. Datelined "New York," this unnamed writer put Jim Thorpe, Hannes Kohlemainen and K.K. McArthur as the top three candidates and then offered intriguing and very insightful commentary as to why Kohlemainen deserved top-tier consideration. Kohlemainen won three events: the 5,000 meter run, 10,000 meter run and 8,000 meter cross country run. Thus, dropping

out of the marathon on a brutally hot day, after having
won three other running events, couldn't have been a great
disappointment for Kohlemainen, one suspects. The writer did
not note who these other "experts" were who joined him in this
conclusion.[52]

The writer began:

> *In spite of the fact that the marathon has been
> considered the chief event of the Olympic program,
> McArthur, though unanimously voted a man of
> class, was quickly dismissed by the experts. The
> general opinion was that the extreme heat has such
> an effect on the majority of the competitors that
> the race could by no means be called a duly run
> one. The same conditions prevailed at London in
> 1908 and the winner of that event, Johnny Hayes,
> proved the correctness of the fluke victory by never
> winning an important race after that memorable
> victory.[53]*

This seems like an awfully harsh condemnation of Hayes,
who was highly regarded in his era. The sharp reproach
concerning Strobino's ability came next.

The critic continued: "It was cited that all the American
runners except Strobino had evidently run far below their
proper form. There were many in the race whose previous
performances entitled them to finish far in advance of the
Paterson youth, and if they had run to form they would have
been close to McArthur if not in front of him."[54]

Again, harsh castigation of the American "hold back"
strategy was unleashed. Forgotten was the fact Corkery, Ryan

and Kohlemainen all dropped out. Forgotten was how poorly all but one of the front-running Swedes fared. Forgotten was how poorly the English runners, including Lord, did. Forgotten, for heaven's sake, was that one man even died of sunstroke!

The writer continued:

> *Various theories were advanced for the backward position of the American cracks, one being that they had followed the pace of that experienced Marathoner, Mike Ryan, and that the Irish American, not being in form or being affected by the heat, had been unable to keep as close to the leaders as he otherwise would. On the other hand it might have been a mistake in judgment on the part of advisers of the men which resulted in their being left so far behind in the early stages of the contest. It is certain that the Americans as a whole were running faster at the finish than the representatives of any other nation. Gallagher of Yale, for instance, made up so much ground in the last six miles and finished so fresh that those in charge of the team were confident that he would have given the winner a hard race if he had made his effort earlier in the race. Among good marathon runners it is well understood that the time to make use of speed is at the beginning of the race. The very distance of the contest will make all tired at the finish so that, all things being equal, the man with a good lead in the first part of the race can crawl home as well as the man who has failed to take advantage of his speed when he was fresh. The sentiment is strong that a truly run Marathon is impossible while the event is held in the middle of a hot afternoon in July...*[55]

To this last point, modern day runners would surely utter "Amen." The rest of the article broke into a lengthy, often vitriolic discussion over whether Thorpe or Kohlemainen was the greatest athlete. Thorpe, interestingly enough, is ultimately dismissed. The suggestion was made, by the unnamed writer, that even Johnny Garrels of Michigan ("Who?" most moderns would certainly ask) "was another great all-around athlete who could run, hurdle, and put the shot better than the winner of the decathlon." Not satisfied to have completely discredited Thorpe yet, the writer concluded: "...until Thorpe displaces Sheridan's record for A.A.U. competition, experts will be slow to proclaim him the greatest athlete of all time."[56]

A modern reader might wonder if, perhaps, racism was an issue here.

So the unnamed writer, and his equally unknown "experts," settled on the outstanding accomplishments of Hannes Kohlemainen. The writer's logic: "When the performances of Kolehmainen [sic] are analyzed they stand out so distinctively when compared with the champions of old that there is no doubt that the Finn is entitled to be classed as the best long distance runner that ever put on a spike shoe, and this, with his record of winning three Olympic events, clearly entitles him to the honor of being the best individual athlete in the games."[57]

Arguing that running is the "oldest" athletic event of all and that the running competition had never been tougher in Olympic history to date, the writer noted: "...yet Kolehmainen [sic] only was forced in one of the three to run his best...the

5,000." The writer concluded that, "altogether, in trials and finals Kolehmainen *[sic]* went to the post six times in a week and on every occasion was the first man to catch the judge's eyes."[58] In the days that followed Sockalexis joined Thorpe as a man largely unappreciated and, perhaps, unfairly criticized for an outstanding performance.

On Tuesday, July 16, both the *Bangor Daily Commercial* and the *Bangor Daily News* ran the same excerpt from Harold Reynolds' account carried in the *Boston Post* concerning Sockalexis' finish.

The *Bangor Daily News* headline blared out: **"SOCKALEXIS SHOULD/ HAVE WON MARATHON/ Was Held Back Too Long Before/Final Dash, Says Sporting Writer."**[59] The *Bangor Daily Commercial* headline was equally judgmental: **"MIGHT HAVE WON/Poor Judgment Lost Marathon/ For Sockalexis/ BEGAN SPURT TOO LATE/ Americans Were Cautioned to Run Too Slowly at First—Indian Runner Finished Strong."**[60]

But, unfortunately, these accounts don't answer the significant questions many readers and most runners would like to know. Did Sockalexis hold back on his own, or did his trainer Smith tell him what to do, or was he merely following the team strategy?

What if Sockalexis had gone out hard with the leaders, like Kohlemainen, Corkery, Ryan? Would he have merely wound up like them, dropouts? Or would he have found a middle niche, like the unheralded Strobino, to push himself right to the limit to win a medal? Clearly the two South Africans went for broke, "win or die" as McArthur seemed to suggest very literally. Could Sockalexis have run a little faster but stayed back, then pushed to catch McArthur and Gertshaw when they were slowing down – instead of being so far behind that he had to run hard for many, many miles (The descriptions never, ever say just how far off the pace Sockalexis truly was. That important piece of information, too, is missing)? Sockalexis was much better than a 2-hour 36-minute marathon runner – the victor's time – and seemed to have run far better for that day.

The heat was a very significant factor and Sockalexis is a native Northeasterner. How much of a factor was the heat? A runner did die, and at least three possible favorites to win the race dropped out after pushing their way to the front.

So, just how fair was it to second-guess Sockalexis? It seems a real shame that this kind of journalism became Andrew Sockalexis's legacy in the marathon. Forgotten was the fact of how young, how inexperienced, and just how well this 20-year-old man did under extraordinary circumstances.

Actually, "forgotten" should truly be the operative word... Paradoxically, the damning of Sockalexis is largely not a problem at all, because he has all but been forgotten. When the Maine Sports Hall of Fame took until the summer of 1984 to elect Andrew Sockalexis this became abundantly clear. Further evidence came when the *Bangor Daily News* published a story in the 1980s about a man who was an alternate on a mid-1940s Olympic team roster and called him Maine's first and greatest name, until Benoit and Bickford, in track and field. This, of course, is all absurd. But, sadly, on Indian Island and throughout the state, there was no one around to help carry Andrew Sockalexis' banner.

Fortunately there was one final testimony to be recorded concerning the Olympic marathon run of 1912 – for Andrew Sockalexis himself would give his version of the race when he returned to a hero's welcome in Old Town.

* * *

Chapter 8

Hero's welcome at home

The marathon. There was a great deal of fascination
and interest in the marathon run, just before the turn of the
century, most likely spurred by the revival of the modern
Olympic Games in 1896 and the birth of the Boston Marathon
in 1897, which itself was inspired by the running of the
Olympic marathon in 1896.

And through the first few Olympiads of the new century,
the marathon appears to have enjoyed fame as a centerpiece
athletic attraction and a popularity greater perhaps than at
any other time during the 20th century. For even with its
popularity during the so-called "Running Boom" of the 1970s
and 1980s, the Olympic marathon still does not appear to
attract the enthusiastic attention it did back in its earlier years.
It is interesting that, perhaps for tradition's sake, the men's
marathon remains the last event started at each Olympiad. And
it may be that it is the history of the event that still incites the
tremendous interest that attends the opportunity to become the

Olympic marathon champion. As one writer at the Olympic
Games at Stockholm in 1912 observed, running is the "oldest"
athletic event and the marathon, as that sport's most stringent
test, continues to garner extraordinary attention.

The first marathon is much written about. Legend has it
that Pheidippides (his name has been spelled a variety of ways)
was a Spartan soldier and courier, sent in 490 B.C. from the
plains of Marathon back to Athens, with the responsibility
of carrying the news of a great Grecian victory over Persia.
Popular history records that when the exhausted fighter-turned-
runner arrived at his journey's end, he collapsed, but with his
dying gasp announced "Victory!" for the Greeks. An even more
dramatic rendering of the tale has the runner arrive, fall to the
ground and then, with one last Herculean effort, half arise and
gasp the one word "Victory." Then, of course, he immediately
died from his efforts. Over the years varying theories have
been offered, disputing various elements of the story. It has
been questioned, for instance, that Pheidippides was the only
courier – some historians suggest there were three – and still
other historians dispute that Pheidippides was the courier who
died. Nevertheless, the legend was powerful enough to inspire
a tribute run when the modern era Olympics were created in
1896. The 25-mile run, the distance from Marathon to Athens,
was dubbed "the marathon" and the trophy awarded the winner
of the Olympic marathon was a bronze statue of the expiring
Spartan runner. Many, many historically-minded marathoners
since have ruefully cursed Pheidippides and wistfully
wondered why the distance could not have been only 20 miles.
Pheidippides too, perhaps, might have fared a little better.

In its earliest years, the marathon provided some of the Olympic Games' best remembered and celebrated moments, but none was any more heroic or more fittingly in line with the effort of the legendary Pheidippides than the inaugural marathon run, in 1896. When Baron de Coubertin of France proposed the idea of resurrecting a modern version of the Olympic Games, and it was adopted, there was agreement the first games should, logically, be held in Greece. (And thus, for purists, it seemed ridiculous when the 100th anniversary Olympic Games, held in 1996 in Atlanta, were denied to Greece for what many believed were purely financial reasons.)

When the Olympic Games were revived in Greece, it was only natural that the Greek people would seek a local hero to win the marathon and uphold ancient Hellenic pride. According to the often repeated, remarkable story an Attican farmer named Loues became obsessed with the notion that if any of his countrymen could capture the marathon laurels, he was the man. However, Loues was a bit tardy in coming to this realization – the candidates to represent Greece for the marathon had already been determined. Loues, supposedly, talked his way into the run. It is widely written that he went to the Grecian athletic authorities and fervently pleaded for permission to run for the honor of Greece.

Legend has it that Loues boldly and, to our modern ears, melodramatically announced to these officials: "I will win or die." At first, the request was scoffed at by even his fellow countrymen. But Loues apparently pleaded so eloquently, so passionately that the officials relented and his name was placed as a post entry. It turned out, indeed, that Loues was not just being theatrical when he uttered his "win or die" battle cry. Just before the race he had a clergyman give him the last rites of the church; even sports writers of that era readily admitted that such theatrics would have prompted ridicule in most other countries.

But because of the intense excitement created by the resurrection of the games and the national pride attached specifically to the marathon, Greeks embraced such unabashed idealism. To many Greeks, it was as if the destiny of the nation hung upon a Greek winning the marathon. Though there were many well-known runners present, with the champions from America and, particularly, England regarded as the best, Loues raced to the front at the break from the starting line. Described in one account as "a simple, bronzed sun-kissed tiller of the soil (who) knew nothing of husbanding his efforts or the other fine points of the game," Loues had one simple strategy: Get out in front and stay there.[1] At first the other runners paid the little Greek farmer little attention at all. Front runners who "crash and burn" are, in fact, a breed better known to running than politics. They are, for the most part, a laughable lot. Sprinting off to the lead for momentary glory, only to be passed by everyone of quality in the race, front runners almost always draw sneers and scorn from their fellow competitors. It is expected that they will come straggling in or drop out, and no one ever seems to understand what vicarious thrill the front runner gets out of being in the lead for the first few hundred yards or even first mile or two. To the veteran runners from England, who were the favorites of the experts to win, Loues was just another of these. Surely, it would only be a question of a few miles before the poor guy cracked and fell by the wayside.

Yet, on and on, over the dusty, hilly roads traveled by his ancient, revered countrymen, Loues pressed ever onward. He was not alone out there. Everywhere along the course, hordes of his race-crazed countrymen pushed against the roadway in lanes on both sides, shouting their encouragement. He plodded on, stolidly holding his place at the head of the big pack. Half way into the race, and half way into Athens, some of the English runners began to get worried and started to more vigorously pursue the Greek. First one and then another of the English contenders took off after Loues and challenged him for the lead. And each time the courageous Greek answered the challenge with a spurt of his own. He responded to every challenge offered in that first Olympic marathon, clinging to the lead with bulldogish determination until, against all odds, he won.

Obviously, one can only speculate as to whether it was in knowledge of and tribute to Loues that, 16 years later, the South African K. K. McArthur used the exact same phrase and philosophy – a "win or die" mantra – to pursue Olympic marathon glory.

Curiously, it was another little known, completely unheralded Greek runner who is responsible for one of the most stirring victories in Boston Marathon history. For it was in 1946 that Styliano Kyriakides ran to victory over "Mr. Boston Marathon," Johnny Kelley (two victories, 1935 and 1945, and an amazing 61 Boston Marathon runs). Kyriakides urgently sought the victory so he could use the winner's platform to plead for international help to combat starvation in Greece. Kelley reportedly teared up when he learned why the victory was so important to Kyriakides and commented that, under those circumstances, he was glad the tiny Greek runner had beaten him.

In its earliest years, largely because of expenses, the runners coming to the Boston Marathon were largely from the greater Boston area, New York and the eastern provinces of Canada. It would not be until the 1920s that a steady influx of international runners from around the world began regularly making the pilgrimage to Boston for the Patriot's Day run. Thus, the earliest Olympic marathons had no rival as the outright "world championship" for long distance running, and it was the only competition over a four-year period where, truly, all the greatest runners of the era were gathered to compete in one place.

Writers in Boston and Maine believed Andrew Sockalexis had already put his name for all-time into the annals of Olympic history and would one day soon race to even greater glory. Only for one gazing at these headlines so many years later, with a poignant understanding of what a forgotten footnote to running history Andrew Sockalexis has largely become, do these exalted words of praise and homage crumble into sorrowful dust, just as the laughably wrong, boastful claim of immortality appears upon the crumbled, nearly completely covered-up statue of Ozymandias, in the Shelley poem.

Certainly the unnamed writer (one has to believe it was Brown, the editor), editorializing unabashedly in a front page lead story of the Saturday, July 20 issue of the Old Town *Enterprise,* believed Sockalexis was destined for running immortality and, drawing from the critical accounts, should have been the winner of the Olympic race. Under the following headline "**ANDREW SOCKALEXIS/ Not the Winner,/ But A Hero of the Race/ Wins 4th Position**" and a large photo of Andrew Sockalexis running in more local surroundings, the *Enterprise* seemed almost bitter that the Penobscot Indian had been denied the victor's stand.[2] The lead sentence seemed not at all to recognize that the youthful runner, competing in only his fifth official footrace, came in fourth place in a race involving all the best long distance runners in the world: "Andrew Sockalexis shows in his brief career that he is one of the world's best long distance runners, regardless of the fact he obtained only fourth position at the Marathon race at Stockholm."[3]

There seemed to be no masking the disappointment, and very tempered recognition of the feat in the tone of this piece. This seems to be a not-so-subtle slap at the so-called "holding back" strategy employed by the American team. The question raised: Why wasn't Sockalexis willing to risk it all in the early going, to be in position for a try for the win at the end, like others in the race? The piece read:

> *Finishing strong as he did with many of the best of them falling by the wayside and the winner being in a total collapse at the end, shows there was an error in judgment in not having Sockalexis do his best in the early stages of the race, that is, he should have been kept nearer the leader. Where there is only one opportunity in four years to win an Olympic trophy, a contestant should go in with*

the spirit of McArthur of South Africa, 'win or die.'
Sockalexis had every reason in the world to believe
he could stand the pace for the whole distance
from his record, and should have kept nearer the
leaders. The time of two hours and forty minutes
against two hours, twenty minutes and fifty-two
seconds at Boston last spring and finishing strong,
justifies us in our above comments. We want to
see Sockalexis a world-beater in his line, which
we believe he is, and unless he goes into profes-
sional ranks in the next four years, we believe he
will achieve the desired honor. He is young in the
running business and we think he has a great fu-
ture. He had advertised Old Town as it could be
done in no other way, and his many friends here
will give him just as good a reception as they would
if he had won his race. So we say, "All hail, Andrew
Sockalexis, coming Champion Marathon run-
ner of the world," whose ability as a clean athlete
has made him the center of attraction of all ath-
letic lovers. Regardless of the fact that McArthur
of South Africa won this great race, wherever and
whenever this race is mentioned among those who
love the sturdy athlete, Sockalexis's name will ever
be mentioned and remembered. By the time you are
reading this article, Sockalexis will be on his way
home and we do hope we have enough pride in his
achievements to give him a fitting reception.[4]

The arrival of Andrew Sockalexis, upon his return from
Stockholm, sparked great anticipation. The "**Up in Old Town**"
town column, carried in the *Bangor Daily Commercial*, talked
about the "great satisfaction" that the news of Andrew's
marathon finish was met with by locals. The backhanded slaps,
however, continued: McArthur had "only" beaten Andrew by

"about five minutes," which is actually a substantial amount of time even in a marathon race, and was "almost exhausted" while Sockalexis completed the ordeal "fresh." Again, there was this trivializing fixation with appearance at the finish line, leading to this unfair conjecture: "The fact...makes many of the Indian's staunch supporters think that, had he exerted himself more, he might have landed in first place. However, the general feeling expressed is, that to have come in fourth against such a big field, after having been trained largely by no trainer except his father, is a big honor for Sockalexis and the city should be very proud of his achievement."[5]

The *Bangor Daily Commercial* carried photos of the American victors at the games. It was noted that the English sports writers were "daily bemoaning the triumph of the Americans and berating the British team for its indifferent and miserable showing..."[6]

Already plans in Old Town were being enacted for a gala reception for the returning Andrew Sockalexis. It was suggested that Andrew be met at the train by as many citizens as possible, accompanied by the marching music of St. Joseph's band.

Several area newspaper accounts captured the flavor and excitement of a welcome home which, in all likelihood, was not to be matched in the state for a returning athlete until marathon gold medal winner Joan Benoit Samuelson and baseball pitcher Billy Swift were welcomed home to the greater Portland area following the 1984 Olympic Games. In its Saturday, August 3, 1912 account, the *Bangor Daily News* carried Andrew's photo and the following headline: "**Old**

Town Gives Sockalexis A Royal Welcome Home." The lead paragraph read: "Had Andrew Sockalexis won the Olympic Marathon by a mile, he could not have been given a more enthusiastic and general hearty reception than he received when he reached Old Town shortly before 7 o'clock Friday night. Probably more than 2,500 people were gathered at the station and his appearance was the signal for a great outburst of cheers."[7]

The *Bangor Daily Commercial* for that Saturday, August 3, ran this headline: "**OLD TOWN WELCOMES ITS MARATHON RUNNER/ One Thousand Citizens Greet Andrew Sockalexis/ and Show Appreciation of His Work at Stockholm.**" The *Commercial's* lead sentence ran: "Andrew Sockalexis, Marathon runner and winner of fourth place in the Olympic Marathon at Stockholm, Sweden, also the first athlete ever to be sent to these international games by a Maine city, arrived at his home here Friday evening, and was given a reception that could hardly have been more enthusiastic."

According to the *Commercial*, at least 1,000 Old Town citizens gathered at the station when the train coming west from Bangor rolled in. The crowd pressed forward and called out things like "There he is!" and "There's Sock" and "He's coming!" as Sockalexis stepped off the train. He was accompanied by Fred E. Allen, who had accompanied him home from Boston. Cheers greeted him and he shook hands with the head of the police department, Bill Fernandez. Fernandez was credited with being one of Sockalexis' most loyal fans and one of the key individuals responsible for the reception "for the youthful hero of a grilling race under a broiling sun, with the temperature at 90 to 95 degrees, over a course that was more than 25 miles in length," according to the *Commercial*.[8]

The headline in the Saturday, August 10 issue of Old Town's *Enterprise* blared out: "**CITIZENS TURN OUT 'EN MASSE'/ TO GREET ANDREW/ SOCKALEXIS/ One of the Most Prominent/ Marathon Runners/ of the World/ 'SOCK' OWNED THE CITY**." The *Enterprise* lead paragraph read:

> *Andrew Sockalexis was announced to arrive home Friday evening, August 2, 1912 and that was all that was necessary to be known by the citizens of Old Town. Our citizens flocked to the station by thousands and a most sincere greeting awaited him as he alighted from the train accompanied by Fred E. Allan [sic] who went to Boston to meet him. "There he is!" "Three cheers for Sockalexis" were called for and they were given with a will, that must have been very pleasing to the hero of the hour.[9]*

There was "great difficulty" in escorting Andrew to Fred E. Allen's car. Allen was joined in the vehicle by the following Old Town dignitaries: Mayor Charles W. Stephens, ex-mayor G.G. Weld and George H. Richardson, reported the *Bangor Daily News*.[10] The *Commercial* account stated that Marshal Fernandez and an officer Wadleigh made "a path through the dense, cheering crowd" allowing Sockalexis and Allen to get to Allen's car. The *Commercial* reported the following to be in the car: "Mrs. Allen, Mrs. Edward *[Author's note: it should read "Francis"]* Sockalexis, Andrew's mother, and one of his two sisters" *[Author's note: Sockalexis had only one living sister]* were in the back seat; Allen, a chauffeur, Dr. G.G. Weld and Dr. E.M. Marquis were in the front. Presumably Andrew Sockalexis, too, is in the car, although he is not mentioned. "With about all the autos in the city in line" and joined by the St. Joseph's band and an "immense number of admirers," the procession proceeded to city hall for the formal ceremony.[11] The *Enterprise* reported that Andrew was joined in the car by his mother, his sister, Fred "Allan" (name still spelled wrong), and a chauffeur named "Lawrence Allan," which may help to explain all the confusion about the spelling of Allen/Allan. Filling the cars immediately following the lead vehicle were dignitaries who participated upon invitation of the reception committee. They included: Dr. A.H. Twitchell, Mr. Brissette, Ralph Davis, the Hon. Herbert Gray, Mrs. Marie L. Bean, J.L.S. Hincks, Dr. C.B. Porter, Virgil E. Tucker, Dr. A.W. Rowe, Dr. J.R. Varney and George H. Richardson.[12]

The *Bangor Daily News* reported the procession formed in this order. First came the St. Joseph's band and city marshall O.B. Fernandez. They were followed by a car containing the Sockalexis family. Then came about 50 cars with "enthusiastic citizens." On the way to the reception at City Hall, "there was one continuous cheering, sounding of auto horns and general celebration."[13] The *Commercial* stated: "The streets were black with people and gay with bunting, flags and decorations of individual business houses in honor of Andrew Sockalexis, whose heart must have swelled with gratitude to his fellow townsmen for this spontaneous outburst in his honor."[14]

According to the *Enterprise*, the procession "marched up Main St., to Stillwater Avenue, up Stillwater Avenue to Brunswick St. thence down Brunswick St. to City Hall where Sockalexis was escorted to the stage, to receive more plaudits and congratulations of his home people."[15]

The hall, it was written by the *Bangor Daily News*, was "packed to the doors." Sockalexis was escorted inside, to a platform, upon which were seated Mayor Stephens, ex-mayors Weld, William H. Waterhouse and Arthur J. Bradbury, and other prominent citizens. Included in these were Allen and Richardson, Indian Agent Pinkham, John Gould, F. Otis Gould, Alexis Nadeau, F.W. Phelps, Alexis Boushay, Dr. Marquis, city clerk McNamara and others. The *Bangor Daily News* unnamed writer then stated that "the father, mother, brothers, sisters of Sockalexis had prominent places" which, of course, is curious in that Andrew Sockalexis had no brothers and only one sister.[16]

The more detailed *Commercial* account recorded: "Arriving at City hall the auditorium was quickly packed with the people and a meeting organized, with Mayor Stephenson as the presiding officer." On the platform with him were the guest of the evening, "his parents and sister," ex-mayors G.G. Weld, W.H. Waterhouse and Bradbury, Indian Agent Ira E. Pinkham, Dr. E.M. Marquis, George H. Richardson, John W. Gould, F. Otis Gould, Fred E. Allen, Alexis Nadeau, Frank W. Phelps, Alexis Boucher *(Author's note: Different spelling from Bangor Daily News account)*, and city clerk Francis W. McNamara.[17]

The *Enterprise*, acknowledging the role of the runner's father, stated:

> *Andrew Sockalexis and his devoted mother occupied a sofa on the center of the stage and were the center of all eyes. At their right and left was the proud sister and more than proud and happy father who knows what success on the cinder path means and at what a cost it is obtained. He has done everything he was able to do to make his son Andrew what he is. He must look back on his work with much satisfaction and joy. The crude track around their modest and rather beaten home on Oak Hill stand as a mute monument of his love and devotion to his worthy son.[18]*

Stephens, Weld and Waterhouse then made speeches of welcome and praise, which were frequently interrupted by cheers, according to the succinct *Bangor Daily News* account. By contrast, the *Commercial* again offered far more detailed and colorful, if occasionally highly editorialized, observations. "Mayor Stephens opened festivities by a speech of felicitation and welcome, voicing the universal feeling of confidence which Old Town's citizens have in this youthful athlete and their feeling that he ought, under right training in advance have won this great world race."[19]

The *Enterprise* quoted the mayor as saying Sockalexis had "done more to make Old Town known the world over than any other citizen. Brickmore Gall Cure Company takes second position now." Hmmm, one suspects this is a joke... or is it? What about Old Town Canoe? The *Enterprise* listed

Waterhouse as the very next speaker and said he made "a most pleasing speech, drawing from Sockalexis' upright life a lesson which should be useful to the coming generation" of Old Town, an exemplary life from which they should all profit. Then Dr. G.G. Weld "indulged in some most interesting personal reminiscences," having known Andrew's father as a boy, when the two met in wrestling matches and "when, as he modestly put it, the elder Sockalexis touched the mat under the vigorous young Weld's advances." The *Enterprise* said Dr. Weld "...went back to his boyhood days in Olamon when he defeated the wrestling champion from Argyle that was represented by Francis Sockalexis, father of the guest of the evening Andrew Sockalexis." Francis Sockalexis then "publicly acknowledged" the doctor's wrestling ability and the audience applauded.[20]

The third speaker, the Hon. William H. Waterhouse used the speaking opportunity to call to the attention of the young people in the audience that "only by reason of the very clean life of young Sockalexis had his work on the race course been possible and to this end he had been abstemious *[Author's note: Could this be a lightly veiled reference to the not-so "clean life" that destroyed the baseball career of cousin Louis Sockalexis?]* and taken the finest possible care to the growing youth" who may one day compete on this same elevated level of competition."[21]

Sockalexis was called upon to give a speech. He responded, the *Bangor Daily News* stated, "in a simple but graphic language" and told the story of the trip across, the race and other details.[22] The *Enterprise* wrote of him:

> *It is useless to waste words on how he was received; it was in a way which must have pleased him. He made no pretense of being an orator, his modest and quiet way in relating his experiences on the way, at Stockholm and his account of the race was listened too [sic] with much interest. There is no braggadocio about Sockalexis, he related his experiences as he would set [sic] down and tell you about it and then set [sic] down at his mother's side amid much applause.*[23]

In a separate account, in the same issue of the *Bangor Daily News* (August 3, 1912), a first-hand account of the Olympic race from Sockalexis himself, was given under the headline: "**OLYMPIC ATHLETE/ BACK TO HIS OWN/ Sockalexis Attributes Marathon Loss/ to Overtraining and Delaying of Spurt.**" The account opened:

> *Andrew Sockalexis, the Old Town Indian who finished fourth in the Olympic Marathon in Sweden and who incidentally was the first athlete ever sent from this vicinity, arrived in Bangor Friday and was seen by a News reporter as he was about to board the 6:20 p.m. train for his home city where a reception had been arranged for him. Sockalexis appeared the picture of health and said that he never felt better. He still wore upon the lapel of his coat, the small pin that served as a token of admittance to the various Olympic events and upon the front of his straw hat was the national shield which all the athletes affected.*[24]

Then Sockalexis was quoted specifically recounting his race: "If I had started my spurt at the turn, which was about 12 1/2 miles from the finish, in other words at the halfway point, I think I would have won but it was not until the 22nd mile of the little better than 25 mile course that I let myself out. At the finish I was a little faint and my heart was barely beating, but the doctor took care of me and I was soon all right. I lost five or six pounds in the race," stated Sockalexis.[25] His own words seem to indicate he pushed himself to a maximum effort and is being, perhaps, unduly hard on himself.

Sockalexis continued: "McArthur is a fair runner and so is Gitshaw [sic] who finished, but Strobino, the New Jersey man, made his position through luck. He has done nothing but short distance runs. The trouble with the American runners was this: They were overtrained. We were worked on the steamer and on the course. Every day, we ran over part of the road and then walked to get familiar with the lay of the land."[26]

In his book *Marathon*, seven-time winner of the Boston Marathon Clarence DeMar, who finished in a disappointing 12th place at the 1912 Olympics at Stockholm, was very critical as well of the team's training just prior to the big race. He wrote: "The way we were handled in 1912 we might just as well have had only three [marathon runners] on the team, for to have the group train together is like putting all your arrows into one quiver." He continued that the runners did not "race, but neither did we loaf. I didn't feel as carefree and confident as I would with a goal towards which I could aim each day without critical eyes on me. Here I felt I had to make good each day whether I were racing or not. Alone I'd have run much slower part of the time."[27]

Coaches-and-trainers Mike Murphy, Mike Ryan and Johnny Hayes were, apparently, ever vigilant controlling the marathon runners group, to the point when DeMar attempted to go off on his own, he was stopped and reproached. Since the rules were never posted, DeMar noted, with great hostility:

> *...a general notice [of such rules] posted would have prevented such humiliation to keyed-up athletes. One of my maxims has always been: 'If you want men to be champions, then treat them like champions, not puppets.' Because the race was only a couple of weeks away we had to train intensively...I strained every nerve to please the coaches every day instead of using my own foresight as when unwatched. One official said that either Ryan, DeMar, or Sockalexis must win this race for us. So we all got plenty of attention and they neglected poor Strobino who had been put in at the last day as a filler. In view of the way the race came out this is significant to me... Eventually, a week or so before the race, with the nervous strain of trying to make good every day instead of once a fortnight, I went stale—that is, I got so tired that I couldn't freshen up in a day or two. I was very lame and I had ruptured a blood vessel from the strain of too much practice. So with all this trouble I wasn't much of a runner when the race came.[28]*

Sockalexis thought the course was tougher than the Boston marathon course, considerably tougher. He stated: "Is the course worse than the Boston run? Well, I should say so. The Boston road is great but on the Swedish course, there are 54 hills and sprinkled over the ground is small chipped gravel."[29]

It is hard to know whether the reporter was embellishing this account, making Sockalexis' language more formal than he actually spoke. However, the young athlete's basic confidence and ability to let go of the past and move on seem apparent.

Sockalexis continued:

> *Say a good word for my trainer, Smith. He used me all right. I haven't a kick as to the reception that our boys received. The Swedes know how to entertain and they used us royally. A Portuguese and a Bohemian died and during the Marathon race, when the thermometer registered from 90 to 95 degrees, a score of people were overcome by the heat. And think of us runners in that heat? I tell you we suffered. While you might think that the Swedes, being familiar with the course, should do better, they were outclassed by the Americans. Their best man, Jacobson [Jacobsson], finished eighth, I think. I was not ill once and enjoyed every minute of the trip.[30]*

Of course, Sockalexis was wrong about the death count: Only the Portuguese runner died. The Bohemian was said to be hospitalized, but in good condition.

The writer then concluded: "Sockalexis' statement as to the reason for his failure to win bears out the opinion of a follower and admirer of the Old Town boy, given the morning after the race. 'If that boy had let himself out earlier in the game, to Old Town would have come the honor of the classic victory.'"[31]

Sockalexis returned from New York where the Olympic athletes were given a big welcome and reached Boston Thursday on his way home.

The *Commercial* offered some colorful, background details from the runner's speech at Old Town City Hall:

> *When Sockalexis himself was invited to speak, he showed the same modest demeanor that has characterized him throughout his experiences and which, if continued, will, men of brains aver, lead him into the foremost place as a runner of world-wide reputation. At first he was a bit hesitant and shy, but as he warmed to his theme and began to tell, in the graphic language possible only to a participant, of that titanic struggle for first place against an enormous field from the whole world's selection of athletes, he lost his shyness but not his modesty. As one listener put it, there was an utter absence of egotism as he told how he had struggled for the lead. It was not until he reached the 22nd mile mark, he said, while still husbanding his reserve force, that he was advised to spurt for all he was worth in the vain hope of winning.[32]*

No one asked, nor was it ever mentioned in any account whether it was his trainer Smith, or one of the marathon

coaches, or one of the other American runners who so
"advised" him. And how poignant to think of Sockalexis
racing against hope in that terrible heat, and then realizing
he could not catch the leaders. In essence, it really wasn't
that horrifying a miscalculation: Socakalexis ran a 2-hour,
42-minute marathon, falling by 6 minutes against the winner's
2-hour, 36-minute winning time. It remains the dilemma of
every marathon, then as now, for someone who wishes to try
for a victory – run your own race or make sure to keep in
contact with any leader or leaders, no matter how "suicidal"
the pace might seem to be, so no one runs off with the
victory.

The *Commercial* then directly quoted Sockalexis as
stating, "I knew then that I could never overcome the lead
of the leaders, but I put forth every bit of my reserve and
from 14th place crept up until only Duffy, the Canadian, was
between me and the fourth position, in which I
finished."[33]

The *Commercial* reporter stepped in to paraphrase
the tale:

> *As he told of that struggle with Duffy, who was
> determined that he would not let the Indian lad
> pass him, one could have heard a pin drop in that
> crowded hall. Although it was evident that his fight
> was a most heroic one, yet all he told was of Duffy's
> magnificent race and it was left to the imagination
> of his hearers to determine his part in it. His re-
> cital was graphic indeed and as he told of passing
> the man ahead when within a quarter of a mile of
> the finish line, after which he forged to a point 50*

> *yards ahead of the Canadian, all realized how near*
> *he had come to being in the very front rank had he*
> *but understood better the science of racing against*
> *these trained and experienced runners. Better*
> *management might, he admitted, have given him*
> *the race over McArthur.*[34]

Still, he's only 20 years old, with just a handful of official races completed. He admitted how spent he was, from the effort to fend off Duffy at the very end. It's very possible if he would have used up that energy at a much earlier stage, his faintness and barely beating heart at the end might well have caused him severe problems and ended his race as prematurely as the races of Ryan, Corkery, Kohlemainen and others ended. The account seems to indicate he was not severely dejected about the race, just confident important victories were coming soon in his future.

In an irony only understood through full knowledge of Andrew Sockalexis's complete running career, the duel Andrew Sockalexis fought and won over Canada's Jimmy Duffy might well have represented the very same duel required to win the 1914 Boston Marathon, the very marathon Sockalexis ultimately passed up two years later. For it was the colorful Duffy, whose first two requests after winning the 1914 Boston Marathon were for a cigar and a beer, who came away with a fairly easy victory. Sadly, the feisty Duffy would be dead within days of the running of the 1915 Boston Marathon, when his Canadian infantry unit was decimated in a hail of deadly German artillery fire on a battle field in Belgium.

The *Bangor Daily Commercial*, too, spoke to Andrew Sockalexis after he arrived in Bangor and was awaiting his train to Old Town and the big reception. It was stated: "In an interview with the representative of the *Commercial*, who met him at Bangor on his return, Sockalexis spoke most enthusiastically and cordially, of his trip and experience. He said that the treatment which he received while in Stockholm was fine, all the way through and he was well pleased with the way in which the sports were conducted. He had nothing but the warmest praises for those who had the matters in charge."[35] Sockalexis related he had arrived by vessel in New York on Wednesday morning, where all the arriving athletes were given "a cordial reception" by a gathering at the pier. Then, after coming up from New York by train, another big crowd was present to give the returning athletes a fine welcome in Boston. Sockalexis said he "had been unable to stay, if there were any further demonstrations, as he felt anxious to get home." In Boston, he was met by Fred E. Allen of Old Town, "who thenceforce took him in charge and made him feel that he was with home folks again."[36] The pair came by steamer to Portland, then took the train again to Bangor and home. It was noted his coach, A. N. Smith, had accompanied Sockalexis to Sweden but left him on arrival in New York because he had business in Philadelphia.

Sockalexis told the *Commercial* correspondent he expected to "renew their friendship" later on, as Smith was returning to the University of Maine for another year. During this interview with the *Commercial* Sockalexis discussed his interest in running professionally.[37]

"Speaking of the possibility of his becoming a professional runner, Sockalexis said that he should not do that before the Brockton Marathon, in which he came in third last year, but in which, with his added experience and training, he hopes to win first place at this coming fair. The prizes to be awarded this year are by far the finest ever given for a Brockton race and Andrew is very anxious that the one planned for the man first to cross the finish line shall adorn his humble home on Indian Island," the newspaper reported.[38]

Sockalexis then stated:

> *"The next Olympic Marathon will be run in Berlin in four years, but I hardly think that I shall wait for it," he said. "If I get a good offer, a chance to make a generous amount by entering a profes- sional race, I think that I shall then break into the professional class, as I need the money and this is the best time of my life for this work. Much depends on what is offered me, however."*[39]

Allen said the reception for Sockalexis in Boston was extraordinary, according to the report.

He commented, "It was just like Barnum's circus day in Bangor, only a lot bigger. There was a runner from Boston, but it was all Sockalexis, they had eyes only for him and he was all they were crazy to see. Reporters and camera fiends were as thick as fleas. Somebody was snapping him all the time and here and there were men who pulled out pads and drew, offhand, sketches of him. I saw one that a man had and t'was a dandy likeness too."[40]

Allen reported that Sockalexis was invited to attend several important athletic events in the greater Boston area, but declined so he could get home as soon as possible. Sockalexis had a "strong invitation," Allen said, to go to Carlisle, the famous Indian school, to study but refused it. Then Allen stated:

> *He is going to run in the two big Marathons of the coming fall, one in Brockton in October and the other in New York in November. Beyond that he has no plans, but the magnificent prize offered in New York is great incentive and he wants it. It is to be the finest gift ever presented to a Marathon runner in this country and will be worth at least $1,000 so of course the boy wants a chance at it. He will train steadily between now and then, to get into right trim for the event and has high hopes of landing it. Early, the famous runner, and Mike Murphy, whom you know is a great authority, told me Sockalexis is the foremost runner in the world today. He only needs right training and right track generalship to put him where he belongs, at the head of the world's long distance runners.[41]*

Poor Andrew Sockalexis. No matter what he accomplished, it seemed, there was always a greater projection tied right along to the praise or the condemnation.

The *Commercial* then noted that after the speeches, the session was "thrown open" for all who wished to shake Andrew's hand to do so, and "probably a thousand pressed forward."[42] The *Bangor Daily News* concurred with this estimate: The ceremony was followed by an informal reception with, it was estimated, "probably a thousand people" coming forward to shake hands and express congratulatory sentiments.[43]

The *Commercial* added: "Andrew took particular care to reach out and shake the hand of every boy and girl who came forward, at the suggestion of a member of the platform contingent, that they might receive perhaps, an inspiration from his experiences, for years before them."[44]

The *Enterprise* said Waterhouse concluded the ceremonies by "calling for three cheers" for Andrew and then for his father, followed by the hand-shaking opportunity which "about everyone in the hall" accepted. Sockalexis was then escorted to his home on the island by the Penobscot people, with "nearly every man, woman and child on the reservation taking part in the welcome. As he landed on the island a loud salute was fired."[45]

The *Enterprise* stated that headed by the band, Sockalexis was escorted to the ferry. It then stated:

> *The band played two selections, the cannon on the Island which had boomed out so many welcomes to the drivers on their return from the west branch drive in years gone by, announced the coming of one of the dusky heros [sic] from the Stockholm marathon. The ferry boat was decorated with flags and here Andrew Sockalexis was left in the bosom of his family by the reception committee to go to his modest little island home, after being recognized by crowned heads, hob-nobbing with the aristocracy of the continent and Sweden and associating with the best athletes of the world for the last two months.*[46]

The *Bangor Daily News* summed up: "It was a rousing welcome and as said before, had the Indian boy won, as many believe he might have had he used a little different tactics, his reception could not have been more hearty and general."[47]

According to the *Commercial*, a well-known and influential citizen (who went unidentified) who was on the train for Old Town with Sockalexis that Friday afternoon, urged him to attend the big public reception to be accorded the members of the American Olympic team by the citizens of New York City, later in the month. Andrew Sockalexis had an invitation in his pocket, "but modestly questioned whether he could accept it or not." This man started a movement for him to go by presenting him with a generous donation, to be used toward that end. It was then speculated that the Old Town/Indian Island citizens would probably make up the rest of the "purse" he needed to defray the costs of being in New York on August 22nd, so as to be present for a reception lasting two days.[48]

The letter of invitation read:

> **City of New York American Olympic Celebration Committee**
> **Offices, 611 Pulitzer Bldg**
> **Telephone, 4000 Beckman**
> **New York, July 30, 1912**
>
> *Dear Sir—*
>
> *The citizens of New York are to extend a welcome to the members of the victorious American Olympic Team on Friday, Aug. 23, and Saturday, Aug. 24, 1912. The plan at this time, as outlined, is*

*for the team to witness a performance of the Rose
Maid at the Globe Theatre on Friday evening, Aug.
23, as the guests of Messrs Werts and Luescher.*

*On Saturday, Aug. 24, the grand parade will
start from 42nd St. and Fifth Ave. at 10 a.m. The
line of the march will then be reviewed by His
Honor the Mayor.*

*On Saturday evening, Aug. 24, a dinner will be
tendered to the team at a prominent hotel.*

*To facilitate the work of the various commit-
tees, will you please answer the questions on the
enclosed blank and mail it to me as soon as con-
venient?*

*Yours very truly
(signed)
Frederick W. Rubien
Chairman Plans and Scope Committee*[49]

The Enterprise concluded:

*Although he does not come home a winner, it is
the next best, as everyone understands why he did
not come in first instead of fourth. It is and will be
the greatest event of his life, for weeks and months,
he will dream and live his experiences over and over
again and wonder if it can all be true. To be fourth
in a class of sixty-five of the world's best marathon
runners trained to the minute is a position worthy of
one's best endeavors. The applause and cheers of his
friends of his home city will ever ring in his ears as he
goes down life's pathway. May he never deviate from
the straight and narrow way on which he has so excellent a start. There was some attempt at decorations
by the merchants and Hotel Fransway. There was not
much time given to making arrangements.*[50]

* * *

Chapter 9

Some Boston rivals come calling

Following his very successful Boston Marathon and
Olympic Marathon, Andrew Sockalexis was at the height of
his popularity in 1912, the greatest year he would have as a
runner. Yet to anyone talking about him at the time it appeared
the victories and the fame were all just beginning and the
greatest days were yet to come.

He was daily news for the area newspapers, who regularly
reported his comings and goings, and the results of his races
which – to all appearances – seem to have come from
him. The editor's notes column of the weekly Old Town
newspaper, *The Enterprise,* regularly carried one- or two-line
entries about him. In one, at the beginning of August, this
column reported that some idea of the ability of Sockalexis
and the respect he commanded from the sporting fraternity
could be gleaned from the following remark from the man
regarded as the best athletic trainer in the United States, Mike

Murphy, the head coach of the 1912 U.S. Olympic team: "I consider Sockalexis the greatest runner in the world today."[1]

In another *Enterprise* column, it was noted that "... Sockalexis left Friday noon by boat for Boston where he is to be one of the participants in a three-mile sprint..."[2] A three-mile "sprint"? Apparently his long-distance running and marathon exploits were spoiling the locals. And in a "**Locals**" column of the *Enterprise* it was noted that the show window of F. E. Allen's Clothing Company had become a "center of attraction" for Old Town all week long, the first full week in August, because it displayed Andrew's running "outfit" from Stockholm. The display also carried many pictures from the Olympic Games. It wound up by stating: "'Sock' as we familiarly call him has had the center of the stage this week and every one considers him worthy of it. He is the envy of the small boy and many of mature age and while the fever is on we expect to see all the boys trying to make runners of themselves."[3]

Worldwide there were several interesting articles that followed in the aftermath of the 1912 Olympic Games. The English team was vilified by its own press for a poor showing. A German expert offered an explanation for American dominance at the Games, citing "race fusion." Described as a German "physical culture expert" he stated that the Americans won, not just because of superior and efficient training techniques, but "the plain fact is that the American breed is physically superior to the European. The American victories are a triumph of race fusion and a triumph for the

coming race." This is truly a curious and ironic twist on a
vile theme, an odd precursor to another German who would
come along some 30 years later and suggest just the opposite.
This "expert" sharply reproached the German team members,
commenting that "it is impossible to regain in one generation
what others have been a century building up. The 19th century
in Europe was a period of extraordinary intellectual activity
interrupted by a series of big wars. This meant for Europe
physical stagnation."[4]

Also in August Bangor's plans for a big Labor Day
celebration were heralded, which was to include nearly 4,000
working men in line, a grand firemen's muster, a 10-mile
"marathon," with "an attempt... made to have Sockalexis make
an exhibition run or act as a judge for this event."[5]

With thoughts of the big Brockton and New York races
in the fall, and perhaps professional running thereafter,
Sockalexis kept competitive immediately. He went to Boston
where he participated in a special tribute to the Olympic
athletes hosted by the Boston Lodge of Elks at the very
newly-opened Fenway Park as well as a track meet, dubbed
the "Boston Games," featuring many of those same Olympians
as well as local Boston athletes. The reception at Fenway
Park was attended by over 6,000 people. On the front page
of the *Boston Sunday Post*, for August 11, Sockalexis was
photographed with the legendary Jim Thorpe, both clad in
their Olympic uniforms. Sockalexis was entered in a 5,000
meter track race. Sockalexis took second place in the race
and the *Commercial* for August 12 headlined his effort as a
"sensational sprint."[6]

In this 5,000 meter race, there were 10 starters, including the surprise third-place finisher at the Olympics, Gaston Strobino, and well-known local runners, Clarence DeMar, Dick Piggott and Israel Saklad. Joe Silva and Oscar Hedlund, both of the Boston Athletic Association, were listed as "being the two scratch men." H. Howard of the Quincy YMCA and E.W. Mitchell of Medford, both described as "high mark men," took the lead after the starting gun.

Silva and Hedlund, as "the scratch men," were considered the favorites and had to surrender a variety of different handicaps to all the other men in the field. As the weakest members of the field at this distance Howard and Mitchell were granted the largest margin and, thus, were in the lead at the outset. Both Sockalexis and Strobino started with a 120-yard margin over Silva and Hedlund, and G. Goldsmith had a 100-yard margin. A well-known middle distance man, Saklad of the North Dorchester A.A., settled into third place, with Andrew Sockalexis right behind in fourth. Then, in order, came: Goldsmith of Arlington, Strobino, Piggott, DeMar, Silva and Hedlund. Saklad took the lead in the second lap, with Sockalexis remaining content to bide his time in fourth place. Goldsmith, Strobino and Piggott held their places. Silva had pulled about 10 yards in front of Hedlund, but DeMar fell further back in a distant last. As the third lap unfolded Goldsmith put on a spurt, pulling into second place and in hot pursuit of Saklad. The rest of the positions remained the same, except that Silva had stretched his lead to more than 50 yards over Hedlund, who quit during the fourth lap. Silva began to narrow the gap between himself and the leaders.

As the runners began the fifth lap, Saklad, Goldsmith and Sockalexis were running first-second-third, bunched tightly and leading Silva by at least 100 yards. Approximately 75 yards behind Silva, Strobino and Piggott ran closely together, barely five yards separating the two. DeMar was described as "hopelessly far behind and losing ground all the time." Early in the seventh lap Silva took command of the race, passing Saklad, Goldsmith and Sockalexis. Silva lapped DeMar in the early stages of the eighth lap and built what looked like an insurmountable lead over the rest of the field. Goldsmith, in second place by a scant margin over Saklad and Sockalexis, trailed Silva by as much as 125 yards. On the back stretch of the ninth lap Sockalexis took over third place, passing Saklad. Goldsmith was described as still "hanging in," showing no tendencies toward dropping back and cutting small pieces from Silva's big lead. Strobino and Piggott still remained together, about 150 yards behind Saklad.[7]

In the 10th lap, the account stated: "Sockalexis began the first of a series of brilliant spurts in the first few yards" of that lap. He passed Goldsmith and went into second place. The others were now ostensibly out of the race. Saklad had dropped back and was a good 75 yards behind Goldsmith. Strobino had finally shaken Piggott, and was comfortably alone in fifth place. These several "spurts" Sockalexis unleashed over the 10th and 11th laps reportedly put him into striking distance of Silva when the runners began the 12th lap. Silva, however, was described as looking strong. Again, he opened up the distance between himself and his followers, so that when the

leaders moved into the final lap Silva was described as leading
Sockalexis by a margin of approximately 100 yards.[8]

The *Commercial* account of the original Boston-based
story concluded with this paragraph:

> *Right here the Old Town Indian began a daz-*
> *zling spurt, and slowly, almost imperceptibly at*
> *first, began to gain on Silva. As the runners passed*
> *the centre field bleachers, Silva's advantage had*
> *been cut down to 70 yards. Sockalexis uncorked*
> *his last desperate spurt as the runners sped down*
> *the back stretch and ate up nearly 50 yards of the*
> *distance before the last turn was reached. Silva, al-*
> *though fatigued and leg weary, kept on with dogged*
> *persistence and broke the tape a scant eight yards*
> *ahead of the sprinting Sockalexis in a sensational*
> *finish. Goldsmith was third, over 100 yards behind*
> *the Indian.*[9]

Unfortunately, the unnamed correspondent provided no
finishing times for any of the competitors, so it is not recorded
how fast Sockalexis and his rival Silva ran the 5,000 meters.
Surely, Sockalexis must have taken some satisfaction in
"dusting" off Strobino, the so-called short-distance runner
who had beaten him at Stockholm; in this handicap race they
began together with the exact same handicap over the two
favorites. It had been stated Strobino's strength was in these
shorter distances. Certainly, it comes as no surprise that
DeMar was not competitive in this "sprint." He epitomized –
and was the best of – the so-called "plodders," the long,
long distance runner, winning 20-milers and marathons,

and even a 44-mile run from Providence to Boston. And, as famous as DeMar was, it is curious how many times his name is misspelled as "De Mar" by the unknowing, unnamed writers. Here, it happened again. Finally, there is the irony of Sockalexis' strong finish, only to take second place. It seems as though he was fated to be remembered as a man who looked for-all-the-world like a winner but was always destined for second prize. It had happened at the 1912 Boston Marathon... and this Boston 5,000 meter race was, tragically enough for Sockalexis, almost a carbon copy script for the race he would run at the 1913 Boston Marathon.

Another event at the "Boston Games" featured black sprinter Howard Drew, the high school sprinter from Springfield, Massachusetts who easily dispatched a huge field of 30 runners in a 100 meter race. As the "scratch" sprinter, he had to surrender a handicap to most if not all of the other competitors. It's hard to imagine how Drew could very comfortably blast his way through the whole field in so short a race, but the *Boston Post* account claimed he "walked through the 100-metre race showing his heels" to the rest of the competition. Drew and Andrew Sockalexis struck up a friendship during their time together as Olympians; sadly, Drew pulled a tendon on the eve of the finals of the Olympic 100 meter sprint and was unable to compete.[10]

Next up for the finely-tuned Sockalexis, his long-range plans for Brockton and New York still very much in focus, was a five-mile race "for a cup," set for the 29th Eastern Maine Fair in Bangor, which coincided with the Queen City's Labor Day festivities. This was announced in the *Bangor*

Daily Commercial and headlined an article about a number of activities planned for the celebration. Referring to the race as one of the key "drawing cards" of the fair, the article went on to characterize Sockalexis as "one of the best long distance runners of the country and the fact that he comes from near home arouses the local interest of all."[11]

Leading into the weekend before this race, the *Commercial* ran several articles about the special ceremonies to honor the Olympic team. Whether Andrew went to New York was not reported in the local Bangor and Old Town newspapers. The *Commercial* in its Thursday, August 22 issue, reported Jim Thorpe, Olympic "all around champion athlete" would be accorded an "honor post" in the New York City parade, set for that Saturday. Saturday evening's edition of the same newspaper carried a story telling of the "monster parade" through Fifth Avenue and Broadway, attracting an estimated 10,000 people to line the streets and honor the victorious athletes.[12] Each car in the parade carried two athletes and the names of those athletes were written on a large line running across the windshield of the vehicle. The following Tuesday another article told of a celebration in Philadelphia. Ten team members, plus ten more from the State of Pennsylvania, attended, including "Thorp" [sic] and runners Gallagher and Tewanima.[13] Finally, the August 28 edition of the *Commercial* contained a photo and caption showing Jim Thorpe receiving a congratulatory handshake from the mayor of New York, carrying this sorrowful racist description: "It was noticed that Thorpe bore himself with the typical attitude of his race and seldom looked to the right or the left. If he was embarrassed by the attention he received he did not show it..."[14]

In Bangor it was announced that Sockalexis' run at the Eastern Maine Fair would be one of the popular "challenge" or "match" races of the era.[15] Sockalexis and North Dorchester A.A. rival and fellow Olympian Tom Lilley would be the sole two competitors in a five-mile run on the track. Matching up two quality opponents, in races of all types of distances, was popular in this era for one big reason – betting. It was the driving force behind the popularity of professional running, and match races between amateur runners, too, frequently drew fans. The *Commercial* heralded the Monday matchup between Sockalexis and Lilley as one of the major features of the Labor Day celebration. It was to be held on the track at Maplewood Park, "a high line drawing card" of the day's events: "The superiority of these men has been in doubt for some time in the minds of many and this race will settle their relative ability and in view of the fact that there is a real rivalry, every inch of the five miles will be hard fought and a record for the distance ought to be made."[16] A second running event scheduled for Labor Day was a 10-mile "marathon," featuring Valissio Vambra of Fort McKinley, identified as "the champion runner of the Army and Navy" (who reportedly had beaten Italian runner Dorando Pietri, the man who nearly won the 1908 Olympic marathon). It was also to feature a number of local college runners, plus Arthur Neptune and Sylvester Francis from Indian Island. This run was scheduled to begin at the Winterport line and finish with one lap around Maplewood Park (now known as Bass Park) in Bangor.[17]

The *Bangor Daily News* for August 29, reported a fine start to the Eastern Maine State Fair. An aviator named Paoli put on an aeroplane exhibition, traveling far over Brewer and extending nearly to the business section of Bangor, according to the headline. A second part of this headline announced an exhibition run featuring Sockalexis. The fair's second day had produced one of the most successful days in its history, with a reported 15,000 people said to be on the fair grounds, making for a "glorious opportunity for pickpockets, and they made the most of it," as apparently the police had five or six complaints. There was also some local boasting about traditional fine weather for the Bangor fair. A sudden shower had struck but reasonably quickly dissipated: "Now, had this been the Lewiston fair, it would probably have kept right on raining until the end of the week; but this is the Bangor fair..."[18]

Harness racing and a baseball game were athletic attractions for the third day of the fair, "but the appearance of Andrew Sockalexis excited the most interest during the day." At 4 p.m. Andrew Sockalexis raced three miles against a team of two other Penobscots, Arthur Neptune and Sylvester Francis, in a match race. Sockalexis set off at the start, matched against Neptune. At the end of the first half-mile lap, he led by a yard. At the end of two laps, and the one-mile mark, the Olympic star led by 100 yards. Completing his duel with Neptune, Sockalexis completed the third lap and half-way point in the run, nearly an eighth of a mile in the lead. At the end of the fourth lap, he maintained roughly the same advantage – only this time over a fresh, new opponent, Francis. Over the course of the final two laps, Sockalexis stretched his lead and finished nearly a quarter of a mile ahead of the Neptune-Francis tandem. Sockalexis was given an ovation as he crossed the finish line, and his time was recorded as an excellent 13 minutes and 48 seconds for the three-mile run.[19]

On the day (Saturday, August 31) of Sockalexis' match race with Lilley, it was announced that "a big marathon" was being planned for September 14, to feature Sockalexis and other Olympic runners in a 20-mile race from Old Town to Bangor. To be sponsored by the Old Town Athletic Association, the race was to begin at Allen's Store in Old Town and come up Route 2 to Bangor, finishing with the last five miles run on the track at Maplewood Park and crossing a finish line in front of the great grandstand. In addition to Sockalexis, officials of the association announced that several other performers from the Stockholm Olympic marathon and from the greater Boston area were expected to appear. They included Clarence DeMar, 1912 Boston Marathon winner Mike Ryan, Thomas Lilley, Dick Piggott, Israel Saklad and others. The B.R. & E. announced it would send special trolley cars along to accompany the runners, on the road from Old Town down to the park, providing an excellent spectator vantage point. Other sporting events to be built around the great race included a 100-yard dash, a mile run, various other track and field events, and a baseball game.[20]

For all the hype the *Bangor Daily News* and *Bangor Daily Commercial* tried to build for the Sockalexis-Lilley 5-mile match race, it turned out to be a very easy victory for the hometown favorite. Interest in Sockalexis, indeed, remained great. The crowd surged to the track at first, reportedly necessitating work by the police to push them back and allow the runners to set off. After only eight laps, Lilley gave up, leaving Sockalexis running alone on the track. "At no time was there any doubt of the outcome" stated the *Bangor Daily News* account. Sockalexis ran the five-miles in a very creditable 26 minutes and 40 seconds.[21]

According to the lengthier *Commercial* account from September 2, the two runners entered the track, in front of the grandstand, around 2:30 p.m. Fred Allen and W.C. Rattray served as starters, with Benjamin Sproul appointed judge. At 2:36 p.m., the starter gave the word and Lilley took the lead, with Sockalexis just a step behind him. They held these positions for the first two miles. The time for the first mile was five minutes, and there was a slight drop in speed over the second mile, with the duo covering the distance in 10 1/2 minutes. At the end of the fifth lap, the half way mark in the race, Sockalexis began to pick up the pace. He took the lead from Lilley as the sixth lap began, right in front of the judge's stand. The time for the leader for the first three miles was reported as 16 minutes. On the seventh lap, both men continued to run close together, with Sockalexis failing to gain any significant ground on his North Dorchester A.A. club rival. But on the eighth lap, Sockalexis reportedly began to sprint. When he passed the judge's stand to complete the eighth lap and fourth mile he was a full 300 hundred yards ahead of Lilley. Sockalexis' time for four miles was called out as 21 minutes. Apparently Lilley felt, for all intents and purposes, the race was over...and so he walked in. Sockalexis ran a strong ninth lap, passing the grandstand looking strong and running all alone. He completed the final lap, for the fifth mile, in 26 minutes, keeping his own time with a stop watch in his hand.[22]

Just before the match race, an announcement was made from the grandstand about the proposed "big marathon" set for September 14. The Labor Day crowd at Maplewood Park Monday was said to be second in size only to the audience which gathered there for the previous Wednesday at the fair, Governor's Day. There were varied sporting programs and booths, which offered a weighing machine and the opportunity to shoot balls "at the African dodgers."[23]

Not long after Sockalexis crossed the finish line, runners began to come on to the track for the conclusion of the 10-mile "marathon" run, begun in Winterport. Sylvester Francis, a 16-year-old from Indian Island who was reported to be a "pupil" of Sockalexis, took first place, beating a field of six competitors. According to the *Commercial*, Labor Day "'twas Indian Day" when Sylvester Francis, "the young Indian whom Sockalexis picked up on the island a short time ago and trained," won the 10-mile race in one hour and one minute, following a "pretty duel" with Harold Barton of Bangor.[24] The competitors were given rides from the fair grounds out to the Winterport line but several of them encountered the embarrassment of suddenly discovering there was no place to change into their "running costumes." The changing, however, was "made possible through the kindness of a neighboring farmer, who tendered the use of his barn." Once the race was under way, Barton, who had won the Orono "Marathon" held during the town's Carnival Week, took the lead with Francis right behind him. They raced neck and neck, swapping the

lead. Francis tossed in one surge, but Barton immediately
made up the distance. At one point, the pair passed a
cemetery and the unnamed *Commercial* reporter joked that
they remained in a "dead heat." Then "as the boys hurried
by Prout's store," Francis began to break Barton's will. He
steadily pulled away, leading "by 15 yards, then 20, then 30
to the good." By Engel's Mill, Francis' lead was described as
at least 50 yards. "He (Francis) kept turning his head back as
he increased his advantage to 120 yards. The race was beyond
question..." It was an interesting scene as Francis suddenly
burst into view and began to circle Maplewood Park track:
"Into the park and onto the track, smashing up a 100 yard dash
just about to start, Francis sprinted. He had gone half a lap
when Sockalexis, his instructor, told him to end it quickly and
the boy did, coming under the wire a winner."[25]

Following these two races, a number of shorter races
were held on the track, for both amateur and professional
participants. After their five-mile duel both Sockalexis and
Lilley jumped into amateur sprints. Lilley entered the
100-yard amateur dash but did not finish in the top three. That
event was captured by C.B. Haskell of Pittsfield, in a time of
11 1/8 seconds, followed by Tarbox of Bangor, second, and
George Graves of Brewer, third. There was also a 100-yard
professional race, which was won by William A. Curran of
Bangor, followed by Edward Duffey of Augusta, second, and
Frank Miller of Bangor, third. This must surely be the same
Frank Miller who attempted to defend Sockalexis' honor
against the braggart who challenged the amateur runner to
a race for money before the Olympic Games. No times were

given. Sockalexis entered the 220-yard amateur dash. Haskell and Graves, first and third in the 100, returned to take first and second places, respectively, in this event. Sockalexis was third, followed by W.E. Johnson of Brewer in fourth. Again, no times were given, but it was quite an effort by Sockalexis considering that he'd completed a hard five-mile run just a short time before.

Originally scheduled for Saturday, September 14, 1912, the 20-mile race announced for that date was postponed for one week. On September 14 the *Bangor Daily Commercial* ran an article announcing that the "Marathon" race, featuring Sockalexis and many Olympic runners, would be run Saturday afternoon, September 21, from Old Town to Bangor. To be held under the auspices of the Old Town AA, the run was just one of several events planned for the day. There were also to be some baseball games and a band concert at Maplewood Park, while spectators awaited the stellar runners. It was announced that the distance to be run would be 20 miles, starting at Allen's clothing store in Old Town and following the trolley line to Bangor and Maplewood Park. The trotting track at Maplewood would be used for the final five miles of the race, offering a unique mix of road race and track race, the latter aspect certainly having appeal to spectators who wished to see the famous runners dueling to the finish. At this point the promoters were advertising the following participants, joining the already advertised Sockalexis, DeMar, Piggott and Lilley: Festus Madden, well-known rival of DeMar's who was a favorite to win the 1912 Boston Marathon; Anastus "Sturgess" *[Author's note: it's really "Sturgis"]*, an outstanding runner, victor at the last 10-miler at Manchester, N.H. on August 17, who would win the upcoming Brockton Marathon; "Joseph" *[Author's note: it's really "William"]* Fallon, another North Dorchester AA club member and the man who would ultimately marry Sockalexis' sister in 1913; "John" *[Author's note: it's really "James"]* Henigan, a tremendous middle distance runner, the "accredited" 10-mile champion of New England, who failed many, many times to win the Boston Marathon but finally did, in a very popular 1931 win; and Israel Saklad, another well-known standout from the North Dorchester AA.[26]

Clearly, Sockalexis' reputation and personality had served him well with his fellow North Dorchester track club members for them all to make the long trip from Boston up to Bangor to compete. Local runners W.A. Johnson of Brewer and Arthur Neptune from Indian Island were also mentioned as competitors for the event. It was further announced that the race was "under the sanction" of the New England Amateur Athletic Union, and would be a strictly amateur event. The Old Town promoters had planned to put on a race for professionals, which the event creators had hoped would attract more spectators (spectators, potentially attracted by the lure of betting, who would then be willing to pay admission into the event). The promoters had already raised, they reported, over $100 in prizes. But, because no professional events could be held in conjunction with an amateur event – without leaving the amateur competitors subject to suspicion that they had competed with professionals – the New England Amateur Athletic Union told the Old Town organizers they must drop the professional race idea if they desired sanction for their event.[27]

So, in place of the professional race, Allen opted for two baseball contests, some dashes, one-mile and three-mile runs, and music by the St. Joseph Band. The running events were to start at 1:30 p.m., with the 20-miler set to start at the same time in Old Town. Allen invited entries for all the running events, noting that amateurs must be registered with the New England Amateur Athletic Union, at a cost of 25 cents which had to be in the hands of a gentleman at a Cambridge, Massachusetts address. Allen gave an Old Town post office box for people to enter.[28]

Chapter 10

DeMar beats Sockalexis in
Old Town- to-Bangor race

During the week before the big 20-mile race on September 21, 1912, the area newspapers carried further announcements about the anticipated outstanding runners coming to Bangor.

The Tuesday, September 17 *Bangor Daily Commercial* identified the same earlier core of outstanding talent: Sockalexis, DeMar, Madden, Henigan, Lilley, Saklad, Sturgis and Fallon of the North Dorchester Club, and spelled Sturgis' name right as well.

New on this stellar list were Gaston Strobino, the New Jersey runner who had taken third place at Stockholm, and another member of the North Dorchester club, R.F. Pickard, plus some local runners, including Sockalexis' protege from Indian Island, Sylvester Francis. A number of runners who would challenge for the prizes in the dashes and shorter track runs were also announced.

Promoter Allen continued to try to hype the event, boasting that some of "the best and fastest men in the country" would be competing in the 100- and 220-yard dashes, as well as the one-mile, two-mile and three-mile races. William McVicar of the Boston AA was coming to compete in "his specialties," the one- and three-mile runs. Also, a "J. Powell" was coming, billed as "the colored Boston 100-yard dash man, one of the fastest in the country." Several Indian Island "boys" had registered, including Theodore B. Mitchell who signed up for the 100- and 220-yard dashes. Tickets for the event were to go on sale that Wednesday at several sites in Bangor.[1]

On Friday, September 20, the *Commercial* boldly proclaimed:

MARATHON SATURDAY
Twenty Mile Road Race, Old
Town to Maplewood Park
STROBINO VS. SOCKALEXIS
Notable Gathering of World Famous Athletics for This and Other Events at Maplewood.

The lead sentence bluntly boasted: "What promises to be the greatest meeting of the world's famous athletes ever held in Maine will come off Saturday afternoon at Maplewood Park, under the auspices of the Old Town A.A."[2]

Yet, in point of fact, the statement was arguably true: There had not ever been, and would not be again for many decades after Andrew Sockalexis left the scene, the same kind of running talent amassed for one event like that which lined up for this 1912 20-mile race in September. And such a comparable array of athletic talent – certainly running talent – was probably not seen in Maine again until 1980, when world-class middle distance runners and marathoners like Bill Rodgers, Greg Meyers, Bruce Bickford, Randy Thomas, Bobby Hodge and others from the Greater Boston Track Club came up to honor Joan Benoit at the Cooks Corner 5-miler in Brunswick. Or when Larry and Gary Allen, Mickey Lackey, Marc Violette, Mike Gaige and others of the Bangor-based Downeast Striders Track Club hosted a series of Benjamin's 10-K road races in Bangor in the early 1980s, featuring some of the top talent from around New England. Presently Joan Benoit Samuelson has been annually hosting the Beach to Beacon 10-K in her hometown of Cape Elizabeth, which attracts a world-class, international field of runners.

In addition, the positive impact Sockalexis was having on the Penobscot tribe was apparently enormous. The *Commercial* noted:

> *No athletic event that has ever been held in Maine has given such an impetus to athletics among the younger members of the Penobscot tribe as this...All the athletic youngsters of the island have awakened to their opportunity... A surprisingly large number of the Indian youth have entered for the lesser events, so that the Penobscot tribe will be represented at the meet, better than in any event held in Maine for many years, if indeed ever.*[3]

Even though he had recently soundly defeated his more successful Olympic rival in that Boston 5,000 meter race,

Sockalexis was said to be "eagerly awaiting his opportunity race" against Strobino, although he was not directly quoted as saying any such thing. This sounds like just more race hype from Allen. Based on his own remarks at the reception following the Olympics, Sockalexis did not seem to regard Strobino as much of a threat to his own success. The *Commercial* reported that because Sockalexis regularly trained on the road from Old Town to Bangor, having made it his "track for practice runs" and thus knew the terrain "like a book," the diminutive Penobscot Indian runner was confident of victory over all his well-known rivals.[4]

The final paragraph of the *Commercial* story asked those who chose to accompany the runners in their automobiles "to keep well out of the way, as even if there is no dust to fly and disturb them, the conditions will be hard enough even with a clear road."[5] There were 15 runners registered for the 20-miler, the latest entry being Oswald Sparson from Lewiston.

The *Bangor Daily News* had a brief story trumpeting the appearance of Strobino, under the headline: "**STROBINO, GREAT RUNNER, COMING.**" In this Friday, September 20 account the New Jersey runner was described as being a small man, only 5-feet-3 and weighing just 116 pounds...but "a very pretty runner...known the world over for his endurance and pluck." DeMar, described as "not up to form on the other side" (in Sweden), had written to say that he had run several fast races recently. And, according to the *News*, DeMar predicted victory, stating that he would win despite the fact that Strobino was running faster than ever before. The hype in support of the hometown favorite continued, with the *Bangor Daily News* noting that "all Bangor and Old Town is pulling for a victory" for Sockalexis, and that "Sock declares himself to be in pretty good condition and has his heart set on winning this big event."[6]

It was more of the same Saturday morning. The *Bangor Daily News* listed the Olympic and Boston-area stars again and noted the marathon was set for Maplewood that day. Sockalexis was quoted as saying: "This is one race that I must win and although I expect a hard race I feel confident that I will win. I was never in better shape in my life." Sockalexis was termed, by the newspaper, as "a heavy favorite and his many friends are pulling for him to bring home the bacon," a $150 silver cup to be presented to the winner.[7] However, one week later, in the *Enterprise* of Sepember 28, it would be reported that "Sockalexis had suffered all day from a splitting headache which interfered with his work of the day but he had in De Mar *[sic]* 'a foeman worthy of his tell.'"[8]

What may have been the most stellar field – and there were only eight runners! – ever to run the roads of central Maine was said to have departed from Old Town at about 1:30 p.m. before a large crowd. Actually, it was after 2 p.m. The *Commercial* also erroneously reported there were "15 runners toeing the line when the starter fired his pistol."[9] Clearly the *Commercial* did not have an actual representative at the start and, perhaps, gambled that all the anticipated runners had arrived and the event started on time. The *Bangor Daily Commercial* had an early afternoon deadline, which also may have contributed to its difficulties in covering this event. The newspaper did note that a short distance ahead of the run officials and newspapermen rode in a big touring car.

The corrected version of the start, in the second *Commercial* account, noted:

> *Although the start had been scheduled for 1:30 p.m., it was nearly 2 when the scantily clad runners appeared in front of Allen's clothing store on Main Street in Old Town and lined up in the mud, waiting for the signal which would send them on their long run down the river. A drizzling rain was falling. The runners danced up and down to keep warmed up in the cold. It was exactly 2:06 when the crack of starter Allen's pistol sent them bounding on their way. A crowd of several hundred watched the start.*[10]

The *Bangor Daily News* commended Allen and Fernandez for bringing greater Bangor "a run worthy of the Boston race." The unnamed writer said it was "unfortunate" about the weather, noting that the runners "slid through mud and hurdled pools of water and when they reached Bangor varied the monotony by dodging autos and electrics. However, in the minds of many that rendered the event more interesting. One thing is sure, this marathon is one that will be talked over for time to come."[11]

The *Enterprise* stated: "The runners were well received all along the line the people turning out in large numbers to see them go by thus evincing their interest in one of the great sports of the centuries."[12]

The *Bangor Daily News* noted that DeMar "handily" won the 20-mile run, which was "nearer 19 miles in length."

The *News* account said it was "a pretty race," witnessed by "throngs" of people, estimating that between 400 and 500 people watched the eight starters leave at 2:06 p.m.[13]

The second *Commercial* account estimated that several hundred people witnessed the finish at Maplewood, and that the streets through which the runners passed were lined by thousands. Nearly the entire student body turned out at the University of Maine, it was reported, and cheered the runners as they passed the campus. An estimated 20 automobile parties followed the field along the road from Old Town to Bangor. The race was under the direction of F. E. Allen and O.B. Fernandez, managers of the Old Town A.A. and, "from a spectacular standpoint, it proved a great success." Dr. E.M. Marquis and Herbert Danforth of Old Town and Patrolman Frank J. Rogan of Bangor acted as timers.[14]

It is very unclear how the *Bangor Daily Commercial* so erroneously documented the start, yet covered the details of the first half of the race, presumably until the newspaper was forced to suspend coverage to meet its afternoon deadline. Was the correspondent late getting to the start and then joined the press vehicle for the first half of the race? Did the correspondent somehow just take details of the race in progress from an eyewitness? It seems hard to believe an area writer would not be suspicious of world-class runners taking an hour to run from Old Town to Orono! Yet, based on the times published in the *Commercial* in its first account, that is precisely what the newspaper was suggesting to its readers with no explanation! The explanation, simply stated, was a 36-minute delay in starting the race.

The *Bangor Daily News* stated that at about 2 p.m., the runners left the Hotel Fransway in Old Town and "strolled" to the starting line, in front of Allen's clothing store. A slight rain, it reported, was falling, but cleared just after the start.[15] The *Enterprise* stated the start was delayed until 2:06 p.m. because of the shower and that, because of the extremely muddy conditions of the roads through the towns along the way, the runners used sidewalks as well as streets.[16]

The *Bangor Daily News* reported it was announced, at the starting line, that Strobino, Piggott and Madden had not arrived "and nobody waited for them."[17] Neither of the local daily newspapers reported about the reasons for any of these absences. Did they all cancel at the last moment? Or were their names merely used at the outset by promoter Allen to create local excitement and sell tickets? No explanation was forthcoming. One auto, with the officials, led the way. A second carried the runners' belongings, and a third, driven by Lawrence Allen, contained the newspaper reporters, with John Ormiston and Gordon Beatty as aides for the race.

Led by Jimmy Henigan, who would win the Boston Marathon in 1931, the runners reached Orono at just before 2:30 p.m., reported the *Bangor Daily Commercial* in its first account – with no explanation of why it would take an hour, according to its erroneous listed start time, for world-class runners to run only four to five miles. Actually, it only took 24 minutes or so. A bunch of runners were packed just behind Henigan. The runners were described as covered with mud but running hard and showing the extra effort to slog through the mud and "sticky" conditions. Following Henigan was Saklad,

Sturgis *[Author's note: The Commercial continued to misspell his name as "Sturges"]*, Lilley, DeMar *[Author's note: The Commercial continued to misspell his name as "De Mar"]*, Sockalexis, Fallon and Sylvester Francis, the young Penobscot runner. Sockalexis was described as "apparently saving himself for the other end of the race," for he was said to be at least 25 yards behind the other runners.[18]

In its second account, the *Commercial* stated that Fallon took the early lead, closely followed by Henigan, Sturgis, DeMar, Saklad, Lilley, Sockalexis and Francis. The mud proved thick and difficult to contend with until the runners were well out on Stillwater Avenue on their way to Orono. From there to Bangor the road was described as comparatively good, with the exception of occasional puddles. The worst footing, the *Commercial* reported, was experienced from the Eastern Maine General Hospital in Bangor on up to Maplewood Park.[19]

The *Bangor Daily News* account offered a few more colorful details. It reported Fallon took the early lead, and Sockalexis stayed to the rear. At the Indian Island Ferry, a group of friends waved encouragement to Sockalexis. As the runners "trotted" up Academy Hill, Sockalexis had "dropped to last," trailed only by his "little pal" Francis. A mile had been covered, and Sockalexis' timer gave his time as six minutes. Stillwater Avenue, where "bunches" of spectators applauded, found Henigan now in the lead, followed by Fallon. Francis was said to be at least 75 yards behind Sockalexis. By the time the University of Maine was reached Henigan was in the lead, followed by Saklad, Sturgis, DeMar, Fallon, Lilley, Sockalexis and Francis, in that order.[20]

With the exception of "little Francis," who dropped some distance far to the rear, there was, the *Commercial* reported in its second account, "hardly ever a distance of more than 100 yards between the leader and the trailing bunch of white clad figures."[21] The *Bangor Daily News* reported: "With Maine students cheering," all the runners were "within earshot" (except Francis). The runners came into Orono, crossing Kelley Road. Francis was seen dimly in the distance. At the seven-mile mark, Sockalexis passed Fallon. On the way from Orono to Veazie, the relative positions of the runners changed slightly. Saklad reportedly began to feel an acute pain in his left side and ran for some distance with a hand pressed tightly against his intestines. "I'm all right," he called out to the race judge when his motor car drew up alongside.[22]

Despite the fact that nearly 20 automobiles followed them the runners experienced "no inconvenience from the machines," the newspaper reported, stating that the drivers were careful to give the runners the right of way. Every now and then a crowded trolley car passed by and a cheer came from the passengers.[23]

By the time Veazie was reached, Lilley had taken over first place and DeMar followed close behind, in second. Henigan, who was now "plainly in distress," had dropped back to third, but very little distance separated all the runners. Sockalexis, Sturgis, Saklad and Fallon followed. Young Francis was described as "somewhere in the rear, among the automobiles."[24]

The *Bangor Daily News* continued: "Veazie furnished nearly seven spectators for the race, as Lilley swept by, followed by DeMar, Henigan, Sockalexis, Sturgis, Saklad. Fallon was somewhere back and where, Oh where, was Francis. Answer, he was somewhere but you couldn't prove it by the writer." The unnamed correspondent reported it took the lead runners one half hour to run from Orono to Veazie. They reached Veazie at around 3 p.m. and the checkpoint was marked by a change in the order, with Lilley coming up from fourth to first and DeMar, who had been hanging back in fifth, moving into second place. The two leaders, the *News* reported, were barely a yard apart, and both described as "running strong." Henigan, who had led through Orono, fell back to third.[25] Sockalexis "had begun to quicken his pace," the *Commercial* stated, and instead of being well to the rear of this lead pack he had now pulled into fourth place. Saklad, who was second to reach Orono, had dropped back into fifth.[26]

In Veazie Henigan, making a determined drive to get back into the race, took the lead again. Just before Mount Hope Cemetery was reached, however, Henigan dropped out of the race and was taken into the judge's automobile. The *Bangor Daily News* reported: "Passing the bridge, Jimmy Henigan had taken back his first position prize and soon the 10-mile mark was in sight. Henigan stopped at Mt. Hope Cemetery. 'Pain in my side,' he panted. Mr. Allen bundled the young fellow into his auto..."[27]

Henigan, it was written, was a 10-mile runner and a generally-accepted theory about him was that he had been sent into the race to set the pace for the first half of the distance in the hope of drawing Sockalexis out. It is not clear if the local media representatives had specifically heard about this strategy from the Boston-based visiting contingent or it was analysis offered by local observers. It is possible the travelers from Boston designated one member to establish a pace for the rest of them, but there is no evidence offered anywhere that the strategy was created specifically to ruin Sockalexis. If it was, obviously, it did not work.

By the time the pumping station alongside the Penobscot River had been reached the race had settled down to a contest between the four leaders. Going up Hichborn Hill DeMar was pressing Lilley hard for first place, and Sockalexis and Sturgis were neck and neck a little over 100 yards to the rear of the two leaders. As the race developed further, the *News* reported Lilley had the lead, with DeMar 100 yards behind, Sturgis another 100 yards behind DeMar, and Sockalexis, 50 yards behind Sturgis. DeMar reportedly pressed Lilley on the hill beside the hospital hill, and Sockalexis pulled even with Sturgis, the two runners pacing side by side. Lilley, reportedly, was using the sidewalk on State Street.[28]

The runners reached Bangor, according to the *Commercial*, around 3:15 p.m., passing a specific landmark, Gallagher's store, at 3:20. The order passing Gallagher's put Lilley in first, DeMar in second, and Sockalexis in third. Somewhere, out of nowhere, the *Commercial* placed the absent Strobino (clearly mistaking him for Sturgis) in fourth place here, never having mentioned him earlier, nor to mention him again![29]

Lilley still reportedly led DeMar by 100 yards when he turned on to Main Street, passing the *Commercial* office. DeMar remained second, with Sockalexis trailing and Sturgis (not Strobino) immediately behind him in fourth place. Sockalexis and Sturgis were again reported as running close together.

Then, because the *Commercial* had a late afternoon deadline to meet, the account came to an abrupt end without the report of the conclusion of the race. The newspaper simply reported that the runners entered Maplewood Park in the same positions that they had passed the *Commercial* office "just as the *Commercial* went to press."[30]

The *Commercial*'s next-day account recapped the race a little and then continued: "There were crowds on State street and the men ran in and out of stream of teams, automobiles and trolley cars. Going down over State street hill the pace quickened and the leaders forged ahead. Lilley had turned Robinson's corner on his way up Main street when Sock was opposite French street. The runners had covered 13 miles."[31]

The *News* noted that by Exchange Street, Lilley had stretched his lead to 200 yards. As the crowd along the route kept up its cheering, the police were trying to untangle traffic and keep a path cleared for the runners. At this point Maplewood Park was still a mile away and the runners had five miles to negotiate on the track after reaching the park, for a total of 19 miles.[32] One of the unnamed correspondents commented that "it began to look as though Sockalexis had given the Massachusetts runners too much of a lead, if he expected to win." Lilley still maintained a small lead over DeMar when the runners first appeared on the track at Maplewood Park. An estimated quarter of a mile behind Lilley came Sockalexis, "to all appearances running easily and strong." Then followed Sturgis, Saklad, Fallon "and – far in the rear – Francis, the gamey, young Indian who had found himself in the fastest company he had ever attempted to travel with." [33]

Israel Saklad quit at the 15th mile, not long after he reached the track at Maplewood. Complaining he was "greatly bothered with an acute pain in his side on the way from Old Town," according to the *Commercial*, he "kept on gamely, nevertheless."[34] According to the *News*, Saklad quit after doing his first mile on the track because of "stomach troubles."[35]

On the first lap around the track DeMar wrested the lead from Lilley, who was described by the *Commercial* as "plainly showing exhaustion."[36] Terming Lilley "a tired lad," the *News* said "his pace grew slower and slower and, ultimately, both Sockalexis and Sturgis passed him, leaving him with a fourth place finish."[37]

At the finish line it was DeMar, winner of the Boston Marathon in 1911, who defeated Sockalexis by one minute in the 19-mile run from Old Town to Bangor's Maplewood Park. Though the local newspapers and citizenry had believed Sockalexis, the local favorite, would be the winner the race was never in doubt once the runners reached Maplewood Park. The *Commercial* reported of DeMar, "the Massachusetts man was never once in danger after he loped on to the Maplewood track, and took a quarter of a mile lead, for most of the last five miles (done on the track). The winner's time was 1 hour 54 minutes."[38]

The *News* account commended DeMar for his running prowess and also for "the modest manner" in which he acknowledged congratulations. As DeMar sped around Maplewood Park in "that light tread and long stride amid the plaudits of the spectators a constant smile was evident and when he finished was as fresh as a daisy." Sockalexis crossed the finish line just a minute later. Six men finished out of the field of eight who started. The final results showed: Sturgis, 3rd; Lilley, 4th; Fallon, 5th; and Francis, 6th. Henigan and Saklad dropped out.[39]

The *Commercial* assessed the performance of Sockalexis as follows: "It would not be true to say that Sock lost the race by deferring his spurt too long, but it is nevertheless certain that he showed more strength on the track than any of the other runners. DeMar's lead of a quarter of a mile was too great a distance for the Indian to overcome, but he nevertheless showed much stamina and cut down the advantage of his opponent to a single minute – a remarkable feat in view of the circumstances."[40]

The *Bangor Daily News* contended: "Sock should not feel downcast for he ran a good race and in coming in second accomplished a good deal as it was." He was said to have "cut down the advantage of the leaders greatly" but that DeMar's lead when the track was reached – one-quarter of a mile – was just too much. "Of course there are a lot of 'ifs' but De Mar [sic] proved himself the best man and there is no dishonor for the others because they failed to attain the premier position." DeMar, the *News* also noted, "finished strong and was running easily at the finish."[41]

Both newspapers praised the performance of the "plucky little Francis." The *Commercial* noted: "His running was little short of professional for a boy of his years. His gameness in finishing was commended on all sides. It seems likely that he will make his mark as a distance runner within a few years."[42] The writer for the *Bangor Daily News* said essentially the same thing, using almost the same phrasing: "Francis, the 16-year-old Indian, a pupil of Sockalexis, finished sixth and was commended upon all sides for his gameness. He should be heard from later."[43]

In his autobiography, DeMar briefly discussed the race, though his memory failed him about the distance run on the track. He remembered the race as a 20-miler, with only the last mile run on the track. He had been experimenting with a strictly vegetable diet for a whole year, through the Olympic competition, and had recently come to the conclusion to "discontinue the experiment. While my failure at Stockholm had been in no way due to the diet yet I could not see that self denial did one iota of good and it was a tremendous bother." Now, he stated, he "ate as circumstances permitted." Since he had worked at his newspaper printing job the evening he was to depart for the race, he ate a cheese sandwich and a piece of apple pie with "inky fingers, while working." He then noted he took the overnight train, departing from Boston's North Station at 10 p.m., up to central Maine. DeMar recalled: "I ran a good race the next day beating the field, including Sockalexis, who had been fourth at Stockholm. So much for being fussy about what you eat for any particular race!"[44]

DeMar was awarded a silver cup valued at $150. Sockalexis received a gold watch, valued at $25, for second prize. The third place prize for Sturgis was a silver tea set, valued at $20. For his fourth place finish Lilley received a mantle clock, valued at $15. Fallon's award, for fifth place, was a traveling bag, valued at $10. And a set of gold cuff links, valued at $5, was the prize for Francis for sixth place. If there had been a seventh place finisher the prize would have been a safety razor, valued at $5...but there wasn't.

So, once again, Andrew Sockalexis took second place. As part of the pre-race "hype," promoter Allen had apparently told the area newspapers that this race meant a great deal to Sockalexis to win because it was in front of his hometown friends and neighbors. Yet, again, Sockalexis had finished second and again media representatives had blamed him for failing to "let him self out" in pursuit of first-place honors.

The original list of runners scheduled to compete had included 15 names at various times. They were: DeMar, Lilley, Henigan, Saklad, Piggott, Sturgis, Sockalexis, Strobino, Fallon, Neptune, Madden, Francis, Jenkins, Johnson of Brewer, Sparson of Lewiston.

But Piggott, Madden and Jenkins, all from Boston, and Strobino, from New Jersey, did not appear for the race, and, Maine locals Neptune, Johnson and Sparson did not show up either. A week after the event, in the Old Town *Enterprise*, dated September 28, the race was praised and reviewed. "Fred E. Allan *[sic]* and Orman B. Fernandez of this city, managers of the Old Town A.A. pulled off Saturday, September 21, 1912 here and at Bangor (Maplewood Park) the greatest athletic stunt that has ever been the good fortune for Maine people to see." It was noted the promoters deserved "great credit for their courage, for they stood to lose a great deal of money and as it was, it rained days before and up to the minute of starting, yet everything went as advertised and everyone was satisfied." The *Enterprise* noted that "the majority" of the talent showed up and every race was well contested, with "not a kick" of complaint from anyone. It was noted that the three Olympic stars – DeMar, Lilley and Sockalexis – were "the center of interest."[45]

The *Enterprise* stated "space does not allow us to go into detail of the race suffice to say it was interesting all the way..." That seems a rather strange statement to make, especially if this was, indeed, a "race of the centuries."[46]

The *Enterprise* praised the visiting runners, exclaiming they were "most pleasant and gentlemanly young men, everyone being glad to meet them and have them in our city." Several of the runners, it was reported, visited Sockalexis' home on Sunday – where one of the few remaining photographs of Andrew and his famous fellow marathoners was taken with Andrew's father and mother. The runners also toured the island. The runners stayed at the Hotel Fransway in Old Town and were "most complimentary in speaking about this new up-to-date hotel" and the hospitality of the proprietor, a man named Perro, and the hotel clerk.[47]

Allen and Fernandez were reportedly "not disheartened from the financial results of the event but have already signed all of the participants of Saturday for a larger and better carnival to be held May 30, 1913 when it is hoped better weather will attend them."[48] There was no mention made, in any of the local newspapers, about how much the event cost or how many paid spectators there were at Maplewood Park; apparently the promoters lost significant money on the race.

The newspapers did provide a list of winners of the other events on Saturday at Maplewood Park. The *Commercial* reported: 1-mile run, with six starters, won by William McVicar in 4:48 (UMaine's Roger Bell, second, and Mike Kelley, third); 100-yard dash, with four starters, won by William Mennix, BAA, in 10 1-5 seconds, followed by "J. Powell (colored),", N. Dorchester AA, second, and George Morse of UMaine, third; and 3-mile race, with a big field, won by McVicar, in 16:18, with Cantalo, second, and Powers, third.[49]

A short blurb in the *Bangor Daily News* for September 21, the day of the big race, noted that in Pittsburgh, at Forbes Field, amateur and senior athletes were competing in a major Amateur Athletic Union (AAU) event. In the 100-yard dash "attention is directed toward H.P. Drew, the fast colored youth of the Springfield, Mass. High school" and in the five-mile race Hannes Kohlemainen, "the Finnish runner who made an international reputation at Stockholm," would be competing.[50] In 1914 Drew would make a special appearance in Bangor on behalf of Andrew Sockalexis.

On the Monday following the 19-miler from Old Town to Bangor, the *Commercial* carried the news that "manager" F.E. Allen of the Old Town Athletic Association was announcing that "all the athletes who competed on Saturday had signed to enter a similar marathon and athletic meet on April 30 next." So it worked out that the *Enterprise*, which announced May 30, and the *Commercial*, which announced April 30, had the same information about another big race – but conflicting dates. The *Commercial*, too, alluded to a financial loss for the promoters: "Although Saturday's meet was not altogether a success financially the management feels that it was through no fault of the meet as an attraction"...[51]

In this *Commercial* article Allen noted that he had received late communications from Joseph Silva, who had taken third place in a Pittsburgh 5-miler the week before and was Sockalexis' big rival in the 3,000-meter track race in Boston right after the Olympics, and Joseph Cook of BAA, both of whom, reportedly, wanted to be in the race Saturday. He said he received their letters after the race had been run.[52] There still was no explanation about the absences of Strobino, Madden and Piggott, nor would there be in the local media.

Then it was reported that Andrew Sockalexis complained of a headache the day of the big 19-miler. Perhaps this was the first step in the decline of his health.

For the *Bangor Daily Commercial* of Thursday, October 3, 1912 carried its usual Old Town news column, called "**UP IN OLD TOWN**," and it carried the following headline above two very diverse items of concern: "**Andrew Sockalexis Has to Withdraw From All Racing/ Peeping Tom Reported Abroad Again**." It was reported that Sockalexis, who had had "his heart set" on competing in the Brockton, Massachusetts marathon in October and then a new big race scheduled for New York in November, had to set those ambitions aside and "retire from all racing for the season and probably for at least six months." Sockalexis got that advice from a physician who recently examined him and bluntly told him that any further racing might have "serious effects" on his health. Sockalexis spoke to a *Commercial* representative on Wednesday and said he felt fine, but "as the examination by the doctors had shown him that he was doing too much immediately after acquiring a severe cold, he felt that it was only wisdom to follow their advice and refrain from all racing for six months."[53]

Sockalexis was quoted by the *Commercial* as saying: "At the end of that time I shall have their promise that I shall be better than ever and next year I shall be running again." Sockalexis had expected to leave the next Monday for Brockton, the place where he first made his regional reputation as a marathon runner, and where he had "high hopes" of winning. The *Commercial* account concluded: "The exhaustive results of his big effort on Labor Day, which left him completely used up for a time emphasized the need of skillful medical care and he went to Bangor for an examination, resulting in the doctor ordering him from the track for the next six months."[54]

On October 4, 1912, the *Commercial* carried the headline: **"A.K. STURGIS WINS THE BROCKTON MARATHON,"** and a short piece noting that Sturgis had captured the event in 2 hours, 30 minutes, 8 2-5 seconds. A William Galvin of Yonkers, N.Y., was second in 2 hours, 41 minutes, while Israel Saklad of Roxbury was third, in 2 hours, 53 minutes, 25 seconds. Fallon and Lilley were also in the starting field. The weather was said to be unusually warm, with the runners facing a breeze for part of the distance. A comparatively flat first 10 miles led into the Blue Hills with three very stiff hills to climb.[55] Having just dusted Sturgis in the race in Old Town, Sockalexis could not have been very happy with the news.

The *Bangor Daily Commercial* carried another article about Sockalexis' failing health on October 7, 1912. It reported that the runner was "to pass six months in the Maine woods, in an attempt to recover his health which has been somewhat affected, presumably by the terrible strain that he had under gone in his marathon racing." There was a curious interpretation of these events by the unnamed writer who stated: "Even the runner trained to the minute finds the marathon a terrific test of his endurance, the more especially if in his striving to win his pluck and courage carries him on even when his flagging energies utter a vain protest."[56]

In late October, the *Commercial* announced the Thanksgiving run, which Sockalexis had won the year before, would be held again, and on November 29, the 5-mile "marathon" was held again. The winner was E.P. Cutler of the Bangor Theological seminary in a time of 31:15. Harold Hardy was second in 31:55 and H. L. Haines of the seminary was third, in 33:50.[57]

In the *Commercial* account of the Thanksgiving Run, the following item about Sockalexis was offered: "An added interest was given to the race by the appearance of Andrew Sockalexis, the Old Town Indian, whose place among the Marathon runners of the world is a high one. Sockalexis made an exhibition run over the course finishing in 29 minutes, 6 seconds. The distance covered is estimated to be some in excess of five miles."[58]

***

Chapter 11

Sockalexis judged tardy for win at 1913 Boston Marathon

Andrew Sockalexis' name temporarily disappeared from the sporting pages, not to be seen until the Boston Marathon of 1913. There were 84 names which dotted the entry list on the April 19th morning of the big race. Veteran Harry Smith led a large delegation from New York, with a batch of New Yorkers representing a group called the "Bronx Church House." With the exception of a few Canadians there were no international names in the field. And Andrew Sockalexis was the only Native American. The North Dorchester A.A. had a pile of representatives with the now familiar names of Madden, Saklad, Lilley, Sturgis, Fallon and Cliff Horne present, along with Sockalexis.

Also in the field were two men from Minneapolis with duplicate-sounding surnames: John Karlsen and Fritz Carlson.

For this 17th running at Boston, Sockalexis wore Number 26. A photograph, published in the *Boston Post*, of a group of favorites for the race included Sockalexis, Madden, Lilley, Samuel Pavitt of Somerville, and the great Canadian champion, Jim Corkery. Curiously, Corkery's name was not included in any of the pre-race publicity, nor did it appear in the lineup of runners the day of the race, so he may have dropped out at the last minute.

The day just previous to race day *Boston Post* columnist Arthur Duffey reported Sockalexis had dropped by the newspaper office and "looked as fit as the proverbial fiddle." Duffey noted: "Andy had little to say about the great race, but after much coaxing let loose and stated that he was afraid that Festus Madden would win the big grind this year." According to Duffey, Sockalexis said: "Madden is the only runner I am afraid of...but of course in a Marathon race anyone is likely to spring the unexpected. Madden and myself had the race out between us last year, and I figure that, if I can beat Madden again, the race will be mine."[1]

Like his famous baseball-playing cousin, Louis Sockalexis, Andrew Sockalexis seemed to have no trouble finding his way to newspaper offices and receiving favorable publicity.

Just below that Duffey column was this *Boston Post* headline and story:

SOCKALEXIS HAS
BRIDE TO CONSIDER

The story noted that Sockalexis, one of the favorites in the next day's Marathon, had "far more at stake should he win than the bronze statuette presented by the BAA. It is a bride, an Indian maiden from the Maine village, that will be

Sockalexis' reward if he breaks the tape tomorrow but a foot ahead of the second man."[2]

Acknowledging the notation about Sockalexis visiting the *Boston Post* offices in Arthur Duffey's column, it seems reasonably obvious this story most obviously came from no one other than Andrew Sockalexis. Yet later, after the race, Sockalexis would say he had no comment to make about that race-victory-leads-to-marriage report. But here, two days before the run, it almost seems in effect Andrew Sockalexis is confidently predicting a win. It seems highly likely it was this story which set up Penobscot Indian maiden Pauline Shay to ride with the journalists, so she could follow the race and so the journalists could write about her reaction to the race in progress.

The writer of the story predicted spectators would "see some great running tomorrow, and, with the road in any sort of condition for fast work and the weather favorable, it would not be surprising to see last year's record for the distance clipped by a few seconds."[3] Had Sockalexis boldly predicted a possible record too?

The *Boston Post* reported Sockalexis had arrived in Boston the day before and "appears in fine fettle for the battle tomorrow. He has been training for weeks for the long grind, and shows it."[4]

In his preview of the marathon for the *Boston Post*, which appeared the morning of the run on April 19, Arthur Duffey identified three specific favorites – one of whom was Andrew Sockalexis – and wrote, very compellingly, about his respect for marathoning.[5]

"**Arthur Duffey's Column**," the titled column he wrote
under, was penned by a man who had been a great sprinter in
his time. In the column he alluded to this ability, noting that
"when I was an athlete some years ago I was credited with
running 100 yards in 9 3-5 seconds. At the time it was said
such a performance was a terrific strain on the heart and other
muscles." But, he argued, the marathon, to his way of thinking,
was "the most grueling contest known to sport." He dismissed
football, baseball, rowing, boxing and other sports said to be
"a great strain on the body," requiring the strictest of training.
His admiration and respect for marathoners was unbridled: "A
marathon runner must go through the most arduous siege of
training. He must be prepared to stand the gaff for over 2 1-2
hours of the most nerve racking experiences. He must have
untold nerve, strength and endurance. There is no chance for
the quitter in this game. Yes, no matter what may be said, a
marathon champion is a champion of champions."[6] Duffey
exclaimed that Boston itself would be well represented "in
the great race today," and then furthered the compliment by
suggesting it would be "the greatest representation that ever
competed." Duffey chose four regional runners as his favorites
for the race, including Andrew Sockalexis; the other three
were greater Boston runners Festus Madden, Anastas Sturgis
and A.G. Horne.[7]

Duffey agreed with Sockalexis that Madden was the
man with the greatest chance to win. Calling all four of these
runners "great marathoners," Duffey added, "Madden perhaps
the best of them all. This husky local runner is a freight
handler by trade. His daily work keeps him hard as nails. He

has competed in so many marathons that it is second nature for him to go through the grind of such a race." Duffey noted that Madden had finished third in the 1912 race, behind Sockalexis. The only damning concern about Madden for Duffey: "...on past performances the favorite rarely wins the race and this is said to be against him."[8]

Duffey then made his case for Sockalexis, referring to him as "Andy" although no one else who wrote about him ever shortened the name from "Andrew." Duffey characterized Sockalexis' chances as follows: "Andy Sockalexis is another runner who is well thought of by all the Marathon followers. Andy is one of the most natural runners that ever run [sic] in the Marathon game. His record also is one of the best." After recounting Sockalexis' narrow loss in record-breaking time to Mike Ryan in 1912, Duffey also mentioned his Olympic appearance but mistakenly placed him as finishing fifth, rather than fourth. Duffey wrote: "On the dope of the race Andy should be the logical favorite from last year, but somehow or other the tip is going the rounds that Sockalexis has been sick and is not in the best of shape."[9] Apparently word of Sockalexis' six-month respite ordered by a doctor had leaked, or perhaps Sockalexis told the columnist about his illness himself. But just the day before Duffey had seen Sockalexis himself and judged him very fit, so it seems a strange and sudden contradiction.

With Madden suspect merely for being the favorite, and Sockalexis suspect for having had a long illness, Duffey reported that Sturgis was now seen as "the dark horse," based on some outstanding showings in area 10-mile races and his win a few months earlier in the Brockton Marathon. According to "the wise ones," Duffey reported the Sturgis "youngster" was the one "to look out" for, the one "sure to be well backed" by the betting crowd because "he has a splendid chance to win." Duffey added that Sturgis was "built right on Marathon lines and resembles the former Olympic champion, Johnny Hayes, in more ways than one." As almost an after thought, Duffey noted that Tom Lilley and A.G. Horne were also "well thought of" and expected to make good showings.[10]

But, for all of his trying, Duffey had not ferreted out the eventual winner, demonstrating once again – as it has occurred so many times over the years – that no "expert" on this sport can ever really know whose day it will be. The year before it had been impossible to measure the heart of Mike Ryan, in the last couple of miles, a man who reportedly had failed many times before at Boston. This year no one knew the pain, the fierce desire to be avenged, that Fritz Carlson carried with him on to the Boston Marathon course.

Up in Maine, on the day of the marathon, the *Bangor Daily Commercial* reported in its headline that it was a "smaller field" that was set to run the marathon, with Sockalexis "trying again" for the big bronze trophy of the BAA. The article characterized the field as "smaller but more select." It added weather conditions that Saturday morning "were not as favorable as in former years because of a heavy rain during the early part of the day." The estimated crowd to watch the marathon every year, according to this article, was 200,000. They formed lines along "the undulating ribbon of roadway between Ashland and Boston" for the 25-mile race. It was reported that of the first 10 finishers at the 1912 race, only two were absent, including winner Mike Ryan who had retired from running the Boston Marathon. The favorites listed in this article, along with Sockalexis, were Madden, Lilley, Harry Smith, Harry Jensen of New York and John C. "Karlson" of Minneapolis.[11] This time a journalist had chosen a "Karlson," but it was the wrong one – and he spelled that Karlsen's name wrong as well.

On Monday, April 21, 1913 the *Bangor Daily News* front-page headline blared out:

SOCK SECOND IN BOSTON MARATHON
As in 1912, Indian Might Have Won If
He Had Made His Sprint Earlier

A simple three-paragraph summary noted that Fritz Carlson had won the 17th annual, 25-mile run, beating a field of only 60 runners to the finish line at the BAA clubhouse on Exeter Street. Carlson's time was 2 hours, 25 minutes, 14 4-5 seconds.

The account from Boston stated: "Andrew Sockalexis, the Old Town, Me. Indian, running under the colors of the North Dorchester Athletic Association, was second. He was reported to have one lung affected, but his time was 2 hours, 27 minutes, 12 seconds." It was said that Sockalexis was "pulled" by McInerny of Philadelphia and the first-place leader for most of the race, Harry Smith of New York, before Massachusetts Avenue was reached. But Sockalexis was "600 yards behind the Minneapolis runner at the tape."[12]

Right under this *Bangor Daily News* story is the exact same story published earlier in the *Boston Post*, using the headline:

"Think Sockalexis Should Have Won."[13]

In summary, the *Post* noted that Carlson, the fifth finisher in the 1912 race, was "regarded as a good man" but had not been "generally considered as likely to...earn the palm of victory" although another good finish among the leaders was anticipated of him. That his time was a few seconds faster over his previous year's time showed that he had "carefully planned his entire race and ran even better than his year-old schedule."[14]

There had been a falling off in entries. Only 60 men lined up for the start; more than half of those finished. But for "its sultriness," the weather, it was said, could not have been better the morning of the race. Still, as start time drew near, it grew warmer and warmer as "the hot rays of the sun began to snap." Prospects for records that seemed good earlier, seemed near impossible just before the race got underway, it was reported. The *Post* writer felt it was a race of significant events "from start to finish." He started with Carlson, calling the Minneapolis lumber man's finish "splendid."[15]

"Chief" among these momentous events, the unnamed *Boston Post* writer stated, "was the gallant fight made" by Sockalexis. From the start of the race, until he and the other leaders had passed Coolidge Corner, Sockalexis remained a "top heavy favorite, and rightly so." After the second-place finish a year before, with nearly a course record-breaking performance of his own, and then the fourth place experience at the Olympics, Sockalexis seemed ready. As the writer said: "...with the experience of a veteran and a bride to be his prize, the time certainly seemed at hand when he would be the first to break the tape in Exeter Street."[16]

The writer expressed his overall assessment of Sockalexis' race this way:

> *Like the winner, the Indian had his race planned for the entire route, so as to bring him in ahead, but the best laid plans often go awry. This was the case with Sockalexis yesterday, for the spurt which he had determined upon, came too late. Had he begun it at Reservoir corner instead of waiting until Coolidge Corner had been reached, he might have been able to have pulled down the lead of the Swedish-American in front of him, and passed that runner before the final dash for the worsted.*

> *But as in the case of his run last summer in Sweden, the Indian held back a few minutes too long, and second place was the best the game little representative of the Penobscot tribe could do.*[17]

The race also went very badly for Madden, who failed to finish. Pushing the pace in the early stages, Madden was in third position and feeling a lot of pressure from the Canadian star Fabre. Before reaching the halfway point in Wellesley, Madden was said to have "begun to go to pieces." Madden momentarily stopped, to rest a few minutes, and then attempted to resume; but he had gone only a few steps when he

was faltering anew. Shortly he would find it impossible
to continue, and took a ride in an automobile to the finish
line. Later, he would say his stomach "went back" on
him.[18]

Winner Fritz Carlson waited patiently to spring his
surprise at the 1913 Boston Marathon. Just prior to the start
of the marathon, the runners convened at a local hotel in
Ashland, headquarters for the race. Here, they received
the large, bold and heavy numbers they would wear in the
race. They were also furnished with trainers, on bicycles, to
accompany them "on the long grind in cases where those they
had engaged failed to put in an appearance."[19] Sockalexis, too,
had a trainer named Bob Fowler, a former fine marathoner
himself who had predicted Sockalexis would win the Olympic
marathon in a syndicated column. Fowler received much
criticism for his handling of Sockalexis after this race. At
noon, George V. Brown, the official starter, fired the pistol
sending the runners away. In the time-honored tradition
of many of these races over the decades, someone looking
for that special moment when he can say he led the Boston
Marathon dashed into the lead. For the record, in 1913, he was
James Cleary from Worcester. Also, for the record, like so
many others who clamor for this short-lived fame, Cleary did
not finish the race.

The first leaders, grouped in a close-knit pack, featured
favorites Madden and Smith, along with runners Stark, Lordon
and Harrop. Smith and Victor Wirtanen of Ashburnham
led the way into South Framingham. Wirtanen captured the
interest of journalists later in the race when it was discovered

that he covered the distance from Coolidge Corner to the finish line on Exeter Street in his bare feet. No reason "why" was given. After Smith and Wirtanen came McInerney and Fabre. Then there was a gap of 100 feet. The next cluster of runners included Madden, Lucas and Horne. To the rear of this group, there was a "big gap in the line, with Sockalexis running all by his lonesome in the middle of it, and well ahead of Carlson, the next nearest runner..."[20]

In a first-person account written after the race that very day for the *Boston Post*, Carlson said he saw things at the start this way:

> *When the race started I let the rest hit up the pace. I took things easy. I saw Smith, Jensen, Madden, Allen and Fabre get away with the first bunch. I lay back and watched Sockalexis. He didn't show any inclination to forge to the front. I reckoned if he didn't see any great necessity for hurrying that I could lay back. He won second last year, too, and I figured that he would be well worth watching. But to my mind he held back a little too long. I went ahead of him a short distance from the start.[21]*

Thus, it was left to Harry Smith to be the catalyst for the Boston Marathon. Running a blistering pace, his running was compared to that of John J. Gallagher from the year before (Gallagher had blasted into the lead at South Framingham in 1912, and held the lead up until Coolidge Corner, until he had "shot his bolt" and was overtaken by the field). Nearing the 10-mile mark in Natick, Smith had taken a 20-yard lead. Into Natick, a light rain fell, "reviving the men somewhat." By Natick, Smith had established a commanding lead, "with a full mile between him and the very last man." It was Smith, then a 100-foot leeway, followed by two Canadians, Fabre and William Allan. Then, McInerney and Horne. Two hundred yards further back was Madden. "Sockalexis was the 20th man, never changing from the pace he struck at the very outset."[22]

According to Carlson: "By the time I had gotten to South Framingham the weaker runners were beginning to fall back toward the rear. I was simply plugging along at this point as I figured that the stiff pace the leaders were setting would diminish after the first of those big hills would be encountered." Coming out of Framingham Carlson was in 12th place and joined by his trainer, William Hicks on a bicycle. Carlson would not be passed again in the race and, while agreeing the leaders had a big start, he claimed it was an exaggeration that they were ever three-quarters of a mile ahead. He said he did not believe that he was ever more than a half mile behind.[23]

Smith comfortably led the way through the half way point, Wellesley. He was "given a cheer by the Wellesley College girls, who had assembled at the campus entrances to greet the runners, an annual custom and a pretty one..." Smith's lead, at this point, was estimated to be nearly one-quarter of a mile. Fabre followed, then Allan, and then there was a large gap. McInerney was said to be leading "the second division," with Horne in fifth place and Madden, nearing his Waterloo, in sixth. Carlson was now in eighth place, having moved up from

11th position at the Natick checkpoint. Sockalexis, too, had also "worked somewhat in the front, passing six and getting into 14th place."[24]

At Wellesley, Carlson reported seeing Madden. And it was not a pretty sight. Carlson said that Madden "seemed to be having trouble with his heart. He was in great pain evidently and made two attempts to resume before giving up. He was the only runner I noticed suffering real distress, but there were other hills to climb and I knew that I would pick up the delinquents one by one."[25] Indeed, he did. By Auburndale he had bettered his position considerably. He had passed Sturgis and a few others. He said he kept hearing people "urging me to hurry." Carlson continued: "Still I didn't worry. I remembered that big hill in Newton some two miles after you swing into the boulevard. I know what a terrible handicap it was last year. That's the reason I didn't do any sprinting in the earlier part of the year...or in the earlier part of the race. I wanted to have something in reserve by the time we reached there."[26]

Up the long hill at Newton Lower Falls, Smith "paced like a war horse, and, swinging into boulevard a few minutes later, he went up the heartbreaking Fuller street hill at the same pace," Duffey wrote. Smith was successfully holding off Fabre at this point in the race. Fuller Street hill "has wrecked more than one Marathoner who had looked good up to that point. And it wrecked several hopefuls" that day...but not Smith or Fabre who, reportedly, passed through showing "little effect." Allan still held third place, but Carlson was on the move.[27]

Carlson, "who up to this time had not been receiving particular attention," had worked up from his eighth position at Wellesley, to reach fifth position. It was McInerney who stood just in front of him now, in fourth.[28]

Beyond the Fuller Street hill on the boulevard came the shorter, sharper rise – just after crossing Walnut Street – the Grant Avenue hill, termed "the bugaboo of every Marathoner."

As usual, the hill claimed its victims, but Smith was not one of them...or so it seemed. Smith moved through Grant Avenue hill, another killer two miles beyond, "still in the lead and looked a winner." Smith, it seemed momentarily, "was not to be set back by hills." Neither, however, were Fabre, Sockalexis, Carlson or McInerney. But Smith apparently had paid a toll. He was slowing up. On reaching the top of Grant Avenue hill, Smith was not more than 50 yards ahead of Fabre.[29]

The use of the wording "heartbreaking" earlier, by writer Duffey, is charmingly ironic for one of the middle of the famed four Newton hills. For, in 1936, *Boston Globe* editor and columnist Jerry Nason would observe Tarzan Brown prove too strong for Johnny Kelley and "break his heart" on the last, "bugaboo" hill, en route to victory. The phrase caught on, and the last of the four hills in Newton, leading directly to the sharp downhill into Cleveland Circle (beside the "Reservoir") is now world-famous as "Heartbreak Hill." In his account of the race Carlson also used the phrase "heartbreaking" for the very hill which would ultimately be known for doing this to leaders who went out too hard and lost their chances at victory year after year on this same hill.

Carlson continued to slowly work his way to the front, "his eye on the leader's back and the firm determination in his heart to pass the New Yorker." Back at South Framingham, Carlson had been in 11th place, and "as the line had then strung out for more than a mile, there was nothing about him except the fact that he appeared to be taking things very easily and at the same time holding his own which would indicate him as a possible winner." By Natick, Carlson was still 11th; however, at the Wellesley square he had worked his way into eighth place and, by the boulevard, was in fifth. "He was now dangerous, though few in the crowds along the route at this point, who had been giving Smith and Fabre cheers, recognized the fact." At this juncture, Carlson would move from fifth to third.[30]

At the time McInerney was in fourth. Allan, the Canadian, had been a dangerous contender up until he had reached the boulevard hills; now, he had fallen far behind, his feet giving out. Allan would finish, though tormented by every step he took from the hills until he reached the finish line. Carlson's strategy for the hills worked to perfection. He knew Boston's hills were often the undoing of the lead runners. He had passed Allan. Then came McInerney. Wrote Carlson: "McInerney was pretty well spent as I passed him, heat and the big incline had proved too big a combination for him...yet all of us were considerably ahead of the field, and I figured that we would all finish well to the good."[31]

Before the race Sockalexis had said Madden was his key concern. Madden, of course, had proven not to be much of a factor at all. Now, both early-favorite Harry Smith and the dangerous Canadian contender Fabre were struggling to maintain pace and

ripe to be overtaken. Sockalexis seemingly had all of them right
where he wanted them, but for the "unexpected" Carlson who was
making all those right moves...just ahead of him.

For it was Carlson overtaking Fabre, with the leader
Smith only a short distance ahead of him. At the reservoir,
about four miles from the finish the positions of the leaders
shifted. After descending the short hill there, Carlson crept
up past Fabre and McInerney, closed upon and "measured"
Smith for a few moments, and then shot past the New Yorker
en route to victory. Smith led the way down the short hill into
the reservoir, with Carlson "nipping at his heels." Then the
Minneapolis runner, nearing the foot of the incline, "turned
loose a spurt and all in a twinkling he had breasted Smith
and passed him, never again to be headed." The thousands of
spectators gathered in this area saw the rapid shift in leaders,
and gave both men cheers.[32]

This is how Carlson saw this climactic part of the race:

> *From time to time I was able to catch glimpses*
> *of the two leaders in the dim distance...Smith and*
> *Fabre, the latter cutting the former's lead down...*
> *But from the moment they struck the big hill I was*
> *sure that the pace, the heat and the heart-breaking*
> *climb were bound to tell. Yard by yard I drew*
> *closer. A quarter of a mile to the other side of the*
> *reservoir I got Fabre. He was drenched with per-*
> *spiration. Previously both he and Smith had left*
> *the hard oiled roadway and taken to the grass.*
> *I was certain that their feet were bothering them,*
> *and that being the case my task was made the eas-*
> *ier. Just as we were passing the pumping station*

> *I drew up on even terms with Smith, who was ap-*
> *parently too tired to give me much of a fight. I took*
> *the lead inside of a few seconds without dispute.*
> *From that time on I knew the race was mine.*[33]

Sockalexis, however, was not out of the picture, though Carlson would never see him or, apparently, know it.

Boston Post columnist Duffey wrote passionately about the decisive spurt employed by Carlson to break from Smith, noting that from Coolidge Corner to Massachusetts Avenue, and from the avenue to Exeter Street, the homestretch to the finish line, Carlson forged ahead, "yard by yard until more than a quarter of a mile separated" him from Smith. "And while they were fighting it out, a new factor, one present from the start of the race, entered into the romp for the finish, Sockalexis, the Indian." From 20th place at South Framingham, Sockalexis had worked his way to 14th place by the halfway point at Wellesley. By the boulevard, at Auburndale, he had moved into 9th place. Wrote Duffey, "He took the boulevard hills fully as easily as the others." Upon reaching the reservoir, Sockalexis, "urged on by his trainer and the cries, 'Oh Andrew, you must win. Brace, Andrew, brace,' from Miss Pauline Shea *[Author's note: it should be spelled "Shay"]*, his bride-to-be, who was following him in an auto, began to quicken his stride."[34]

Carlson, in the meantime, was pulling away from the others and finally reached the Coolidge Corner timing station in 2 hours, 8 minutes, 22 4-5 seconds. Sockalexis' time, just one year before, had been 2 hours, 6 minutes, 21 seconds. At

Coolidge Corner, Sockalexis passed Fabre and "soon began to menace Smith," who struggled to hold his position. Knowing Sockalexis was pressing him, Smith courageously forced himself into a spurt. But Sockalexis also began surging, and it was he "who was now decidedly running the better of the two." Despite Smith's efforts to hold second place, Sockalexis was gaining with every step. Half way between Coolidge Corner and Massachusetts Avenue Sockalexis pulled close behind Smith, and then was racing, stride for stride, with him. "For a few moments, it was neck-and-neck, but Smith was a defeated man," Duffey wrote.[35]

Sockalexis sped on. Carlson was now the only man between Sockalexis and victory. But Carlson had "a splendid lead," too great to be overcome in the distance that remained. Still, Sockalexis chopped away at it.[36]

However, by the time "the gallant little runner" was swinging on to Exeter Street from Commonwealth Avenue, Carlson broke the finish line tape and received the cheers of the crowd in front of the BAA clubhouse. Both men, it was reported, "finished strong." McInerney and Smith had a great battle for third place, with Smith finally holding the position to the finish.[37]

Carlson saw the conclusion of the race this way:

> *I was feeling terribly tired, of course, as I raced between those two long lines of applauding spectators all the way down towards the city. But I saw that the end was in sight. I could see the dome of the State House gleaming more brightly all the time. It was only a question of my ability to keep it*

up. Oh, but it felt good to know that the race was approaching its end. It's a fearful grind, in spite of all the glory attached to the winning, and my legs were getting fairly numb. It was too hot for comfort, and I could feel the perspiration running in rivulets down my back. A mile from the finish Mr. Brown of the BAA and some of the officials passed us in their big car. My trainer, Hicks, called out and asked them if there was any chance of breaking the record. We were told that we had five minutes in which to do it, but Hicks would not let me speed it up. The day was too hot for speeding at the end of such an exhausting run. Besides, we were satisfied to win first without setting any new mark. It is glory enough to beat the field over this wearisome course.

That last 50 yards was the longest of the race. When we drew into Exeter street and I could see the red tape in front of the clubhouse it seemed as though I would never reach it. I was minutes, seemingly, in going this short distance. I was ready to drop when the great roar went up. I knew I had won and I felt as though I could drop right there on the sidewalks and go to sleep.[38]

The story of Andrew Sockalexis' finish, to the *Boston Post*, became as much the story of Pauline Shay, his fiancee, as it was his. The story made for great telling in the *Post*. The headline read:

Indian Is Second but Wins Bride
Plucky Oldtown Girl as Proud of
Sockalexis as Though He Had Finished First

The account opened with the remark that when Sockalexis, the "sturdy little Indian runner, staggered" across the finish line, "sick from the terrific exertions he had made during the last seven or eight miles of the grind, he was no nearer collapse than was Miss Pauline Shay, his bride-to-be and the girl who had promised that her heart and hand would be given to him should he breast the tape ahead of all the other entries in the field." Shay was a poignant figure in the story, depicted as seen "all over the course, now in front, urging (Sockalexis) to greater efforts, again in the rear and struggling vainly to catch a glimpse of the Oldtown *[sic]* brave as he plugged along far in the rear of the leaders." The unnamed writer noted "the girl who had come all the way from Maine to cheer her lover on to victory was praying hard that her Andrew should achieve this signal triumph."[39]

From her seat in the "big touring car," which carried her and members of the press over the course, "the girl watched every move in the struggle. When the leaders pulled away well out in front, Miss Shay was fearful that Sockalexis was lingering too far behind. Three different times between Ashland and Wellesley the car in which she was seated loomed up in front of Sockalexis, and Miss Shay called upon her lover to hurry. 'Faster Andrew,' was her appeal. 'The others are away ahead of you. You'll never catch Smith unless you brace up.'"[40]

The *Post* writer noted that atop the hill in Wellesley the car pulled up while the clearly disheartened young girl looked far back onto the course "without getting a glimpse of her lover." And with each runner who plodded by, she became more and more nervous. "Each second that passed served to increase her anxiety. A flimsy handkerchief torn almost to shreds in her nervous clasp. But still she did not lose courage."[41]

Here, through Pauline Shay, the *Post* writer revealed the strategy Sockalexis was employing for the 1913 race:

> *'Andrew knows the course,' she kept repeating. 'He told me that there are lots of big hills before the course ends and this is where he expects to make up the difference. He told me the other day that he intended to hold back for 18 miles and then start to speed up. Still, he had better hurry up. He is in great shape for this race. The last time he ran down in Maine he did 28 miles in three hours, then got into a canoe and paddled for over a mile.'[42]*

The *Post* writer then vividly described how disconsolate Pauline Shay was visibly growing:

> *Mile after mile went by, runner after runner entered the stretch without the lithe form of the Indian coming into view. When Newton Lower Falls was reached, and a terrible gap was evident between the first and second divisions, Miss Shay first began to abandon hope. 'Poor Andrew is going to lose after all and I did so hope that he would win. He has his heart set on winning, too. That Smith is running too strong; Sock can never overtake him now.'*

> *The first glimpse of encouragement was obtained at the Reservoir when, at the head of the second division, appeared the little Indian. A cheer greeted his appearance. The car held up for a moment till the Oldtown [sic] lad drew up even.*

> *Grasping the bunch of roses pinned to her breast, the girl tore them away and threw them at her sweetheart. 'Hurry Andy boy,' she cried tearfully. 'If you are going to win you must run as you have never run, now.'[43]*

The press car then sped ahead, moving quickly in order to be in time for the finish at Exeter Street. Pauline Shay again grew visibly discouraged as she saw how wide the gap was that separated Sockalexis from Smith, who at that moment was barely ahead of Carlson. The *Post* correspondent wrote: "Then Miss Shay resigned herself to the inevitable. 'He held back too long, he has not a chance left to finish first' was her true sizing up of the situation."[44]

At the finish line the young girl made a particularly poignant sight for the *Post* writer:

> *Sadly, and silent, the plucky girl from Oldtown [sic] stood beside the entrance to the BAA and heard the roar of acclaim tendered the plucky Swede as he staggered through that lane of humanity and received the accord given the winner. 'Those cheers should have been for Sockalexis,' was her thought. Still she stood there, waiting to see her hero, forced to be content with a fourth or fifth, apparently. But*

> a roar shook the crowd, and the drooping spirits
> of the maiden braced when she heard the name of
> Sockalexis passed down the line.

> 'Here comes the Indian,' was the cry.
> 'Sockalexis finishes second.' Down the street
> plugged the tired Indian. With just strength enough
> left to pass under the wire he finished his great race
> second for the second successive year, then stag-
> gered toward the clubhouse where willing hands
> caught him before he fell. The girl stood so close
> that she might have touched him as he was carried
> into the entrance.

> Yet Sockalexis, utterly spent, was too far gone
> to see the maiden or read the message of love and
> sympathy in her eyes. Then for the first time she
> gave way. Willing hands supported her to a neigh-
> boring hostelry where she at length gave way to the
> tears that would not come before. 'It was so unex-
> pected,' she explained. 'I thought that he would be
> left far behind.

> That he would finish second seems too good
> after the terrible lead that the others got on him.
> I am as proud of him as if he finished first for I
> know that he must have put up a grand fight to pass
> those others as he did. Tell Andrew that I will be
> waiting here after he gets ready to go home.[45]

The *Boston Post* writer concluded his extraordinarily
different perspective on the race this way: "The message was
conveyed to the plucky Indian and half an hour afterward

Andrew Sockalexis, Marathoner of Oldtown *[sic]*, Maine, undoubtedly received a welcome more dear to him by far than the winning of a great race in which he had just participated would have been."[46]

Several very short accounts of the race neighbored this story. One, under the headline of "**FAILURE OF MADDEN SURPRISE OF RACE**," carried a few sentences concerning the fate of Festus Madden, a runner who was considered a major favorite to win the race. Madden, it stated, began showing "distress" signs just before the half way mark in Wellesley, "faltering in his stride and stopping running momentarily." The report noted that he "resumed the pace again and had only traveled a short distance when he was again overcome, and decided to retire after having covered 17 miles. He explained afterwards that his stomach "had gone back on him."[47]

Another brief report, again by an unnamed correspondent, was highly critical of Andrew Sockalexis. The headline ran: "**THINK SOCKALEXIS/ SHOULD HAVE WON**." The account stated:

> *Sockalexis finished in second place, running with every evidence of having plenty of running in reserve. It was generally believed that he should have won the event if he had started to get out in front a little bit earlier. With a better display of judgment it is more than likely that he would not only have outdistanced his field but would have come dangerously near the record.[48]*

In his first-person account written for the *Boston Post* following the marathon, Fritz Carlson told both a poignant and uplifting tale, in relating his perspective on the victory.

Like Mike Ryan the year before, Carlson was a veteran runner, nearing the end of the trail who had long hungered to win at Boston. Like Ryan too, he had a particular, special reason to really want the victory. For Ryan, 1912 had been the last attempt; he had come and failed a number of years before and determined that he would not come back again – this year or bust. Carlson also could not expect too many more chances, but it was revenge and the chance for vindication that also drove him to deeply desire a win.

Fritz Carlson explained this in a very straightforward manner:

> *I am the most delighted man in Boston to-night. I have won the big Boston Marathon—done something I have always wished that I might be able to do. I can hardly realize that of all those 80-odd [Author's note: it was only 60] starters, the picked long-distance men of the country, I was really the first to break the tape at the finish. I have achieved a long-cherished ambition and the win gives me a double satisfaction. For besides winning this big American classic I have proven to my friends that I have the right stuff in me. Perhaps now the AAU may come to consider that they did wrong in barring me from the races in Sweden [the Olympic Games] last summer.*

*You know, I finished fifth in this same event
last April. The course was strange to me then and I
had the effects of a long journey and a big change in
climatic conditions to contend with. But I thought
that the way I finished then would entitle me to
consideration as a distance runner in the Olympic
games, particularly as I went over to Sweden without any help from the AAU. But I didn't have the
money necessary to enter. I had no influence and
I couldn't afford to pay the AAU enough to be allowed to compete. I can prove this when the right
time comes if anyone desires the proof. So, by winning this big Marathon event, I have proven to my
friends that I have the stamina that might have
enabled me to help in the point winning in those
Olympics last summer.*[49]

Fritz Carlson noted that after he finished fifth in the 1912
Boston Marathon he was initially selected by the American
Olympic committee to represent the United States at
Stockholm. He stated he made the trip to Sweden but not with
the Olympic team – having made the trip over beforehand.
Then, he claimed, owing solely to the fact that he "did not
officially sign an American Olympic entry, according to
prescribed Olympic form," he was declared ineligible to
run.

How tough this must have on Carlson, if it happened just
this way: After traveling all that way, anxious to compete
against the best in the world, he was disqualified on a
technicality. Carlson was respectful of Sockalexis at the start,
even determined to watch him closely and do-as-he-did for

awhile, but dropped that strategy fairly early when it became apparent to him that Sockalexis was not keeping close enough to the leaders to suit him.

Carlson wrote:

> *...it was a grand race to win because of the number of fast men I had to compete against. I knew before I started that I would have my work all cut out for me. I knew that Soxalexis [sic], the Indian, Harry Jensen, Smith and Festus Madden were all likely candidates for first place, besides two or three runners from Canada, who had their eyes on the coveted trophy. I knew that whoever won, it would be only after a bitter struggle and I prayed last night that the weather would not be too warm. A run of 25 miles over dirty or muddy roads in the heat takes life and strength out of anyone.*

> *I didn't map out any particular plan for the race. Just the same, I made up my mind not to try and set pace for a field at the start, at least. You see, I am 29 years of age, considerably older than lots of the others who were entered in the race. I made up my mind to let the youngsters do the pace-making. I felt sure that I would fit when the time came.*

> *When the race started I let the rest hit up the pace. I took things easy. I saw Smith, Jensen, Madden, Allen and Fabre get away with the first bunch. I lay back and watched Sockalexis. He didn't show any inclination to forge to the front. I reckoned if he didn't see any great necessity for hurrying that I could lay back. He won second last*

*year, too, and I figured that he would be well worth
watching. But to my mind he held back a little too
long. I went ahead of him a short distance from
the start.*[50]

In Arthur Duffey's wrap-up column on the marathon
he evaluated the performances of the lead runners. Calling
Carlson's victory a "great win yesterday," he termed the
Minneapolis lumberman a "practical unknown" and that the
"ease" with which he took the victory surprised the most
ardent followers of the event. Duffey expressed the opinion
that had Carlson been pressed at all he might have broken the
course record and that "had he been allowed to start in the
last Olympic games no doubt he would have been close to a
winner..."[51]

Of Sockalexis, Duffey had this to say:

*Andy Sockalexis, the Old Town Indian's great
showing in the race, should not be overlooked.
Sockalexis showed enough class yesterday to win
a hundred such marathons, but it was not his day.
The Maine Indian was never in such condition for
a Marathon race. In fact I doubt if there ever was a
marathoner who stepped to the mark at Ashland in
finer fettle than Sockalexis. The redskin did not run
the race with proper judgment. Had he run a more
head race, especially at the beginning, perhaps he
might have overtaken the Minneapolis champion.
At any rate the Indian finished in better condition
than any other runner in the contest.*[52]

Duffey acknowledged the criticism many had for Sockalexis' trainer for the event. "Bob Fowler, the veteran Cambridge runner, who coached Andy Sockalexis in the local race, came in for much criticism after the contest for the manner in which he handled the Indian in the big race. Many thought Fowler's coaching was responsible for the Indian failing to land the first prize. After the race, though, the Indian absolved Fowler from all blame."[53]

According to Sockalexis, no one was to blame for his failure but himself. He said: "I felt a little rocky about the middle of the race, and it was there that I lost my real burst. My failure to win was only one of those little incidents which are apt to happen in any Marathon race."[54]

In his remarks about the other heroes of the race, Duffey praised Smith for his "great" effort, noting that Smith was better at shorter distances, like 10 and 15 miles. The columnist noted that the North Dorchester club had shown real well, taking five of the first 12 places – Sockalexis, Sturgis, Gaskill, Brown and Pavitt.[55]

Carlson impressed Duffey for taking the win so matter-of-factly. Apparently he told the *Boston Post* writer that he "had only two days' real running for the great race. Now that I have made good I will be back to work bright and early Tuesday morning on my job in the lumber yard, and if there are any more Marathons I will try to keep up to my record."[56]

A couple of days later, the *Bangor Commercial* reported remarks attributed to the Indian runner in the *Boston American*. The comments were published in the "**Up in Old Town**" column:

> *The many admirers of Andrew Sockalexis,*
> *who were sorry to see him come in anywhere, but at*
> *the head in the Boston Marathon, will be interested*
> *in what he said to the Boston American about it:*
> *'I believe that I should have won this race as I*
> *was in the pink of condition. The only trouble that*
> *I experienced was cramps in my legs. This bothered*
> *for the last part of the race. I think that they were*
> *tied up. I came down here believing that I would*
> *win, but outside of that I have little to say. Carlson,*
> *who won, is a grand runner and he used his head.*
> *Owing to the hot weather conditions I thought that*
> *I would stay back. The rain seemed to me to be very*
> *oppressive and at times it weighed me down. The*
> *only thing that bothered me was the dusty air that*
> *was laden with gasoline fumes. I believe that I will*
> *smell that bad air for a week to come. I suppose*
> *that they cannot keep the automobiles off of the*
> *course, but it is too bad for the runners certainly*
> *have to suffer. I will not retire from running after*
> *this, as many have suggested. I am only 20 years*
> *of age, why should I? I have nothing to say just*
> *now about that story regarding my engagement*
> *to a young lady. I tried hard to win but I suppose*
> *I must credit my defeat to a misjudgment of*
> *pace.'[57]*

The *Commercial* carried a brief editorial note, in that same issue of April 21, 1913, stating that Sockalexis has "again established his claim to a high position" among the marathoners of the world. Terming his second place finish as "a very creditable performance," the newspaper concluded by stating: "Had he captured the first honors his win would have been a very popular one as he is a favorite competitor."[58]

Chapter 12

To turn professional...
or not to turn professional

Strange, sad turns in fortune were in store for Andrew Sockalexis following his second straight second-place finish at the 1913 Boston Marathon.

Maybe it was just the time for such tales. A national article in the *Bangor Daily Commercial* a few weeks after the 1913 Boston Marathon told a poignant story about the sad fortunes of Lewis C. Schilling, a penniless, 81-year-old Civil War veteran who was said to be the last living survivor who had been at the Alamo. He was identified as a 4-year-old child whose life was spared when Santa Anna and his troops made their final assault on the San Antonio mission, wiping out all its defenders. Schilling had been adopted, it was reported, by Kit Carson. Now, living in a shack in Reno, he had been robbed of every cent of his savings of eight years and was said to be living on crackers and water.[1]

A little later, on April 28, a story appeared concerning 1908 Olympic marathon champion Johnny Hayes' announcement that he would return to running as a professional. He had been coaching Irish-American runners for several years but had determined that he could make a comeback. He reportedly had sent in his entry for the 15-mile professional race to be held at the Monument games at Celtic Park on May 4. Hayes, according to the article, "thinks he can pass Longboat, Billy Queal and Willie Kohlemainen in the Monument games in the same manner that he defeated Dorando in the historic London Marathon." Hopefully, Hayes was not expecting them all to collapse before reaching the finish line and be disqualified, which is what happened to the poor, little Italian runner Dorando Pietri, presenting Hayes with the victory.[2]

In the *Boston Post* on May 3, Arthur Duffey had a column blurb on Hannes Kohlemainen's brother Willie and the professional runners. Duffey noted the pro runners were "down for their inning tomorrow afternoon at Celtic Park, New York," where runners like Tom Longboat, Billy Queal, A.E. Wood, W. Kolehmainen, Ted Crooks, Johnny Hayes and others were to compete for the 15-mile professional championship. "Kolehmainen is picked to defend his honors as the world's professional long-distance champion." Later, for one brief day, Andrew Sockalexis would claim to have taken third place in this very race, as his professional debut, finishing behind Kolehmainen and Queal.

On May 7, 1913, newspapers carried the story that Jim Thorpe had been stripped of his Olympic medals, for having played minor league baseball for money. The headline simply read: "Thorpe's Medals/to go back." The Thorpe case came up in a private session of the Olympic committee which "discussed it in all its phases." Thorpe, who confessed to having played professional baseball after the games at Stockholm, was the winner of two "much coveted trophies," the Viking ship offered by the emperor of Russia to the winner of the decathlon and the bronze bust of the king of Sweden offered by the king to the winner of the pentathlon, both all-around competitions. These trophies would now go to the respective runners-up, H. Weislander of Sweden and F.R. Bie of Norway. The committee unanimously adopted the British proposal to send congratulations to the Amateur Athletic Union for the "sportsmanlike manner" in which the American organization had handled the case. All the delegates, it was reported, "regret the Thorpe affair, but praised the Americans for their promptitude in making amends..."[3] It would be more than a half century and well after the death of Jim Thorpe before this injustice was rectified. A "confession" for athletic professionalism? What Thorpe was really guilty of was being a poor Native American who had played a handful of minor league baseball games for a few dollars. No one asked just what baseball had to do with track and field. And it would be far too many years before the governing Olympic body would drop the whole charade of attempting to maintain letter perfect, pristine amateur standards and futile tries at determining what was appropriate "professional" involvement. Thorpe was banished in total disgrace; however, for decade after decade, the hypocrisy of allowing athletes to be subsidized as "amateur" athletes for years on end by their countries, or paid for celebrity appearances or clinics, was perfectly acceptable.

On May 9, **"Arthur Duffey's Column"** in the *Boston Post* had a blurb announcing that Tom Lilley, Festus Madden, "Andy" Sockalexis, Cliff Horne, and Clarence DeMar, all of the North Dorchester A.A., were expected to participate in the *New York Evening Mail* modified Marathon race in New York on May 10. And, "in spite of the fact that DeMar has been away from the Marathon game for some time," many local followers were predicting that DeMar would be "a strong contender" for top prize.[4]

The Boston area runners and Sockalexis, if they all indeed went to the race, apparently got shut out. The *Post* carried this account on May 10: **"RECORDS GO/IN MARATHON... Kolehmainen Smashes 12 in New York."** The account reported that Hannes Kolehmainen, of the Irish-American A.C., won the third annual Evening Mail modified Marathon. He "smashed" 12 intermediate records and "his wonderful pace" brought five other runners beside himself, ahead of the best mark for the 12 3/8-mile course. The Amateur Athletic Union timed "the flying Finn" breaking the finish line tape at the City Hall in 1 hour, 5 minutes and 15 3-5 seconds. He bettered the previous record by 3 minutes and 12 6-10 seconds. Familiar names taking second and third, respectively, were Harry Smith of the Bronx Church House and Gaston Strobino of the South Paterson A.C., topping a reported 1550 starters.[5]

Shortly after the 1913 Boston Marathon Andrew Sockalexis entered into the snarled web of trying to decide

between professional versus amateur running status. It is
impossible now, obviously, to know what he was thinking. It
is more than likely that being poor (he was a basket maker
by trade), Native American Andrew Sockalexis simply left
the amateur running game early because he felt the need
to support himself by taking money, rather than trophies
and trinkets, for his skill. Rather than continue running in
pursuit of some "pure amateur" ethic so treasured by the
sports writers of the day – who, of course, would not dream
of writing about sports "just for the love of it," not unless
there was a paycheck attached – the better runners of the day
quickly faced a quandary about whether it was in their best
interests to pursue prestige (strictly amateur events like the
Boston Marathon or the Olympics) or dollars.

Perhaps the legendary Canadian Indian Tom Longboat,
after winning the 1907 Boston Marathon, left the amateur
scene so quickly for no other reason than he was poor and
wished to use his ability as a runner to support himself.

Perhaps an impoverished Andrew Sockalexis saw the
professional ranks as simply a way of making athletics pay.
Perhaps he was disappointed, maybe even a bit bitter about
his repeated runner-up finishes in the amateur ranks and the
continuing criticism he received for not taking first place. He
was only 21 years old; perhaps immaturity was a factor.

The newspapers are the only gauge there is today for
assessing him, and there is little about his thinking and driving
motivations about this decision that is clear and not completely
baffling. From this point on, however, from the newspapers'
perspective, Andrew Sockalexis was no longer going to appear

as unquestionably admirable. From their view, he appears very self-centered, manipulative and money-hungry. The only thing that seems clear is how confusing the professional-vs.-amateur situation was for Andrew Sockalexis: He did not seem to know which way to go.

On May 7, 1913, the *Bangor Daily Commercial* carried a letter from Boston Marathon rival and North Dorchester teammate Festus Madden, which carried a surprising tone of hostility. Was it real animosity Madden felt towards Sockalexis, or was he merely trying to build up a promotional following? The headline read: "**A Challenge to Sockalexis.**" And Madden's statement bluntly said: "I, the undersigned, do hereby challenge Andrew Sockalexis, the Old Town A.A. Indian, to run a match race of 15 miles or over. I ran second to the Indian last year in the BAA Marathon and this year, owing to having a bad toe which bothered me in the race I did not finish. I want one more chance against the Indian and I am sure I will defeat him. I will run him any time, at any place." It was signed: "Festus Madden 114 Regent St., Roxbury, Mass."[6]

Three days later the *Commercial* had an announcement about a track and field meet, plus that planned big "marathon" promised by the promoters of the 19-mile run in the fall. Allen was back, announcing that he was receiving, daily, letters from athletes intending to compete. The meet was set for Maplewood Park on Memorial Day.[7]

Howard Drew, the black sprinter from Springfield (Mass.) High School, wrote Allen to promise his participation, stating he would compete in both the 100- and 200-yard dashes. At the time Drew held the world record for 70 yards indoors and was optimistic that he could set a world record in the 100 as well. The field in the dashes appeared very strong. Returning were Bill Meanix, who had won both the 100- and 200-yard dashes in the meet at last year's Memorial Day meet, plus Powell, who was second in the 100, and another noted sprinter, Irving T. Howe, from English High School in Boston.

Also W.H. McVicar, a winner last year, planned on returning and repeating his good work. McVicar had won the one-half mile New England championship and also was a champion at the 1-mile, 5-mile and 10-mile track races, holding the New England record for these distances. McVicar, while at Exeter Academy, had set the world record for 1000 yards indoors in 2:17. Runners Roger Bell and Dick Power, both of the University of Maine, felt confident they could capture the 2-mile race.

For Allen's big "Marathon," the North Dorchester club promised to have the following: DeMar, who'd won the race last year, plus Madden, Lilley, Sturgis, Tom Brown (eighth place in the 1913 Boston Marathon), Saklad, Pond and Fallon, as well as local hero Andrew Sockalexis. It was also reported that "a committee is in correspondence" with Fritz Carlson of Minneapolis, the BAA winner, to come. Carlson, ultimately, did not come.

Further, promoter Allen was stating that Joe Silvia and a number of other Boston Athletic Association champions would also be competing in the different races.

On May 26, the *Commercial* carried a large photo of Sockalexis, with DeMar and Lilley and American flags.

Allen worked to build up the event: "All indications point
to a record-breaking record at Maplewood Park" due to all
the "crack runners" from around the country for the second
annual amateur marathon. The event was sponsored by the
Old Town AA. There was to be one notable change made in
the design of the long-distance run: The runners would not be
traveling from Old Town to Bangor; the entire race was to take
place on the track at Maplewood Park.[8]

Apparently there had been some trouble with gate-crashers
the year before, with men as well as boys getting into the
park "through, over and under the fence." Supposedly, the
management at the park was arranging for a number of special
officers, who were "to watch every section of the big board
fence and the man who gets through without paying admission
is subject to an interview with the authorities." Special rates,
for would-be audience members, were made with the local rail,
the Maine Central, from all points east of Lewiston and from
the entire B&A system.[9]

On Tuesday, May 27, there were more listings of entering
competitors in the *Commercial*. Thomas J. Halpin, the New
England half-mile and 600-yard indoor champion who was
also reportedly the half-mile national junior champion of
America and the quarter-mile champion of the United States
and Canada, was announced as coming.[10]

For the "marathon," now announced as a 15-mile track
run, the listing of luminary starters, all from the North
Dorchester club coming to race against Sockalexis, read:
DeMar, Sturgis, Henigan, Lilley, Fallon, Joseph Marino,
Brown, Saklad, Joseph Lordan. One could not help wondering,

after the recent challenge he had made to Sockalexis, where Madden was. Others listed as signed up to participate included Sockalexis' protégé, Sylvester Francis, as well as Sockalexis himself.

Registrants for other events included: 2-mile – Henigan, McVicar and Bell; 1-mile – McVicar; half-mile – Halpin; 200-yard dash – Halpin, Howe and Drew; and 100-yard dash – Howe, Drew and Powell.

It was at this point Andrew Sockalexis apparently reached a running career crossroad crisis: To turn professional, or not to turn professional. It appears he first went into the *Bangor Daily News* and announced that he had turned professional, had already run one professional race recently (supposedly finishing third to Kohlemainen and Queal) and would be leaving town to run another one; thus, he could not participate in the amateur race on Memorial Day.

Since he would ultimately completely deny all the information the *Bangor Daily News* account contained and would actually run in the Memorial Day race one can only be baffled by this story. Was it Sockalexis' uncertainty about the idea of rejecting his amateur status and actually running professional races that caused these two conflicting headlines? Perhaps he thought by making an announcement like this he could push himself over the edge and take the big step into professional running. Or was it disenchantment with local promoters for exploiting him and a desire for a share of the profits that prompted his actions? Perhaps he was trying to get under-the-table money from Allen to appear in the Memorial Day race – as was alleged by Allen later.

First, on Wednesday morning, came the *Bangor Daily News* story, on May 28, 1913:

OLYMPIC ATHLETE NOW PROFESSIONAL
Andrew Sockalexis No Longer Ama-
teur—Goes to New York for Big Race

The account read:

> *Andrew Sockalexis, the Old Town Indian, noted as the Olympic runner, called at the News office Tuesday afternoon on his way to New York and contributed two bits of information, one of which is extremely important. Sockalexis has become a professional. And, naturally, he will not participate, in fact, he cannot, in the marathon race from Old Town to Bangor on Memorial Day. Though known to but few, the fleet Indian became a professional runner when he raced Queal and Kolehmainen on the night of May 10 at Celtic park. Sockalexis finished third. His amateur career ended when he took part in the modified marathon held under the auspices of the New York Evening Mail in the afternoon of May 10. Sockalexis has recently returned from New York and left Tuesday night for the big city to get in readiness for the professional 20-mile run on the track of the National ball league grounds in Brooklyn, on Memorial Day. Others running will be Kolehmainen, Queal, Longboat, Crooks and Johnson.[11]*

After the *Bangor Daily News* story came out in the morning, Sockalexis apparently immediately contacted the office of the *Bangor Daily Commercial* and completely denied the *News* account.

On the afternoon of Wednesday, May 28, 1913, the afternoon paper, the *Commercial*, carried this story:

MARATHON ENTRIES
Those Who Will Compete at
Maplewood Memorial Day
SOCKALEXIS IS IN IT
Denies Story That He Has Already
Become a Professional—Some Promising Contests

The *Commercial* account read:

Notwithstanding the broad side of the News to the contrary, Sockalexis, Old Town's plucky little Indian runner, is not a professional, according to a statement by Andrew Sockalexis himself to the Commercial, Wednesday noon. 'I wish,' said he to this paper, 'to contradict the article in this morning's News. I will enter the Memorial Day Marathon as an amateur, as I am just as much of an amateur now as I ever was. I shall not go to New York for Memorial Day.'

Sockalexis thus sets at rest all speculation as to whether he will, or will not, be in the races of Friday as an amateur, as in fact the only Maine amateur who took part in the world-famous Olympic games at Stockholm, Sweden.

For some time the little red man has planned to enter the professional lists, but has purposely deferred until after this race in Bangor should be out of the way.

> *Sockalexis is in excellent condition and ex-*
> *pects to give a good account of himself in Friday's*
> *Marathon. He did 15 miles to Greenbush and back,*
> *Wednesday afternoon, following the Greenbush*
> *road out of Old Town and return.*[12]

Understandably, the *Bangor Daily News* was furious at this terrible attack upon its credibility. Why hadn't the *Commercial* asked Sockalexis why he told the *News* all this false information... or ask him where did he think it came from? Someone must have finished in third place at Celtic Park in that professional race. Where did that story come from? What was behind these two very different stories coming from the same man to two different newspapers on back-to-back days?

The headline alone, the very next day, showed the *Bangor Daily News'* anger with Sockalexis, on Thursday, May 29, 1913:

"If Sock Could Run As Fast As He Can Change His Mind There Wouldn't Be A Chance for Any Other—See?"

The story branded the unnamed *Commercial* writer as an "amateur" and sharply attacked Sockalexis' character and his alleged unsportsmanlike remarks and intentions.

This account read:

> *If Andrew Sockalexis could run as fast as he*
> *can—well, change his mind, he would soon gather*
> *enough wampum along the distance trails to keep*

him and his tribe fat and happy until the resurrection of Orono and Madockawando and all the other copper-colored colonels who bossed things along the Penobscot in days long past and gone. But he can't.

Neither can anybody else. On Tuesday Sockalexis came into the News office and volunteered the information that he had shed his amateur shoes and had become a professional; that he was even then on his way to New York to take part in a twenty-mile run on Memorial Day, and that he would not appear in the Old Town A.A. event here, never having entered for that race. He said a lot more, which was omitted from Wednesday's News in the interest of sport and good feeling.

Then, on Wednesday, he telephoned to the Bangor Commercial a flat contradiction of his statements made to and published in the News— about three inches of type, which the Commercial's enterprising and wide-eyed amateur describes as a 'broadside.' He denied that he had become a professional, that he was going to New York or that he had decided not to run in the Old Town A.A. race. The News is not...anxious about Andrew Sockalexis, his movements, opinions or sudden changes of base, but so long as the erratic Indian has seen fit to hand this paper a plain and unsolicited statement and then contradict it in another paper it seems about time to tell the facts and put Sockalexis in the class where he belongs. Anybody has a guess at the name of the class.

WHAT SOCKALEXIS SAID

*On Tuesday afternoon, Sockalexis en-
tered the News office and asked for the sporting
writer. Soon he was engaged in earnest conversa-
tion with a reporter. 'I want something put in the
paper,' Sockalexis stated. 'I'm not going to run in
the Memorial Day race and I want you to put that
statement in great, big type in the paper. I have no
use for the people who are managing the affair and
I want you to spoil it.' The reporter answered that
he would state that Sockalexis would not participate
in the race but thought that he would not attempt
to 'spoil' the event. 'Of course, I am a big drawing
card and would be in this race. The people running
the race know that and that is why they have advertised my name. They never asked me if I would
run but started to advertise that I would. They had
my picture in the Old Town Nickel but I had them
take it out. I'm all done with that crowd. I am
going to New York to run in a professional race on
Memorial Day. On May 10, I ran in a professional
race with Kolehmainen and Queal. I finished third.
It was kept quiet so that nobody knew that I had
become a professional. This was after I ran in the
Evening Mail marathon. Now I'm a 'pro.' 'You are
going to get the money now?' 'I am.'*

WHAT HAPPENED?

*It appears that on Wednesday someone 'saw'
Sockalexis. It was not president Allen of the Old
Town A.A. for on Wednesday night Mr. Allen
told the News that he hadn't seen the Indian that*

day and knew nothing about his sudden change of heart. It was someone else. Mr. Allen did say a whole lot of things about the Indian's methods, which would not look well in type, but which may be printed later. As affecting the Indian's standing as an 'amateur,' however, it may just as well be stated that Sockalexis had demanded $180 for starting in the Memorial day race here and that he had been demanding money all winter from Allen, who has a contract to manage the runner as professional after the race here. That contract probably never will be carried out, as Allen is just a trifle tired of Sock's methods and his ideas of sporting ethics.[13]

Well, at least in this account there is some hint about where all the conflict lies. No different from skilled athletes in any era, Andrew Sockalexis apparently believed promoters and outsiders were the ones most profiting from his abilities. Perhaps it became a battle of promoters, between Allen and the mystery person who allegedly "saw" Sockalexis on Wednesday. Perhaps, Sockalexis saw others cashing in on event money (promoters), appearance money (unscrupulous competitors), or betting money (promoters and spectators), and he wanted his share. Perhaps racism, too, was a part of the equation as greedy white promoters thought they could take advantage of a poor Indian. Or, perhaps, Sockalexis himself had now evolved into a manipulating, greedy athlete.

Sockalexis, from Allen's perspective, had either become a difficult nuisance who pestered him for money and was no longer worth the effort or, perhaps, Allen recognized he was losing a valuable commodity to other money-hungry promoters and was now trying to destroy the little Indian's credibility.

Had some promoter from the professional ranks contacted Sockalexis and he was now confused as to which way to go? Was there a new mentor in his ear, or was he himself being manipulative for merely greedy reasons? Unfortunately, there is no way to know. The only known outcome of all of this is that Sockalexis remained an amateur and ran the Memorial Day race, and then shortly thereafter declared himself a professional runner and ran several professional races during the summer of 1913.

On Thursday, May 29, the *Commercial* reported that it was hoped the weather would be good the next day for the 15-mile "marathon." It had rained hard most of that day but weather predictions were good for Friday. Here, it was announced that the race would, indeed, be entirely run within the confines of Maplewood Park, rather than run on the roads and brought on to the track for the finish.[14] The same press release essentially appeared in the *Bangor Daily News* the morning of the marathon. An update on the weather revealed that it was still raining hard at midnight; however, it was stated that the Maplewood track "is but little affected by rain and the races will be pulled off this afternoon."[15]

Bad weather, however, did affect the event. The *Commercial* reported that a cold wind blew across the park and the rain clouds persisted, limiting attendance to around 400 people at Maplewood Park on Friday afternoon, May 30. The unnamed writer said about 200 were scattered through

the grandstand while the rest were lined up on either side
of the track. The track races were late starting, because the
participants were late in arriving, and "much delay was caused
in dressing." The St. Joseph's band of Old Town had arrived
early, and "did what it could to relieve the monotony of the
long wait."[16]

The assessment of the track being able to withstand
the elements apparently was very wishful thinking. The
Commercial reporter wrote: "The conditions for the races were
most unfavorable. Thick mud covered the track and in many
places there were large pools of water. On the upward stretch
the heavy wind struck the runners square in the face, greatly
hindering their progress."[17]

The first event was a 1-mile run with four participants.
Oscar Hedlund won in 5 minutes 1 second, beating Saklad and
McVicar, with Johnson of Millinocket dropping out. In a
100-yard handicap race, Drew won in 9 3-5 seconds, with
Meanix in second and Howe, a close third.

How did the handicap work in a 100-yard dash?
Apparently Drew and Meanix ran from scratch, or the actual
starting line, while Howe's "handicap" lead was a one-yard
advantage at the gun. Drew's run was considered remarkably
fast, considering the unfavorable conditions. "This time ties
the world's amateur record for the 100-yard dash, and it hardly
seemed probable that the track at Maplewood would permit
such speed in the condition that it was in Friday. However,
there was a strong wind at the runner's back, which may have
aided a little, and Drew is regarded as fast a man as there is
in the country, winning a place on the last Olympic team,

but being unable to compete in Stockholm because of an accident."[18]

Halpin of the Boston A.A. won the half-mile in 2 minutes 17 and 3-4 seconds with Morris of Old Town A.A. in second, and Morriston of North Dorchester, third. At this point, the meet was still in progress as the *Commercial* went to press.

The rest of the events leading up to the 15-miler went like this: Drew also captured the 220-yard dash, in 21 3-5 seconds, with Howe, second, and Meanix, third. Hedlund, too, was a repeat winner, taking the 2-mile run in 10 minutes 54 seconds.

The *Commercial* reported: "The races were all clean and interesting, and there was no doubt about the decisions, although many doubted the accuracy of the time in several instances."[19]

The Saturday, May 31 issue of the *Commercial* announced the victory of Cliff Horne in the 15-mile race and also carried the shocking news that Sockalexis had collapsed on the track and not finished the race.[20] The headline ran:

Clifton J. Horne Winner of Marathon
Memorial Day Races Marred By Soggy Track
Sockalexis Dropped on Track at 10th Mile
The Preliminaries Furnished Some Good Sport

The 15-miler was won "easily" by Horne, another of the outstanding North Dorchester Athletic Association runners from the greater Boston area. His time was 1 hour, 33 minutes and 13 seconds. Lilley was second, followed by William Brown, third, and Sturgis, fourth. Sockalexis protege Sylvester Francis finished fifth, with William Johnson of Brewer, sixth. Clarence DeMar, about to go into a lengthy, several-year hiatus from serious running competition, finished only seventh in this visit up to Maine.[21]

All the other events had been held. The *Commercial* reported that the attendance figure of 400 had bulked up to about 1,000 for the start of the 15-mile, solely-on-the-track race. The track conditions were described as "most unfavorable," with the track itself "wet and soggy."[22]

Horne, the *Commercial* account stated, took control of the race from the outset and held the lead throughout the entire race. "Not once did any of the other runners get close enough to give him any worriment, and the calm manner in which he went lap after lap, without changing his pace except in the finish evoked rounds of applause every time he passed in front of the grandstand."[23]

At the beginning, Sockalexis, Fallon, Johnson, Sturgis, McCarthy, Francis and Saklad followed behind Horne, with others strung out further behind. The *Commercial* reported that at the end of the third mile, the runners were in the following positions behind Horne: Saklad, Sockalexis, Lilley, Sturgis, Francis, Brown, Fallon, Thibodeau, Johnson, McCarthy, Pooler.[24]

The newspaper reported: "Horne gradually crept away from the others and the contest." The pace or Horne's lead apparently proved too much for Saklad, who dropped out in the fourth mile. In the fifth mile some more runners began to weaken and drop further behind Horne's relentless, steady pace. Lilley was now in second place, but Sockalexis relinquished his third place spot to Brown, followed by Sturgis, on the next lap. With Horne firmly in control of the race, Lilley held second, with Brown, Sturgis and Johnson following. For a short while Lilley appeared to shorten the distance between himself and the leader, but gradually he fell back.[25]

At the crack of the pistol for the final lap for the leader, when he had completed his 29th lap, Horne started to sprint and was nearly a quarter of a mile ahead of Lilley.

What happened to Sockalexis? The *Commercial* described it this way: "In the tenth mile, Sockalexis, who had not been holding his own after the fifth, was seen to be running under difficulties and when he was rounding the upper stretch of the track staggered and fell upon the track."[26]

Others who did not finish the race were Saklad, Fallon, Edward Thibodeau, Michael J. McCarthy and Aldman Pooler.

On the Monday after, the *Commercial* carried a short, untitled piece in its city notes column:

> *There was a persistent report about Bangor Monday morning to the effect that Sockalexis, the Old Town marathon runner, had dropped dead from the effects of Saturday's race. It proved to be without foundation and many anxious inquiries on the Commercial telephone were answered to that effect. Sock left Old Town Monday morning for Brattleboro, Vt. where he will participate Tuesday in a ten-mile marathon under the auspices of the Valley Fair association. He was feeling fine when he left Old Town and it is not known how the rumor started.*[27]

* * *

Chapter 13

Sockalexis turns pro and takes a wife

Early summer, 1913. Interesting times. Nathaniel
Hawthorne's son, Julian, was jailed and had served two
months of a one-year sentence for complicity in a mining
promotion swindle. His problem, he claimed, was "a family
curse," the result of his ancestors' cruelty in the Salem witch
hunt days... Another article noted that Paul Revere's ride was
"not that famous or known about" until the Longfellow poem...
"Helen Keller Socialist" was the title of the speech (and the
speaker) to be featured before a sociological conference at
Sagamore... At newly built (1912) Fenway Park in Boston, the
Red Sox put up their championship flag from the previous
baseball season... The legendary Shoeless Joe Jackson, usually
very mild mannered, was indefinitely suspended for "his
trouble" with umpire Egan in a game Saturday... And future
Hall-of-Famer Napoleon Lajoie, a man who had entered
professional baseball in 1897, the same year as Andrew
Sockalexis' second cousin, Louis, was said to be about to leave

major league baseball. His dissipating skills had forced him
to the bench "until he loses weight and grows faster on the
paths." It was suggested that the "greatest batter of his time"
might prefer to retire than sit.

In track and field news, Cornell's John Paul Jones "sailed"
to a new mile record, running 4 minutes, 14 2-5 seconds...
Noted trainer Michael Murphy, who was head coach of the
U.S. Olympic team in 1912 despite failing health, died... On
July 7, 1913 Jean Bouin, a French runner, set a new world
record for distance running in one hour: 11 miles and 1,413
yards, beating Alfred Shrubb's previous record of 11 miles,
1,136 yards set in 1904... It was reported from London that a
new world record for running 50 miles had been set: E. W.
Lloyd's 6 hours, 13 minutes, 58 second run eclipsed the old
record of J. E. Dixon, 6 hours, 18 minutes, and 26 1-5 seconds,
which had stood since 1885.

In Arthur Duffey's column in the *Boston Post*, Arthur
Smith, the University of Maine trainer who accompanied
Sockalexis to Stockholm, was congratulated for his work as
coach of the track team which won the Maine Intercollegiate
competition. Duffey said Smith "deserves much credit
considering the limited material he has to work with..."[1]

Also in his column, Arthur Duffey acknowledged Howard
Drew's excellent 100-yard dash in Bangor on Memorial Day.
He noted that Drew, the Springfield sprinter, had run the
race in 9 3-5 seconds. "As Drew was not timed by competent
timers, and as Billy Meanix was the runner who finished
second to the colored flyer, it is doubtful if the mark will be
recognized. However, Drew is a remarkable performer," wrote

Duffey, who himself was a champion sprinter and once ran the 100-yard dash in 9 3-5 seconds in the Intercollegiate Athletic Championship at Berkeley on May 31, 1902, the "original" world's record for an amateur. Duffey did not explain what the problem was concerning Meanix's participation, nor did he explain why it was "too bad" Drew was not eligible for college competition. In the professional running ranks, Duffey reported Willie Kohlemainen had been suspended for failing to file an expense bill for his appearance in Paterson, N.J. Kohlemainen was reinstated one week later.[2]

For Andrew Sockalexis the month of June, 1913, may have been his biggest trial period yet, in deciding when and where he should turn professional runner. It seems clear after the Memorial Day race, it was only a matter of time before Sockalexis joined the professional running ranks. Perhaps he was still trying to work out a deal with another manager or a professional promoter, since his relationship with his previous manager, Allen, was clearly destroyed by the events surrounding the Memorial Day race. Sockalexis did not go to a professional race held June 15, 1913 at the Dorchester Day Meet at Celtic Park in the greater Boston area. Well-known runners like James Powers, Abel Kiviat, Gallagher and others competed...but there was still no runner named Andrew Sockalexis among their ranks.

On Tuesday, June 24, 1913, the *Boston Post* and "**Arthur Duffey's Column**" announced: "Andy Sockalexis, the Old Town Indian, will make his debut among the money chasers in the 10-mile open professional race at the Scotch games. Andy is down to meet Billy Queal, Abbie Wood and Al Shrubb, who will go after the big prizes."[3] So, as late as June 24, he still had not turned professional runner but no explanation was offered why he had passed up several apparently prestigious and potentially lucrative professional races to remain an amateur.

Yet, Sockalexis was not competing in amateur races either. For instance, he was absent from a big amateur competition, the 1913 New England Track and Field Championships. James A. Powers of the BAA won the 1-mile in 4 minutes 10 2-5 seconds; Joe Silva of the BAA won the 5-mile, in 27 minutes 22 1-5 seconds; Drew took the 100-yard race in 10 seconds; and Howe won the 220-yard race in 22 1-5 seconds.

Another professional "showdown" race, was reported by Duffey on July 5. He noted that in a recent match race, between Shrubb and Longboat, Shrubb won the 5-miler in 26 minutes 10 seconds. Another 10-mile professional race, scheduled for the Scotch Caledonia Games at Caledonian Grove, was announced for Aug. 2.

On Friday, July 11, the *Boston Post* reported the following: "Andy Sockalexis, the Old Town Indian, is being favored to win the 10-mile professional race at the Scotch games Aug. 2. Although such competitors as Al Shrubb, Billy Queal and Tom Longboat are booked to start, the marathon runner is picked to beat them all."[4] But Duffey did not mention who was promoting Sockalexis as the favorite to beat such proven, outstanding runners; nor did he even mention that Sockalexis, to date, still had not declared himself to be a professional runner. Shrubb was identified as a coach at Harvard, and another outstanding professional runner, Jimmy Powers, was a construction iron worker. Powers and a man named Kiviat were being matched in a special 1-mile race at the Scotch Clans games.

On July 14, a blurb in Arthur Duffey's column about professional running appeared in the *Boston Post* announcing that "nearly every local 'pro' runner" was expected to start in the 10-mile relay marathon at Rocky Point, Providence, on July 27. Among those identified were "well-known" professional runners Sam Meyers, Pat Dineen, Bob Fowler, Prouty and Bart Sullivan, who were set to make the trip. Duffey also stated: "Judging from the way Rhode Islanders are turning out for the professional running events in that little state, it looks as if the days of the money chasers are gradually coming back again."[5]

Another Monday, July 14, article about the 60th annual Scotch games mentioned Sockalexis and a big professional race. Heralding excellent prizes for both the amateur and professional races, the blurb said these prizes would be "the most valuable ever given in New England." The Irish-American A.C. vs. the Boston A.A., in nine events, was seen as keen competition, with all the competitions set up as handicap events except the 3-mile. "In the 10-mile professional race, that will be held after the amateur events have been completed, Billy Queal, Ted Wood of England, Andrew Sockalexis, Alfie Shrubb and at least 2 Canadian Indians will be among the starters."[6] Again, there was no explanation concerning who was promoting the entry of Sockalexis into this race or a statement definitively announcing that he had become a professional runner.

In a July 17 column *Post* columnist Duffey wrote:
"Andrew Sockalexis, the Old Town Indian, should make
good in the professional running events around the Hub this
summer. With Billy Kolehmainen *[Author's note: it's "Willie"
Kohlemainen]* in England and with the rest of the money
chasers not showing their usual paces, the redskin ought
to fit in pretty well among the big purses."[7] One wonders if
Andrew Sockalexis himself was back visiting newspaper
offices offering this information himself. He still had not run a
professional race. Duffey also speculated about another match
race among the professionals, featuring Billy Queal against
Bart Sullivan, sometime after the Scotch games.

On Tuesday, July 15, the *New York Tribune* carried this
blurb about Sockalexis under the headline "**Training for
6-Mile Race**." The account stated: "Andrew Sockalexis, the
famous Indian runner, who recently turned 'pro' has begun
hard training for the 6-mile team race, one of the features of
the three-day carnival of sports to be held at Ebbets Field,
Brooklyn, on July 26 and August 2 and 9. The Oldtown *[sic]*
(Me.) boy, who finished fourth in the Stockholm Marathon,
will have Tom Longboat as a teammate. They will race against
Fred Meadows and Alfred Shrubb."[8]

Becoming a professional runner was becoming an "in"
thing to do apparently. Betting on running, apparently, was
growing even more popular and promoters had better offers
to make to lure the amateur runners away. Under the headline
"Little spurns Harvard," a Sunday, July 13 story from Raleigh,
N.C. announced that Richard Little, "the self-styled world's
champion one-mile runner," was turning professional runner.

In so doing, Little "gives up going to Cornell, declines Harvard's offer, accepts principalship of a small school and challenges the world." Little apparently had bettered the record for one mile by John Paul Jones "but it was not generally accepted."[9] The reason why was not given.

On Tuesday, July 22, 1913, the *Boston Post* simply stated: "Andy Sockalexis, the Old Town Indian, has not run professionally yet. He is booked to run his pro race in Brooklyn Saturday." On that same Tuesday, July 22, the *Worcester Telegram* carried this headline, "**Sockalexis Joins Professionals**," and ran this short blurb: "Andrew Sockalexis, the Indian marathon runner, Oldtown *[sic]*, Me., has decided to join the professional ranks. He will enter a 6-mile relay race in Brooklyn, Saturday. His teammate will be Tom Longboat, the Indian professional. Their competitors will be Al Shrubb and Fred Meadows."[10]

On Saturday, July 26, the *New York Tribune* announced: "**Games at Ebbets Field/Foot and Cycle Races to Be/Held in Inclosure**." The first of a series of athletic carnivals was to be held by the Ebbets-McKeever Exhibition Company at Ebbets Field, in Brooklyn, that afternoon. The field was available because the professional baseball team, the Superbas, the forerunners of the Dodgers, were on the road. The big enclosure, it was announced, could be used as "an amusement place in other lines than baseball." The *Tribune* noted professional runners Alfred Shrubb, Billy Queal, Fred Meadows, Andrew Sockalexis, A.E. Wood and Tom Longboat were "on edge for their races." It was then, again, announced that "Sockalexis, the Oldtown *[sic]* (Me.) Indian, who has just turned professional, will team up with Longboat in a six-mile race against Shrubb and Meadows." Queal was scheduled to race five miles against Wood. Queal confidently declared he never felt better in his life and was confident of beating his rival. Other competitions included bicycling, matching Joe Fogler (of "six-day bicycle fame") against Alfred Goullett in a series of bike races, a baseball game, a tug-of-war, "and a race between girls."[11]

Andrew Sockalexis' debut as a professional runner came on Saturday, July 26, 1913 at Ebbets Field in Brooklyn, N.Y. As reported in the Sunday, July 27 edition of the *New York Tribune*, Charles H. Ebbets and the McKeevers were given credit in the opening paragraph for making some use and some money from their ball park while the professional baseball team was away on the road. It was noted that English long distance runner A.E. Wood and Billy Queal of Alexandria Bay "furnished the best part of the day's competition...(having) a rousing tussle in a special match race at five miles." Wood opened up a lead in the fourth mile and established "a big gap" to win. However, in an open 1-mile race, later in the day, Queal "came back strong and raced Wood, stride for stride, all the way, finally beating him in the last ten yards by a terrific sprint."[12]

Sockalexis' inauspicious professional debut was described this way in the account:

Fred Meadows and Alfred Shrubb, the former English champion and two-mile record holder, ran a five-mile team race against Tom Longboat and Andrew Sockalexis, who was a member of the American Olympic team last summer and was competing in his first professional race. Sockalexis became ill after running three laps, and the burden of running against Meadows and Shrubb fell almost entirely on Longboat. After resting for several laps the little Maine Indian resumed the race, but could not keep up the pace, though he tried hard. When he finished he rolled on the grass in intense pain, and had to be helped to the dressing room. This left only Longboat to finish, and the best he could get was a poor last. He finished a third of a lap behind Meadows, who did the running in the last lap for the opposing team.[13]

Meadows and Shrubb ran a cumulative 23 minutes, 08 4-5 seconds, it was reported.

In other action Joe Fogler beat the Australian Goullet in the best of three match bicycle races. The Brooklyn man Fogler won the half-mile sprint "over the rough turf course by half a wheel." In the two-mile race, "pedalled on the Australian pursuit plan," Goullet "looked the like the winner until the second lap from the end, when Fogler let out a terrific burst of speed and just caught his man on the line." There was even a women's race: "A 100-yard dash by two pretty girls furnished a lot of amusement for the crowd. They started from a point in centre field and raced in the general direction of the pitcher's box. Miss Julia Downey won by three yards, after having outrun all the way a fair-haired little girl, who, the announcer said, was Miss Hutchinson."[14]

Sockalexis had also expected to compete in the open 1-mile race for professionals, but, reportedly, "was too ill" to participate. The *Tribune* reported that Wood and Queal "made a splendid race of the one-mile run. Six men – Wood, Queal, Longboat, Meadows, Shrubb and Sockalexis – were slated to start, but Shrubb and Sockalexis were not on the line when the starting pistol was fired." Shrubb had "pulled up lame after his part in the team race," and Sockalexis "was still too sick to care much whether there was another race or not."[15]

On Monday, July 28, the great amateur runner Hannes Kohlemainen beat a team of five runners in an exhibition race at the Kalevat Athletic Club games. The "world's greatest amateur distance runner individually beat each of the five runners in this five-mile event," running the distance in 25 minutes, 23 3-5 seconds. According to the account he beat the first, second and third men by 30 yards, beat the fourth man by 10 yards and the fifth man by 6 yards—thus, he beat the combined five-member team by well over 100 yards.[16]

On Saturday, August 2, the second series of sporting events, featuring several races involving professional runners, was held at Ebbets Field. Andrew Sockalexis did not compete in the open 1-mile race or the 4-mile, two-man team race. He did, however, take third place in a one-half mile race. A crowd estimated at 4,000 persons attended this sporting outing which included the bike and foot races again, another women's race (this time with four competitors) and even "an exhibition of Belgian sheep dogs."[17]

Longboat and Meadows nipped a team composed of Shrubb, the famous English professional champion, and Abbe E. Wood, a Canadian. A new "pro" runner, Tad White, was introduced at this competition. White, surely a local favorite from Brooklyn, had been an outstanding amateur runner from a "decade ago" when he won several amateur championships while representing the local New York and Irish-American Athletic clubs. He finished third in the open 1-mile run (with Wood winning and Longboat second). White did win the half-mile run, in 2 minutes, 08 seconds, with Meadows of Canada, second, and Sockalexis third. No time was reported for second or third place.[18]

The 100-yard dash for girls, "who wore bloomers," proved to be "another easy victory" for Miss Julia Downey of Brooklyn. She defeated three other foes this time, however, including Miss Edna McBride of Brooklyn, Miss Hattie Hutchinson of Montreal, and Miss Margaret Holmer. Miss Downey "got off to a good start and was able to hold her lead," although Miss McBride apparently made "a rush" in the last 15 yards and finished only a yard back. Miss Downey "showed the sprinting stride of a man, breaking the tape in 13 1-5 seconds."[19]

On Sunday, August 3, at Caledonian Grove, a 10-mile professional event was held, with Billy Queal, of Alexandria Bay, winning handily. Ted Crooks of Fall River, Mass., was second, followed by James Fitzgerald of Australia, third, and George Hooley, Newark, N.J., fourth. Queal was timed in 56 minutes, 02 seconds.[20] There is no evidence that Sockalexis participated in this race.

Sockalexis was to have participated in a professional race as a part of a field day of events in Worcester, Mass. for Saturday, August 9, it was announced on August 4, but the event was called off. No reason was given. The article, published in the *Worcester Telegram*, stated:

> *Worcester followers of the track game will*
> *have an opportunity to see some of the fastest dis-*
> *tance men in this section of the country perform*
> *at the picnic and athletic carnival of St. Josephs*
> *church, Stoneville, Saturday at Prospect park.*
> *Rev. James P. Moore, pastor of the church, who*
> *has general charge of the field day, announced*
> *that the contemplated professional 10 mile race*
> *between Andrew Sockalexis, the Old Town, Me.*
> *runner and some other runner of equal merit, to*
> *be selected, had been called off and in its place a*
> *10-mile marathon which has been sanctioned by*
> *the N.E.A.A.U. and which will carry with it the*
> *New England championship will be carded. This*
> *event is sure to prove a far bigger attraction that*
> *[sic] the Indian long jaunt artist.[21]*

Representatives from Boston AA, North Dorchester AA, Irish American AA were expected to run, including Joe Silva of the BAA who "fought his way through a big and strong field, Saturday, at the Scotch games at Caledonian Grove" and said he was coming.[22]

The name of Andrew Sockalexis did not appear in the results of the third and final Saturday series of contests at Ebbets Field, on August 9. A Canadian team of Wood and Meadows beat Queal and Longboat in the two-man team race over four miles. Queal won the 1-mile over five competitors, including Wood, Longboat and "Tallfeather, a Wisconsin Indian, who was competing for the first time," and Shrubb. White won the half-mile race, beating Wood and Meadows.[23]

On August 13, according to an article in the *Worcester Telegram*, Hannes Kohlemainen "doesn't care whether it's six men, eight men or four-man team." In an eight-mile match race, he beat a four-man team by two laps and 100 yards, or a 700-yard advantage. He won by 2 minutes, 3 1-5 seconds.[24]

An Old Town *Enterprise* article, on Saturday, August 16, on the front page carried this headline:

Andrew Sockalexis returns from a successful tour of team racing

The article said he was "resting in Belgrade Lakes" after having teamed with Tom Longboat. He claimed 10 firsts, two seconds, one third and one fourth.[25]

The article continued:

The many friends in this vicinity will be pleased to know that Andrew Sockalexis, the world renowned marathon runner, has just returned from a most successful tour of team racing with Tom Longboat as team mate, and Alfred Shrubb of England and Meadows of Canada, champions in their class as opponents.

He has been successful from a financial, as well as a running standpoint. He has won ten first, two second, one third, and a fourth money during this time. He has run in New Haven, New London, Conn, New York City, Brooklyn, N.Y., Pittsburgh, Philadelphia, Pa., Newark, N.J. and Worcester, Mass.

In two races he was taken sick on the track but finished well under the conditions. He is racing for money now and is making good money and getting a fat bank account. He now has more races on

> *hand than he can handle so picks those that show the most money. His longest race on the trip was six miles, which he made in 22 minutes and 25 seconds. His time for one half mile is 1:57, mile 4:36, two miles 9:50, three miles 15:04, five miles 25:55. He is now resting at Belgrade Lakes.*

> *Sockalexis has an ambition to play league ball. Dahlen captain of the Brooklyn League team sees no reason as the following shows. Bill Dahlen, mandarin of the Dodgers, sees no reason why Sockalexis should not make good as a ball tosser. 'He's got the build and all other requisites,' declared 'Bad Bill' after sizing up the young Indian.*[26]

Did Andrew Sockalexis run, and do so well, in professional races in all the cities named above, from his debut on July 26 in Brooklyn to August 16th? The claim, unfortunately, raises some doubts, especially since he did so poorly in Brooklyn and the Worcester event was cancelled. The claims of success and money made to the media is again, clearly, coming from him.

According to a Thursday, August 28, **Arthur Duffey's Column** in the *Boston Post*: "Andy Sockalexis, the Old Town Indian, has cleared up $400 since his advent into the money chasers. As Andy puts it: 'This is more than all the medals and cups won in many years while in the amateur ranks would amount to.'[27]

Also, in this column, Duffey wrote that "Willie" Kohlemainen, the pro runner was returning from Europe, leaving the resident pro runners "quaking" at the thought. However, Duffey joked, prospects still looked bright for the "money-chasers"...because Hannes Kohlemainen was still an amateur.[28]

On August 31, 1913, "**Arthur Duffey's Column**" stated Canadian Wood would go head to head with Finn Willie Kohlemainen for the American Professional Championship at the Scotch Clans games "tomorrow" on September 1, Labor Day. Another story about the Scotch Games, Caledonian Grove, Labor Day announced a 10-mile professional race to include: A.E. Wood, Canada; Ted Crooks, Fall River, Mass; J.J. Fitzgerald, Australia; Bill Prouty and Pat Dineen, South Boston.[29]

Crooks captured first place in the 10-mile professional race at the Scotch Clans games, on September 1. His time was 57 minutes, 14 seconds. Second was Karl Keneemah of Buffalo, followed by J. Whooly of Newark, H. Prime of Boston and Bob Fowler of Cambridge. Fowler, the man who served as Sockalexis' adviser at the 1913 Boston Marathon (and was blamed by some for Sockalexis' second place finish), claimed he lapped Prime. The crowd agreed. Even Prime agreed. But the judges ruled he had not.[30]

On Saturday, September 27, 1913, the *Eastern Argus* (Portland, Me.) reported in a story, under the headline of "**Patrick Deneen Entered in 20-Mile Race at Bayside**," that Deneen was the first entry for a professional race to be "pulled off" at Bayside Park, Portland on October 10. The race was organized by A. Vambra of the 50th Company, Fort McKinley, who was acting as manager of the race. Two more sentences promoted the ability of Deneen and expectations of "a classy field" to develop in the days to come.[31]

The entry of Andrew Sockalexis was announced on Wednesday, October 1 in the *Eastern Argus*: "**Sockalexis Entered In/20-Mile Race Oct. 10.**" The article noted Sockalexis' accomplishments and said Alessio Vambra, "the celebrated Italian runner" who was in charge of the Bayside Run, had received the entry "yesterday." It was noted there would be a special match race of 100 yards between Micky Swisko of Fort Williams and Hoyley of Fort McKinley for the championship of the Portland Artillery District.[32]

On Saturday, October 4, Vambra announced a third entry – Ted Crook. The article stated: "Crook boasts a fine record... having beaten such formidable runners as Queal, Shrubb, Holmer and Longboat." It was reported Crook had finished in third place in the $10,000 marathon at the New York Polo Grounds in 1909 and fourth in the same race the following year. Crook was also credited with winning the international race at Indianapolis and the 10-mile race at Boston Labor Day.[33]

On October 3, headlines in New England newspapers announced that Joseph Lordan had won the 6th Brockton Marathon 25-miler, in 2 hours, 26 minutes, 30 seconds. Lilley had taken second place in 2 hours, 39 minutes, 53 seconds. Oswald Sperson of Lewiston, Maine had finished in ninth place.[34]

By Friday morning, the Portland paper, the *Daily Eastern Argus,* was trumpeting "**CLASSY FIELD FOR 20-MILE/ RACE AT BAYSIDE TODAY**" in its headline. To be staged at Bayside Park that afternoon, the race was now said to have a fourth well-known professional runner, "Prouty of Hyde Park, Mass. who is a veteran runner of many notable distance races."

Prouty was said to have competed for eight years and, with Pat Deneen as a running mate, won the International team race in Madison Square Garden, New York, in March, 1909. At the time Prouty and Deneen had established a new record, yet to be equaled. "With such a classy quartet as Sockalexis, Crook, Deneen and Prouty lined up for the word there is sure to be a grand good race." The article appeared with a photograph of Sockalexis standing behind two of his trophies.[35]

In the Saturday morning, October 11 edition of the *Daily Eastern Argus*, the headline ran: "**PAT DENEEN WAS WINNER/ In 20-Mile Race at Bayside Park Yesterday/ Prouty Was the Only Other Entrant to Start/Sockalexis Showed Up But Crowd too Small**." The story read: "By a fine exhibition of head work, nerve and endurance Pat Deneen, the veteran pedestrian, go-as-you-please man and long distance runner, defeated his younger competitor F.W. Prouty of Boston, in the 20 mile race at Bayside Park yesterday afternoon." A track, measured five laps to a mile, around the football field, was set up. Prouty, a "big man with a long stride," lapped the "gray haired vet" twice inside the first 10 miles. "Perhaps he figured this would be enough for him to come and go on at the finish, but he reckoned without his host." Prouty "died away completely" at the 17th mile, and Deneen, who kept the same steady clip throughout, "gained back both laps between the 17th and 19th miles." With Prouty merely walking around the course, "it was easy for Deneen to pass him" and win by a lap and a quarter. Deneen sprinted home the last 220 yards, got a great hand, and finished the 20 miles in 2 hours, 8 minutes, 36 seconds.[36]

What happened to Ted Crook of Fall River? He wired Vambra that illness in the family prevented him from coming.[37]

And what about Sockalexis? The article stated: "Andrew Sockalexis was at the park, but when he saw that there were scarcely a hundred persons present he refused to run."[38]

Maybe Sockalexis really was making quite a bit of money on the professional running tour and saw this opportunity as not worth his time. Maybe he was not going to get the amount of money promised by the promoter for running. Does this mean that money given to runners, at least at this particular event, really was based on gate receipts? The rejection to run by Sockalexis certainly seems to be based on this concept.

An *Old Town Enterprise* blurb in its "**Local News**" column in late September noted that the ferry over to Indian Island was "a very busy place these pleasant Sundays. There are many visitors from out of town who come to see the island in general and the home of the two Sockalexis's in particular. It never loses its interest for out of town visitors."[39]

On Sunday, November 9, 1913, Andrew Sockalexis married Pauline Shay on Indian Island. And just two days later his sister, and his only living sibling, Alice Sockalexis married William Fallon of Roxbury, Mass. Fallon was also a marathon runner, who had come up to Maine to run previously and had been an amateur teammate of Andrew's with the North Dorchester A.A.

The headline on the Old Town *Enterprise* for Saturday, November 15, 1913 on the top of the front page read:

"WEDDING BELLS/ Ring in the Sockalexis Family for
Two Members."[40]

The article began:

> On Sunday last at the little church on Indian
> Island, at 4 o'clock, Rev. Fr. J. J. Rice performed
> the ceremony whereby Andrew Sockalexis and
> Pauline Shay were united in marriage. It will be
> remembered that Sockalexis' reputation as a run-
> ner is almost or quite world-wide and the wedding
> on this account was much in the public eye.[41]

The new Mrs. Sockalexis was identified as a graduate
of the grammar school in Old Town. She had attended high
school for one year, and later studied both at Hebron Academy
and at a school in "Brooklyn" [Author's note:..it's Brookline]
Massachusetts.[42]

The story continued:

> The little church looked very gay and festive
> with its decorations of evergreens, palms and chry-
> santhemums and the members of the Penobscot
> turned out in large numbers, also many white
> people were present from surrounding towns. The
> couple stood beneath an arch of evergreen decked
> with roses and chrysanthemums, the altar being
> beautiful with flowers and palms. The bride wore
> white messaline, with chiffon trimmings, white veil
> caught with rosebuds and carried a white prayer
> book. She was attended by Miss Vina Attean who
> wore pink crepe de chine with large black hat.[43]

On the following Tuesday morning, two days later, Alice Sockalexis, the only daughter of Mr. and Mrs. Francis Sockalexis, was married to William Fallon of Roxbury, Mass. by Rev. Fr. J. J. Rice. This event was held at 7 o'clock in the morning nuptial mass in the "little church of St. Ann on Indian island." Fallon was identified as "also being a marathon runner who has at different times been Andrew's white rival for running honors." The church was said to be "well filled with members of the Penobscot tribe." Miss Helen Sapial acted as bridesmaid and Philip Lolar was best man. The bride wore pink chiffon with a white hat. The bridesmaid wore a blue suit and hat to match.[44]

The account continued:

> *Following the ceremony the bridal party left for Bangor where their wedding breakfast was served. In the evening they returned to the island to join in the wedding festivities of Mr. and Mrs. Andrew Sockalexis. They will reside on the Island.*

> *The festivities were at the hall on the island where many things of weight and importance have been duly celebrated but this was the greatest event of later times and as such will take rank among the remnant of the once powerful tribe.*

> *The celebration was a revival of old-time tribal dances with all its paraphernalia. There were many white people present who had never witnessed these old-time dances and who were highly entertained.*

> *The pow-wow came first with Joseph Solomon*
> *in the lead; later came the Mic Mac dance also the*
> *snake dance, all the old men making music with*
> *the shot pouch. John Neptune is mentioned as be-*
> *ing also very proficient in these dances. After the*
> *tribal dances the floor was cleared for the wed-*
> *ding dances. The two marathon runners with their*
> *brides led to the music of Frances' orchestra, com-*
> *posed of members of the tribe.*[45]

The final paragraph of the wedding account is pretty significant, in providing some of his schooling, plus some real discrepancies in terms of official times, number of professional races and wins, and his vocation outside of running – manufacturer and dealer in baskets.

The article stated:

> *He attended the common schools and later*
> *took a business course in Bangor. In recent years*
> *he has won fame as a runner at various distances*
> *from three miles to the full Marathon course, his*
> *record being well known to the sporting world. He*
> *was a member of the American Olympic team at*
> *Stockholm last year, where he finished fourth in the*
> *Marathon in a field of 98 men. In the Boston A.A.*
> *Marathon on April 19, 1912, he finished second in*
> *2:21:08 1-4. In the summer of 1913 he took part as*
> *a professional in twelve races, winning eight. His*
> *regular business is that of a manufacturer of and*
> *dealer in fancy baskets.*[46]

According to the actual marriage certificate from State of Maine records, Andrew Sockalexis and Pauline Shay were married on November 9, 1913. He was 22, she was 21. Indian Island was listed as the home address for both. For "occupation," he listed "athlete" and she listed "at home." They were married on the Island by James J. Rice of Old Town. Andrew's parents were listed as Francis, river driver from Indian Island and his mother, the former Sarah Lacoute from St. Stephen, N.B., housewife. Pauline Shay's parents were listed as Sebattis Shay, a laborer, and the former Margaret Ranco, housewife, both from Indian Island.[47]

It is a terrible irony, to look at the *Enterprise* issue of Saturday, November 15 and see the story about Andrew Sockalexis' wedding literally bumping headlines at the top of the front page with a story about the deadly disease killing Native Americans all over the country, the deadly disease which would be responsible for the death of Andrew Sockalexis less than six years later... tuberculosis. The story, about a Maine anti-tuberculosis lecturer from the area, noted that this pastor of an Orono universalist church, had spoken on tuberculosis, termed "The Great White Plague," on 107 nights out of 115 from June through September. Because of his success as a speaker on the subject, he became a full-time member of the association combating the disease in Maine and resigned his pastorate.[48]

Tuberculosis was a continuing national plague. In 1911, estimates of fatalities resulting from TB were set at 94,205. By mid-year 1912, the cost per year to Americans to fight tuberculosis was an estimated half billion dollars, according to figures by the National Association for the Study and

Prevention of Tuberculosis. It was noted by a Yale University professor of economics that the state of Connecticut and other states were paying heavily to "save the lives of consumptives, especially incipient consumptives" (this was considered important because these were the sickly who were able to return to the work force). According to this professor, in a *Bangor Daily News* June 3, 1912 article, "at present about $15 million a year is put into the tb fight in the United States" and he argued that when "several times this amount is invested enough to isolate or, at any rate, educate every one of the million odd consumptives in the US, now spreading infection, we may expect to see the beginning of the end of the great white plague," he said.[49]

Of these individuals, Native Americans were particularly hard hit. It was a real epidemic. In early August of 1912, a third National Tuberculosis Day was set by the National Association for the Study and Prevention of Tuberculosis for October 27th. The year before an estimated 50,000 churches had observed the holiday, and that figure was expected to double this year. It was stated that 10 percent of all church congregation member deaths were caused by TB. Further, over 52,000 of the 33 million communicants in churches in the US were dying from TB every year.

In Alaska, the Indians there faced TB as the "most prevalent and fatal malady" and a doctor, writing in the *New York Medical Journal*, cynically stated that TB was a comparatively new infection among them, "bestowed upon them by the benevolent paleface along with firewater and certain other blessings of civilization. Among these blessings must also be accounted scarlet fever, measles, influenza, whooping cough and diphtheria."[50]

A *Bangor Daily News* article, on December 29, 1912, was headlined: "**INDIANS GOING BLIND/ Trachoma and Tuberculosis Wiping Out the Race**." From a report submitted to the Senate by the joint Congressional Indian Committee, trachoma "threatens the Indian race with total blindness" and "tuberculosis is wiping out the whole race." The committee thought about trying to establish a central TB hospital but that idea, apparently, was met with great "hostility" by Indians not wishing to leave their home areas. Around the world, TB was a problem, with the death rate in Paris said to be three times that of London and two times that of New York and Berlin.[51]

The end of 1913 brought some outstanding sporting achievements: Francis Ouimet, a teen-aged local Boston boy stunned golf fans around the world, doing what has not been done since – winning the U.S. Open as an amateur – when it was played in Brookline, besting two great English professionals... Ty Cobb was leading Joe Jackson in a fierce fight for the batting title at astronomical numbers... Hughie Jennings was showing just how eccentric a professional baseball coach he could be with his "Eyah!" yell in the coach's box... Hannes Kohlemainen came to the U.S. to establish a permanent residence and compete as a professional runner, like his brother Willie, who came too. Hannes Kohlemainen gave handicaps from 290 to 450 yards in a 3-mile race and won... Further, it was announced that Miss Marie Peary and Mr. Don McMillan (offspring of the two Arctic explorers) were engaged...

In Bangor, much commotion was stirred when a famous nude painting, called "September Morn," was displayed in the window of Gorham's Art Store on State Street in Bangor. The "dainty little maiden" had been barred in New York and Chicago ("barred by police and furnishing countless columns for newspapers"...it now "stands smiling and unabashed" here). Bangor folk can "discover for ourselves if the professional town reformers had cause to be alarmed (it was a gold medal prize winner in Paris). Interestingly enough, in Boston the police didn't object to the picture, but did object to the crowd which filled one of the main streets until even the cars were blocked...so again there was official action (New York and Chicago forbade showings of it in storefront windows).[52]

In the *Bangor Daily News'* end of year summary for Bangor it was noted: "Another event in the sporting line was something out of the ordinary for Bangor, the fleet races at Maplewood on Memorial day which brought together the best field of runners ever in Bangor, including Horne, Lilley, Sturgis, Saklad, DeMar and others...Sockalexis started but did not finish."[53]

Chapter 14

Andrew Sockalexis Tag Day

Andrew Sockalexis' name dropped from the area sporting pages from late summer (and his return from summer professional racing) until the spring of 1914. He got sick again. This time, very sick.

On Saturday, April 18, just a day before the 1914 Boston Marathon, a blurb in the Old Town *Enterprise* stated: "Andrew Sockalexis...is fast regaining his old time form. He will be ready for work in July. He has now many dates for August."[1]

Healthy or not, as a professional runner Andrew could not go to the Boston Marathon of 1914, but his 60-year-old father, Francis, wanted to go. However, the elder Sockalexis was denied the opportunity. An *Enterprise* article on Saturday, April 11, carried this notice: "Francis Sockalexis, according to the Boston papers, thinks he has one more race in him in spite of his sixty years and past reputation...He wanted to enter the race of the B.A.A. this month and try and equal his son's record but the powers decided that he had seen the snows of too many Maine winters."[2] A *Bangor Daily News* column, picking up information by an unnamed writer for the *New York Evening Telegram*, reported: "Although the committee in charge of the Boston AA Marathon has rejected the entry of Louis *[Author's note: it should read "Francis"]* Sockalexis, 60-year-old father of Andrew, the famous Old Town, Me. Indian, on account of his age, it is not a sure thing that they were justified. 'Sock' once told the writer the 'old man' could give him a good run for his money."[3]

Arthur Duffey's column in the *Boston Post* for April 19, explained that BAA officials in the early years often restricted entries to just individuals they felt had a chance to win. Concerning Andrew's father, Duffey wrote that he had received a letter from "Andy" who is "particularly peeved at the failure of the BAA committee to allow his father to start in the race." According to Duffey, Sockalexis said: "It is a downright shame. True, father is 60 years old, but he can take the measure of many of the runners in the race. I know he would finish among the leaders. I cite for my reasons the fact that he ran 20 miles with me when I ran a trial for the Mike Ryan race and he was as fresh as I was at the finish." Duffey concluded: "This is going some for a man of 60 years."[4]

Columnist Duffey listed the contenders for victory at the 1914 Boston Marathon as being: 1913 winner Fritz Carlson, Joe Lorden of Cambridge, Jimmy Duffy of Canada, Ed Fabre of Montreal and Festus Madden of Boston. It is easy, through hindsight, to imagine what a wonderful battle might have ensued in 1914 if Andrew Sockalexis had not declared himself a professional runner and returned to Boston to attempt to capture the title that just eluded him in 1912 and 1913. For it was Duffy, the easy winner of the 1914 Boston Marathon, who Sockalexis passed in the last stages of the 1912 Olympic marathon, then held off and narrowly beat to the finish line to take fourth place in the prestigious race.

If it was announced in mid-April that Sockalexis was making a rapid recovery, then it quickly turned around the wrong way. A blurb in the Saturday, May 9, Old Town *Enterprise* reported that Sockalexis left the week before for the Hebron Sanatorium for tubercular treatment. His case, it was noted, "is considered a mild one and an early recovery is expected."[5]

Almost two months later, a "Local News" blurb in the *Enterprise* on Saturday, July 4, included a report from his mother that Sockalexis was "improving rapidly" and expected to be discharged from the sanatorium at Hebron in August. It was also suggested that he might even leave before that date to go to the seashore with his wife.[6]

A short item from the *Maine Sanatorium News* newsletter for July of 1914 listed Pauline Shay as a visitor and may be carrying a parenthetical aside to its famous Indian resident. It noted that the residents celebrated the 4th of July in "a very patriotic manner," with a special dinner prepared for the day. The tables were decorated "with flags and fireworks (No fire-water)..."[7]

And as early as mid-July, it was clear that Sockalexis' status must have changed for the worse, and that the bills for treatment were exceeding the family's means. A short article in the "Local News" of the Saturday, July 18 *Enterprise*

announced that a "big benefit" was being planned for
Sockalexis on August 22 in Bangor.[8] Another *Enterprise*
piece, on Saturday, July 25, stated Sockalexis Day in
Bangor, set to take place next month in August, was "being
extensively advertised and looks as if it would be a success." It
noted: "Sockalexis' former opponents, colleagues and friends
are offering their services, sending money and doing anything
possible for this sturdy son of the forest and hero world."[9]

On August 19, the *Commercial* ran an update on
Sockalexis Day, noting that many well-known athletes from
around the East had entered a number of events to be held. In
its headline the *Commercial* stated: "**Next Saturday Will Be
Notable Day/In History of Maine Athletics—/The Entries.**"
Accompanying the article was a photo of a gaunt-looking
Sockalexis in a suit and the caption noted that the photo had
been taken of him at the Hebron Sanatorium. The event, the
Commercial stated, "promises to be among the very best ever
held in the state of Maine." Long distance running stars like
Madden, Horne, Sturgis and Lilley were scheduled to duel
in a 12-mile race, while a 10-mile match race offered Jimmy
Henigan of North Dorchester AA squaring off against the
unattached Roth. Arthur Neptune led several local entries
for a 15-miler, with others scheduled to participate from as
far away as Massachusetts and New York. Fallon and others
from Massachusetts, New Hampshire and Vermont were listed
for a 25-mile marathon. Howard Drew of Springfield, Mass.
was listed for the 50-yard, 75-yard and 100-yard dashes. The
events scheduled included: shot put, hammer throwing, discus,

bicycle race, motor cycle race, standing and running broad jump, running high jump and standing high jump.[10]

In the *Commercial* for Friday, August 21, an article carried a headline stating that most of the announced athletes had arrived and were in good condition, with a smaller headline that heralded the starting time of events and noted that Howard P. Drew, who had tied the world's record for 120 yards on Thursday, had arrived Friday evening. The appearance of Drew, the article stated "will be one of the most interesting of the events" on Sockalexis Day..."on which there will be numerous athletic events for the purpose of raising money for the aid of the great Indian runner, Sockalexis." Arrangements were said to be complete.[11]

The *Commercial* then offered this poignant news: "Sockalexis, now in a sanatorium, is to receive all the proceeds of the day to aid him in regaining his health. He will probably never run again but he has left an enviable record behind him for some of the ambitious young runners to emulate." It was noted that a collection of the beautiful and prestigious trophies won by Sockalexis was on display in Priest's window, at the corner of State and Exchange streets.[12]

Again, the stellar field of running stars visiting Maine to honor and help Sockalexis was highlighted. Runners like Henigan, Roth, Madden, Lilley, Sturgis, Horne, Fred Faller, Fred Nagle "are...the pick of the Marathon runners in the eastern part of the United States." Irving T. Howe, the fast sprinter brought to Bangor to oppose Drew, "is considered by many to be one of the few men in the country today able to give Drew the race of his life." In other events Bangor was also expected to see "some of the best men in the world in each one's particular event." In the evening a reception and dance, which many of the athletes were expected to attend, was to be held. And, before the dancing, there was to be a war-dance staged by the Penobscot Indians in native costume. All of the events were billed as fund-raising benefits for Sockalexis.[13]

The day-long program, to begin at 10 a.m. and run through 4 p.m., was scheduled as follows: 10 a.m., 5-mile race from Hampden; 11 a.m., log and canoe races; 1 p.m., motor cycle race, from Bangor to Bluehill and back, starting at high school; 1:30 p.m., 25-mile race, from Charleston; 2 p.m., bicycle race, to Old Town and back; 2:30 p.m., field events start, Abbott Square; 3:30 p.m., 10-mile race, two miles this side of Old Town (race for the championship of New England); and 4 p.m., 15-mile run will start from Hudson.

Drew apparently sent a letter to Tom Daley, the organizer, stating that he had recently tied the 120-yard dash world record in Providence, and expected to arrive in Bangor on Friday at 9:25 p.m. Athletes were to arrive and report to the Star Theatre. "**SOCKALEXIS DAY**" was proudly boasted on the front page of the *Old Town Enterprise*, Saturday, August 22, 1914: "This is the great SOCKALEXIS DAY, a day to be filled with athletic events the like of which has never been seen in Maine. All honor the King of the Marathon runners..."[14] It was just four days short of the date Andrew Sockalexis would die upon, five years later in August of 1919.

On Saturday, August 22, the *Bangor Daily News* headline read: "**EVERYTHING READY/ FOR SOCKALEXIS DAY.**" The article immediately offered the purpose of the big athletic meet that day:

> *...the object of which is to bring out a crowd to contribute through the Tag Day scheme for the benefit of Andrew Sockalexis, the only Maine man ever in the Olympic games now fighting for his life in the Hebron sanitarium. Tags will be sold for whatever anyone may feel like contributing. Any sum, small or large, will be accepted. The contribution from the merchants towards defraying the expenses has been comparatively small and this has been applied for the actual expenses of a few of the star athletes and for advertising. Some merchants have been liberal but others have refused altogether, although they have contributed liberally to other much less deserving objects.*[15]

It was explained that how much Sockalexis was aided depended upon the purchase of the tags, for there was no other source of income. The events themselves were all free.

Another section of the article addressed the appearance of Howard Drew. Drew, at the Eagles games, had broken the American record and equaled the world's record in the 120-yard dash, running the distance in 11 3-5 seconds. The article claimed: "He (Drew) comes all this distance, turning down several other offers, for his regard for Sockalexis and gets nothing but his actual expenses."[16]

Because of heavy rains and bad roads, the motor cycle race was canceled. It was announced that the runners would all make appearances at the dance, "to help in every way, and all will be introduced."[17]

Another Saturday story captured some of the results of the day and the color before the *Bangor Daily Commercial* went to press in the mid-afternoon: "**SOCKALEXIS DAY CALLS/ OUT CROWDS OF PEOPLE**." It reported, "Scores of athletes, including several of national fame, gathered in Bangor, Saturday, to participate in the big athletic meet arranged for the benefit of Maine's great Indian runner, Sockalexis, who is now ill at the Maine Sanitarium from tuberculosis." The day was termed "a great success," commenting that "hundreds of people gathered in the streets to watch the various events, all of which were interesting and exciting..." The benefit dance was set for City Hall.[18]

How was money raised? "Pretty little Indian girls from the Old Town reservation were much in evidence for Saturday was 'Tag Day' and few of the spectators got by without donating something towards the fund which is to be given to Sockalexis. The tags were worn by nearly everyone down town before the close of the day, which showed that a liberal response had been made to the request."[19]

Drew, now identified as being from the Los Angeles AA and a student at the University of Southern California, reportedly had first met Sockalexis as a member of the American team at Stockholm "and between the two there has been a warm friendship ever since." Drew had equaled the

world records in most of the dashes and, at the time, held the
world record for 90 yards, sprinting it in 9 1-5 seconds. The
Commercial commented: "Drew came a long distance to be
here, and gets nothing for his trouble, having responded when
he was first invited that he would be glad to do anything that
he could to help the cause along."[20]

A film, apparently, was made from the events of the day.
Two "movie" men were in the city to film Sockalexis Day
and the city's three movie theaters, the Bijou, Nickel and
Star theaters, were reportedly set to have the pictures and
show them on Monday and Tuesday. The cameramen, it was
reported, were "on their jobs all the time..." During water
sports, they filmed from motor boats. Then they ran their
video machines from autos for the long distance running.[21]

The Indian Island band provided music during the day.
Jack Searles, a promoter of the Queen City Sporting Club
and a man who reportedly managed an "excellent" boxing
exhibition earlier in the week, was "right in the thick of the
activities." Searles was termed "a live wire, and he kept things
moving when they were disposed to lag a bit." Searles was
credited with personally taking charge of some of the tags and
going through the crowd, "succeeding in collecting a large
sum for the fund."[22]

In the first event, the Hampden 5-miler, Drew acted as the
starter, sending off just four contestants. Andrew's brother-
in-law William Fallon acted as a judge. Fallon "claimed he
has run in more marathon races than any man in the country
(along with Bob Fowler)." H.B. Mosher won in 30 minutes
40 seconds, then came men named Lee, Lane and Taylor.[23]

That was followed by log and canoe races, with the film makers "capturing the antics."[24]

The *Commercial* carried a large photo of Drew beating Howe in the 100-yard dash, sprinting between two huge, very close columns of spectators under the caption: "Drew's Appearance Feature of Sockalexis Day Finishing in 100 Yard Dash."[25]

On Monday, August 24, the *Commercial* carried the account of the rest of the Sockalexis Day festivities, calling Drew's victory over Howe "the big feature" of the day. Drew, referred to as "the colored champion sprinter," defeated Howe, "another colored runner" from Boston, in the 100-yard dash. Although the runners were considerably impeded by the crowds of people on the street, officials announced Drew's time as 9 4-5 seconds, which equaled his fastest time to date.[26]

The now unattached Festus Madden, a several-time favorite to win the Boston Marathon, won the 12-mile race. Just a year before Madden had challenged Sockalexis to a mano-a-mano race at any distance over 10 miles. Then he ran the 15-mile Memorial Day race and now he'd returned to Bangor again in honor of Andrew Sockalexis.

Jimmy Henigan, who would win the Boston Marathon in 1931 after failing so many times trying, took the 10-mile match race. Both of these races ended simultaneously, resulting in some confusing moments.

According to the *Commercial*: "The 12-mile race and the 10-mile race finished at about the same time with the result that the spectators were mixed as to just who were competing. Hennigan [*sic*] had been matched with A.V. Roth, unattached, for the 10-mile race, but instead Roth was entered in the 12-mile race, and Fred Faller of the North Dorchester club and Albert Payne, of Campbellton, N.B. ran with Hennigan, who won by about 300 yards." Faller was second, and Payne, third.[27]

Madden defeated Roth, second, and Nagle of the North Dorchester club, third. At the finish line, the crowd in front of the public library was "so dense that the runners had to make their own way through the crowd."[28] *(Author's note: This scene is actually very reminiscent of the Benjamin's 10-K races of the early 1980s, finishing right in front of the library with national greats like Bruce Bickford, Joan Benoit and Greg Meyer competing.)*

Drew, apparently, also had a difficult time with the crowd when he tried warming up for the race. It was reported: "Drew had considerable difficulty on account of the crowds, both on Harlow street and Abbott square lot. Even when the race started on the street, there were no ropes and only a narrow lane was secured. Drew won by a foot or two without exerting himself a great deal."[29]

A number of events were scrapped because of terrible weather. Because of the conditions of the roads, the marathons were canceled. Also, the "failure of the participants to appear, with the lack of facilities for handling the crowds in Abbott square" caused the canceling of the field events.[30]

A "large number" of people were reported to have attended the reception and dance after the athletic events. The motor cycle race was held the next day, Sunday afternoon. The race was 37 and 1/2 miles, from Bangor to Blue Hill and back. Two competitors finished, and two did not.

The *Bangor Daily News*, on Monday, August 24, published an account that was almost, in much of its coverage, very close to that of the *Commercial*. The observations were almost identical.

The *News* was impressed, too, by the series of events and the many people attracted to Bangor Saturday. It, too, noted that the "feature of the day" was the appearance of Drew "who took part in the sports that he might aid his friend, Sockalexis..."[31]

The accounts for all the races were virtually the same, for instance: "...the crowd in front of the public library building was so massed that the runners in finishing had to make their own way through the crowd. The course was from Old Town to Bangor."[32]

The *News* coverage on Drew did offer a little more color on his difficulties in dealing with spectators:

> *Drew's appearance in running costume was the signal for the presence of a still larger crowd and the noted sprinter was followed wherever he went. He tried to 'warm up' in the street but the presence of the spectators made it impossible; he hastened over on the open lot across the street, but failed to get any room. There had evidently been some misunderstanding regarding police for none were on hand, two arriving toward the close. Finally, Drew and Howe moved to the street and Sheriff J. Fred O'Connoll and others tried to keep the crowd back. There were no ropes and much delay ensued until a slim lane was cleared. Even then it was a wonder that Drew did not give up but he stuck it out good-naturedly and finally the start was made. Drew won by a foot or two but he did not have to exert himself. The time was given out as 9 4-5 seconds.[33]*

On the Wednesday after the Sockalexis Day, August 26, Sockalexis was in the news again. A headline read: **"SOCKALEXIS LOST/A FAMOUS MEDAL/Indian Girl to Jail for Taking/Olympic Marathon Prize."** It was noted in this *Commercial* **"Old Town News"** column that Judge Knowlton had faced a busy criminal agenda, disposing of three different larceny cases. In each of the cases Knowlton found the respondents guilty.[34]

Stella Mitchell, an "Indian maiden," was brought before the court on the charge of stealing several articles, some of which were found on her person. Among these items was the medal awarded to Sockalexis for his fourth place finish in the 1912 Olympic Games. The medal, however, had not been recovered, but "the court saw the lace collar valued at $10 and the cuffs valued at $2.50 which the accused was wearing when arrested" that accompanied the medal. Mitchell was sentenced to 60 days in the jail at Bangor.[35]

In the August issue of the *Maine Sanatorium News*, Mrs. Andrew Sockalexis, of Old Town, was listed as a visitor on the Sanatorium Register.[36]

On Saturday, September 12, 1914, the **"Local News"** column of the *Bangor Daily News* reported that Andrew Sockalexis had returned to town briefly, because of the death of his father-in-law, Sebattus Shay. He told the newspaper he would be returning to Hebron "for a few months more" citing tubercular problems in his throat. Though he said he was "much improved" in health and expected a "complete cure," he nevertheless added that he "does not expect to train for two years, at least..." He, reportedly, spoke "in glowing terms" of the work being done at Hebron and predicted that, in time, "all tubercular trouble can be cured."[37]

Then, in this *News* account, came this rather shocking revelation: "He (Sockalexis) knew nothing about Sockalexis day in Bangor until about a week before the day and feels as if he should have been consulted. He looks with suspicion upon it, and before he returns will make an investigation."[38]

Was this event legitimate? Did Sockalexis have a right to feel "suspicious" when Henigan, Drew, Madden and so many others came to Bangor for his benefit? Or did that boxing promoter and Daley pull a shady fast deal and make off with the receipts? Certainly, by then, the money should have been put into the family's hands. Perhaps it still had not been presented to the family.

Sockalexis' deceased father-in-law, Sebattus Shay, had been "prominent" in the legislature, his obituary stated, and for 35 years he had had a summer home at Watch Hill, Rhode Island.[39]

An article, on Saturday, December 12, 1914 discussed **"Your Tuberculosis Bill"** and assessed the bill for the father of a family of three, earning $3 a day, who was suddenly taken ill with TB. The cost of a six-month stay and treatment at a sanatorium was reported as $250, care of family at $8 per week for six months set at $192, and the loss of wages for six months, at $3 a day, came to $432...for a total of $874. The article urged "prevention" noting that "an ounce of prevention" (proper care of body), study of available free literature, and stopping of all bodily excesses all came to "00.00" and that a timely examination by a doctor was only $3 and the purchase of 100 Red Cross seals, "as your share in the general preventive campaign against TB," was $1...bringing the total to $4. The disease, this article stated, "was annually killing 200,000 people" and was "presently leaving a trail of a million wounded."[40]

Maine was said to have "lost 1,000 citizens a year from tuberculosis." Each tubercular patient was required to have: own thermometer, sputum cup, hot water bottle, fur coat, blankets. The cost, per patient, was $10-to-12 a week. Encouraged medical advice included the force-feeding of patients with milk and eggs, and "open air life." The Maine Sanatorium in Hebron had been incorporated in 1901 under the canopy of the Maine State Sanatorium Association for Pulmonary Diseases, Greenwood Mountain, Hebron. On Oct. 6, 1915, the Western Maine Sanatorium came under state control, with 56 patients in the institution.[41]

Tuberculosis was not the only bad world-wide news in the late summer of 1914. It joined the start of World War I and the death of Pope Pius X in Rome in the front page headlines of the nation's newspapers.

Chapter 15

The race that did not happen… and death

After this latest illness and Sockalexis Day events in
the late summer of 1914, Andrew Sockalexis' name dropped
completely from public sight from then until his death on
August 26, 1919.

Occasionally a significant name in the running world or
from Sockalexis' past life in the running limelight appeared
in a newspaper headline. Someone named George V. Bonhag,
for instance, was being hailed as "the new American distance
running hero" in a newspaper article in March of 1916... On
April 8, 1916 a short newspaper article announced that Hannes
Kohlemainen, "the best distance runner in the world," would
be making the United States his permanent residence. The
article noted that, accompanied by his brother Willie, also a
professional marathon runner, the Finn had won three recent
races easily... A short but poignant article on August 26, 1916
announced that Howard Drew, the thoughtful, considerate
sprinter who had come for Sockalexis Day just two years

before, had his career as an athlete come to a sudden, shocking
end when the "negro sprinter" was paralyzed as a result of
an injury. Ironically, the date of this newspaper article, to
the day, is the date of Andrew Sockalexis' death three years
later[1]... Arthur N. Smith, the University of Maine trainer, who
worked with Sockalexis and accompanied him to Stockholm,
moved on to Colby to become track coach, according to a
newspaper article that same Saturday, August 26, 1916[2]...
Napoleon "Larry" Lajoie, who came up as a rookie baseball-
playing sensation the same year Andrew's cousin Louis
Sockalexis had done the same, in 1897, was celebrated in a
1916 newspaper article for his nearly two-decade career on
the playing diamond. It was noted Lajoie had played all the
seasons without ever having played on a pennant-winning
team...[3]

Aside from the continuing World War I activities in Europe,
the year 1916 was the year of Mexican revolutionaries Pancho
Villa and Emiliano Zapata – Villa and Zapata "the bandits" or
Villa and Zapata "the liberators," depending upon your nationality
and, particularly, economic status. Villa raised havoc in his native
country and frequently went on marauding raids across the border
in Texas. Following his exploits through the newspapers created
a comical kind of serial adventure. One account, for instance,
would suggest to the reader that Mexican forces (or U.S. forces,
for both were after him) had him trapped, and that his capture or
death were imminent. Then there would be a couple of days of
newspapers in which his name was mentioned not at all. Then,
suddenly, there would be another account of Villa – hundreds of

miles away from the previous account and back on the offensive, pillaging and brazenly defying authorities from two countries.

One article, in the late summer of 1916, analyzed the two Villas, noting that there were, indeed, "two public estimates" placed on the man who had, for more than a year, been carrying a continuous warfare against the Mexican government in southern Mexico. His war was termed one "distinctly...of the classes."

Zapata, or "the Tiger of Ayala," as he was called by his "hundreds of admiring followers," claimed to be "fighting for the freedom of the peon element and the small property owners... who he says have long suffered from tyrannical practices of the government." Zapata was said to be "a product of the Diaz rule...a victim of the system that oppressed many of the lower classes all over the country." He was said to now be paying back the government for all the injuries it did to him. Zapata had been arrested and sentenced to a long term of "exile in hot lands. Few survived but he did." He vowed vengeance, and quietly fomented a spirit of retaliation against the government by the people of his class. He did not quit fighting when the peace compact was signed, believing he still had wrongs to avenge, particularly against the petty municipal officers who had carried out the orders of the government. Emiliano Zapata "is the hero of the common people who wants division of the vast estates which were taken by the merging of small properties," taken either by force or "by semblance of law." A man described as being of "fine physique," Zapata offered one more colorful aspect adding to his legend: "...he was married only a few months ago to a pretty mountain girl, and she has been his constant companion ever since.'⁴ Villa and Zapata, it appears, were the best and most interesting "runners" of 1916.

The year 1916 is said by Michael Ranco (AKA "Michael Sockalexis"), an Indian Island native and a direct descendent of Andrew Sockalexis, to be significant because it is alleged Sockalexis ran one last great race that year.

In 1971 Ranco published a copyrighted story, featuring interviews he attributed to three elderly Penobscots, Arthur "Archie" Neptune, then 84, and Nicholas Ranco and Susie Dana, both 77 at the time. They claimed to know Andrew "as a close friend and teammate." Neptune, a young running protege of Sockalexis, had competed against his mentor in a match race, on August 31, 1912 at the Bangor Fair in which he and Sylvester Francis split the distance of three miles trying to beat the time of Sockalexis who ran the whole way himself. Sockalexis had beaten the two talented youths handily.⁵

According to these three friends as told to Ranco:

> *In 1916 Andrew ran in his last race, a 15 mile battle with Clarence DeMar on the dirt Route 2 from Old Town to Bass Park in Bangor. DeMar brought up his team from Dorchester to run against the Indian Island team consisting of Andrew, Sylvester Francis, Arthur 'Archie' Neptune and Everett Ranco. Prior to the race date, Andrew was suffering from a severe cold and complaining of chest pains. Against doctor's orders he insisted on running, because he was determined not to disappoint his friend DeMar and the fans that came to watch. So in this last race, Andrew ran with a bad*

cold. He was ahead of the field from the start of the race.

Archie Neptune distinctly remembers the smoothness and untiring effort of Andrew's running style. Approaching the twelfth mile, Archie recalls, Andrew was way ahead as they ascended the steep hill near the Eastern Maine General Hospital. Clarence DeMar was some two hundred yards behind but was no threat to Andrew. Andrew crossed the finish line in Bass Park the victor but as he stopped running, he started to cough up blood and collapsed onto the guard railing.[6]

It's an incredible story and a heart-warming story, especially in light of all the disappointments, all the second-place finishes. It would, indeed, be poetically wonderful if Andrew Sockalexis closed out his running career with a courageous victory over the greatest American name in running in his era, and one of the greatest runners of all time.

But there are a number of factors which make this story very questionable.

1. There's no record of it, in either of the two Bangor newspapers, the *Bangor Daily News* and the *Bangor Daily Commercial,* or the *Old Town Enterprise.* And neither the much celebrated Sockalexis nor the equally-heralded DeMar, accompanied by their respective running groups could possibly have gone into a head-to-head competition, and not received any newspaper attention whatsoever. On the two occasions when celebrated runners from the greater Boston

area had come to race against Sockalexis, in 1912 and 1913, there had been many stories, previewing the races, covering the races and analyzing the aftermath of the races. It does not seem possible that DeMar and Sockalexis could have raced each other, with "the fans who came to watch" on the course obviously fully aware the event was taking place, without any attending newspaper coverage. In three phone conversations with the author, who challenged the authenticity of such a race, Michael Ranco stated he had "a newspaper clipping" about this alleged race but said he did not have a date or even the source of the alleged account. Ranco refused to show the author the account or send him a Xerox copy of the account.

2. Equally important, Andrew Sockalexis had declared himself a professional runner during the early summer of 1913 and ran several documented professional races. Thus, after July of 1913, he could no longer compete in the same race with amateurs – that most definitely meant DeMar. That also meant he could no longer compete against all the members of the North Dorchester running club, and all the would-be contenders for the two most prestigious long distance running titles in the world, both amateur-only events, the Boston Marathon and the Olympics. Amateurs who ran against Sockalexis, after he competed in his first professional race during the summer of 1913, would lose their amateur status.

Remember, in 1912, Sockalexis' position on the American Olympic team was momentarily challenged when it was alleged he had participated in a race with a French professional runner. For playing professional baseball, the great Jim Thorpe had recently been stripped of his two Olympic gold medals. By the strict amateur code of the time Clarence DeMar would not have been allowed to participate in any further Boston Marathons after 1916 if he had raced against Sockalexis – meaning he could never have won six more Boston Marathons (victories captured in the 1920s, culminating with his final win in 1930), nor been allowed to compete in the Olympic Games in 1924 (where he took third place and a bronze medal) and 1928.

3. Clarence DeMar had very strong moral, religious and ethical convictions, and it is extremely unlikely he would have attempted to outright defy or attempt to deceive the existing amateur code. He would have known that racing Andrew Sockalexis in 1916 would have meant banishment from racing the Boston Marathon ever again or competing in the Olympics. In his autobiography DeMar discussed the amateur-professional dilemma. He said, candidly, that the only professional offer he had ever received "was not for ten thousand dollars nor one thousand dollars, but just for two hundred dollars, to appear several times a day for a week at a theatre." And that would have also cost him his job in the print shop at the newspaper too. Further, he stated: "Being barred from the good races if not in the Amateur Union, is one of the biggest reasons why most of us prefer to stay 'amateur' unless there is something worth while as a professional. The A.A.U. controls all the important running contests so it is a good policy to get along with them."[7]

4. During these last years of his life Andrew Sockalexis was often very sick with the tuberculosis that would kill him. He had been frequently sick since 1914 and there is no record

he made it back to running more professional races, or races of any kind, after 1913.

5. In 1916, Clarence DeMar was in the midst of taking a major break from competitive, long-distance racing. At the time of the Boston Marathon, on April 19, 1916, he was playing a version of "Capture the Flag," renamed "Capture Villa" in tribute to the elusive Mexican revolutionary, with a group of boy scouts for whom he served as troop leader. In his autobiography he recalled that during this period he would do, only occasionally, a short, local race in the greater Boston area. He was not in the type of shape he would have required of himself to travel out of a state, race 15 miles and compete against a very formidable rival like Sockalexis was known to be. DeMar did not resume his long, long-distance running until the 1920s.[8]

It seems very, very doubtful Clarence DeMar and Andrew Sockalexis raced 15 miles against each other in 1916, with Sockalexis winning and then collapsing at the finish line. As wonderful a story as it makes, it does not come close to adding up. It seems more likely Archie Neptune and the others, if they did indeed tell such a story, innocently had their collective memories fail them, blending a few earlier races together into one magnificent triumph; after all, Sockalexis had narrowly lost to DeMar in a wonderful Old Town-to-Bangor race in 1912 and he had collapsed on the same track at Maplewood Park in a race featuring other Boston rivals in May of 1913.

Perhaps it is they or, more likely, Michael Ranco who is trying to protect the memory of Andrew Sockalexis and is forgetting the last bad stretches of the runner's life. The late

Michael Ranco, who renamed himself "Michael Sockalexis," acknowledged he changed his name and his family's name to "Sockalexis" in the late 1980s because the last individual to be born and die with that prestigious name had died on Indian Island. He said he believed the name "Sockalexis" "deserved to survive."[9]

According to the 1971 Ranco account, soon after the alleged 1916 race Sockalexis first "developed tuberculosis."[10] This is clearly not true. Andrew Sockalexis may have suffered his first bout with it as early as the late fall of 1912. However, certainly after rebounding for Boston 1913 and attempting his first few professional races he became very sick and entered the Hebron Sanatorium in 1913 and the reports of how seriously he was ill with consumption, or TB, was the inspiration for spawning Sockalexis Day in 1914. By 1916 Sockalexis had been battling the disease for several years.

Andrew Sockalexis dropped from public sight. There were no further bold headlines, no stories of triumphs, no stories of comebacks, no stories of what was happening to him at all.

Records indicate he was in and out of the Hebron Sanatorium several times over the last three years of his life. Did he keep running, keep trying to recover his athletic glory? Or was he resigned to his fate? None of the local newspapers offer any information what these last few years of his life were like.

Is it possible he actually became quite bitter, quite cruel, and an alcoholic? According to a petition seeking a divorce,

Pauline Shay Sockalexis identified him as a very cruel and abusive drunk in her last years with him.

On January 4, 1919 Pauline Sockalexis filed for divorce in Penobscot County Court:

> *IN A PLEA OF DIVORCE, wherein your libelant alleges that her maiden name was Pauline Shay; that she was married to the said libelee, Andrew Sockalexis, in Old Town, Penobscot County, Maine on the ninth day of November, 1913, by the Reverend Father Rice, a Minister of the Gospel; that they lived together as husband and wife in said Old Town, for more than one year; that your libelant has always conducted herself toward the said libelee as a true, faithful and affectionate wife, but that the said libelee, Andrew Sockalexis being unmindful of his marriage vows and obligations, has been guilty of cruel and abusive treatment and extreme cruelty toward your said libelant; that he is edicted [sic] to the use of intoxicating liquors and guilty of gross and confirmed habits of intoxication from the use of intoxicating liquors; that your said libelee being of sufficient ability and being able to labor and provide for her, wilfully and without reasonable cause, refuses or neglects to provide suitable maintenance for her; that there is no collusion between your libelant and the said libelee to obtain a divorce. WHEREFORE she prays that a divorce may be granted to her for the causes above set forth, and that she be allowed to resume her maiden name, Pauline Shay.*
>
> *(signed) Pauline Shay[11]*

Pauline Sockalexis' lawsuit was "entered at the April term" of the court when she appeared in person on April 1. The court continued the lawsuit until its next term and "now on the first day of the term, it is Ordered by the Court that the libel be dismissed." According to the late Indian Island historian Glenn Starbird, the divorce became a moot point, for well before the divorce decree could have been declared legal in October, Andrew Sockalexis died.[12] Pauline Shay did resume her maiden name, lived until 1971 and is buried on Indian Island.

Andrew Sockalexis died on August 26, 1919. According to the State of Maine's Record of Death certificate for him, he died in Oxford, just outside the Hebron Sanatorium. He was listed as a resident of Oxford for three years. The cause of death was listed as a two-week bout with Tubercular Meningitis, the final battle of a six-year, "continuing" affliction with Pulmonary Tuberculosis. He was classified as being married. His occupation read "Athlete." He was 27 years, 7 months and 15 days old on the day of his death.[13]

The *Bangor Daily Commercial*'s death notice on August 28, 1919, noted that Sockalexis died at South Paris "where he had been for several months...after a long illness." The only running credit he was accorded was the 1912 Olympics. He was called "Old Town's famous runner who won international fame in the Marathon race at Stockholm."[14]

The *Commercial* continued: "Sockalexis had a great future before him following the sensational race he ran in Sweden, when he came in fourth, but somehow his physical form was not up to the strain of success and

popularity and he was unable to realize further in his
ambitions toward racing fame. His later efforts were not as
promising as that across the seas and before long it was evident
that tuberculosis, the dreaded enemy of the Indian race, had
marked him for a victim and he had failed in health from that
time."[15]

The *Enterprise* obituary notice noted that his death
followed "a long and lingering illness of tuberculosis," and that
for several years he "was in the public eye as a runner of more
than National reputation."[16]

The *Enterprise* continued: "While not a first place runner
in all events his work was always such he was considered a
dangerous competitor. He made the trip to Sweden in 1912,
with scores of other world beaters and made a most enviable
record. His trouble was to *[sic]* short a time to get acclimated.
He was a well known competitor in the Boston Marathon races
for several years. Like his cousin the late Louis Sockalexis
the wonderful ball player he made Old Town known the world
over. He was a young man of quiet and pleasing disposition
and well liked."[17]

The *Enterprise* reported that Sockalexis had been under
treatment at West Paris for over one year and that "his parents
have been with him for several months." But not his estranged
wife. The notice did state: "He is survived by his parents and
a wife who have the sincere sympathy of their friends at this
time..."[18]

Sockalexis died on Tuesday, August 26, and his remains
were transported up to Old Town on Wednesday afternoon,
August 27. The *Bangor Daily News*, too, in its funeral services

notice, mentioned that Sockalexis died in South Paris after a long illness, "where he was spending the summer with his parents." His remains were taken to his home on the island. The *News* notice simply stated he was "survived by his wife and father and mother."[19]

The funeral services were held in St. Anne's Catholic Church on that Friday morning at 9 o'clock, with the Rev. V. Nonorgue officiating. The pall bearers were Stephen Sockabesin, Charles D. Mitchell, Lewie Lois and Henry Sockabesin. Interment was in the cemetery on Indian Island...[20]

Then a young niece, the late Edna Becker had poignant memories of sitting with a crippled Francis Sockalexis, who had lost the use of both of his once wonderful running legs in a logging accident. She would keep the elder Sockalexis company at his home while his wife shopped or went out for a short time. The pair played cards and, Becker recalled, did not talk much. With Andrew's running trophies proudly on display, it was very clear to her, she said, how much Francis Sockalexis missed his son and how proud he still was of him and his outstanding accomplishments as a runner.[21]

Afterward

Is it possible that the man who is regarded as the most revered and, arguably, the most knowledgeable journalist ever to write on the Boston Marathon is responsible for the most damning and unfair criticism of Andrew Sockalexis that exists to this day?

The man is the late Jerry Nason, for years the sports editor for the *Boston Globe*. It is the stuff of legends that Nason was born on April 14, 1909 in a Newton hospital right on the Boston Marathon course and that, five days later, on Patriots Day his mom held him up to her hospital room window so he could see the runners pass by. He covered his first Boston Marathon for the *Globe* in 1933 and then, from 1942 until 1977, Nason wrote the lead story for his newspaper in a stellar career that nearly spanned half a century. Noted Detroit sportswriter Joe Falls dubbed Nason the "Boswell of Boston" in his 1977 book **The Boston Marathon**, and was incredulous that Nason should have but never did pen the definitive history of his beloved marathon.

Actually, Jerry Nason had. For years the *Boston Globe* produced a little blue booklet, featuring succinct summaries of each year's race, beginning with the first one in 1897 and concluding with the previous year's event. Nason summarized, from reports from the Boston newspapers of the day, the earliest years' runs and then offered his own knowledgeable assessments for more than one-half of a century. He died in 1986.

This author has a copy of Nason's booklet, one produced by the *Boston Globe* in 1965, that contains, stuffed inside, a freestanding single page attachment offering his 1966 race critique.

Seemingly when people write about the earliest days of the Boston Marathon and they focus upon the years 1912 and 1913, these writers invariably cite Nason's blunt connect-the-dots-between-the-two-races description: Sockalexis "lost" **both** victories when he went out "too fast" in the 1912 race and went out "too slow" in the 1913 race. But close scrutiny of both races and the actual accounts penned at the time strongly suggest that Andrew Sockalexis doesn't deserve to be classified as "a loser"; Mike Ryan (1912) and Fritz Carlson (1913) deserve far more credit for outstanding victories...

It seems that when Andrew Sockalexis took an extraordinarily impressive 17th finish at the 1911 Boston Marathon, in his very first official road race, he set the tone for what would be an extraordinarily explosive burst, albeit a short burst, of a career.

Yet even at what should have been Andrew Sockalexis' greatest, triumphant moments his stellar achievements were recognized as such but always seemed to carry the same condemning critical analysis: He could have done even better.

Only 20 years old and running just his fourth official foot race, Sockalexis came within seconds of breaking Clarence DeMar's course record at the 1912 Boston Marathon in April; yet when Mike Ryan, who did break the course record, passed Sockalexis in the last two miles of the 25-mile race and beat him to the finish line by only a 300-yard margin, the young Penobscot athlete would forever be damned for his effort by a sports writer who very questionably contended the inexperienced runner had "gone out too fast" in the early stages of the run.

In the searing temperatures of the 1912 Olympic marathon at Stockholm in July, Sockalexis, dubbed the American favorite to win by several columnists, ran to an heroic fourth place finish, passing many of the world's stellar long distance runners in the second half of the race in a torrid heat that directly led to the death of one runner; yet, the American marathon team was vilified for a strategy of "holding back too long," and Sockalexis, specifically, was criticized, in headlines and stories, for being the man "who should have won."

Considered one of the heavy favorites at the 1913 Boston Marathon, the 21-year-old Sockalexis wisely avoided the suicidal pace of Harry Smith, a Canadian named Fabre and other serious contenders for more than 20 miles of the race; yet, when he overtook all of them but one – eventual winner Fritz Carlson – he was Fritz Carlson – he was again doomed to be characterized, in the annals of the storied race, as a second-place finisher "who should have won" but erred in judgment by not speeding up soon enough.

Did Andrew Sockalexis "win" second place twice at the Boston Marathon or did he actually "lose" first place once or even both times? Did he run a courageous Olympic race and just narrowly fail to win a medal or did he fail to win a medal and even fail to win the race because of his own poor planning or poor execution? Sadly, the journalism of the period, even while celebrating his skill damns him for each of these lost opportunities at overall victory. And it hardly seems fair that writers with questionable knowledge of long distance running should, first of all, overlook his youthfulness and inexperience and then challenge his strategy and ability to execute in the last mile or two of the "grueling grind" that the marathon was so often accurately described as then, and continues to this very day, to be so characterized.

Because there is so little history left behind on Andrew Sockalexis – newspaper accounts surrounding his major running competitions comprising the great majority of what little there is – there are many questions left hanging for this author, who spent so many years as a journalist himself.

A major one concerns the controversy when Andrew Sockalexis, following the 1913 Boston Marathon, could not, apparently, make up his mind whether or not to become a professional runner, and run for money, rather than remain a true amateur and receive accolades but only minor material prizes. It was, perhaps, a very confusing time for him – he apparently went to one Bangor newspaper and declared he had turned professional runner and then, the very next day, went to the other daily Bangor newspaper where he said the first story was nonsense and declared himself still an amateur runner.

But after just a couple more amateur races, he turned professional runner during the summer of 1913, sacrificing forever any further chance of winning the Boston Marathon or competing in another Olympic Games. One can not help but wonder what his motivation was. Was it money? Most likely. He was, by trade, a basket maker and he may well have been enticed into believing he could make considerable money in match races that attracted bettors at carnivals and state fairs. Perhaps he had had enough, too, of promoters making money on his appearances. Maybe, he felt he had achieved all he needed to achieve in amateur running.

Sockalexis reported he did very well in pro races, though what little evidence the author could find about his professional race career actually proves the contrary. Frankly, it really does not matter; for Sockalexis contracted tuberculosis and was so severely ill the fall of 1913 that his running career and, indeed, his life were both careening towards their tragic ends.

Left unanswered, too, are the questions about why Andrew Sockalexis said he did not know about the 1914 Sockalexis Tag Day and why he questioned the motives of the participants. Did he ever get the proceeds from the benefit day activities? I was unable to locate a newspaper account that provided these answers.

Another important unanswered question revolves around the story of Sockalexis' alleged last great race in 1916, circulated by Sockalexis' contemporary blood relative, Indian Island native, the late Michael Ranco (AKA "Michael Sockalexis"). One tends to give the benefit of the doubt to the three elderly friends whose collective memories could easily have failed them, connecting any of Andrew's local victories, to his mano-a-mano 1912 race from Old Town to Bangor against DeMar, to Andrew's collapse on the track in 1913 with DeMar significantly behind him in the race. The problem comes with Ranco's insistence, over several decades, that he had physical proof that the race took place.

This author had both telephone conversations and person-to-person conversations with Michael Ranco during the 1980s, 1990s and 2000s, up to within a few months of his death in 2007. On many of these occasions, when challenged about the authenticity of this specific race, Ranco maintained that the race had taken place and that he had a newspaper clipping about it. Politely asked to xerox a copy and mail it, or just meet briefly to show it to the author, to prove the race's authenticity, Michael Ranco always refused.

Challenged by the author with the above factors that make such a race highly doubtful, Ranco grew angry and defensive, but would not even offer the alleged date the race supposedly occurred upon.

Ranco grew even more angry when asked if he was aware of Sockalexis' ill-fated professional running career and the difficult last days of his life, when his wife sued for divorce, claiming her husband was often abusive and under the influence of alcohol. Ranco alleged he knew about these things but omitted writing about them himself because, "There are bad things that happen in everyone's life..." and added in a threatening voice, "There is no reason to write these negative things about Andrew."

As much as this author personally grew to like and respect Andrew Sockalexis through most of what I read, I believe it is imperative to offer every bit of information I was able to find to allow each reader to make his or her own objective judgment about the man and his running career based on all the information available.

Finally, this author is left with one last warm thought about Andrew Sockalexis: I suspect running with his father, from those earliest moments as a young colt of a boy right on through to those training runs when he was a world-recognized running star, may have ranked with his greatest triumphs as the most rewarding and enjoyable running experiences of his life. There were clearly many father-son training runs and one hopes the shared joy of running filled each of them with a spiritual love for the sport more special than any accolade or victorious trophy could bring.

* * *

APPENDIX
WITH
PHOTOGRAPH GALLERY

1	Joan Benoit Samuelson Won Olympic marathon	26	Whitney Leeman 16 New England swimming titles
2	Cindy Blodgett No. 5 alltime in NCAA hoops scoring	27	Kevin Mahaney Silver in sailing at 1992 Olympics
3	Jack Coombs Won 31 games, 13 shutouts in 1910	28	Raymond Lebel Won six Maine amateur golf titles
4	Edmund (Rip) Black Third in Olympic hammer	29	Bert Roberge Maine righty won 12 games in bigs
5	Dick MacPherson Coached Syracuse and Patriots	30	Harold White Bowdoin All-America swimmer
6	Billy Swift Led NL with 2.08 ERA in 1992	31	Jean Roy All-America defenseman at Bowdoin
7	Mike Bordick Shortstop for Maine and Orioles	32	Clyde Sukeforth Helped sign Jackie Robinson
8	Joey Gamache WBA lightweight champ in 1992	33	Robert Aceto Southern Maine All-America pitcher
9	Mark Plummer 10 Maine amateur golf titles	34	Jay Ramsdell CBA commissioner at age 23
10	Bill (Rough) Carrigan Managed 1915, '16 Red Sox	35	Marcus Nash Standout cross-country skier
11	Chet Bulger Two-way NFL tackle from 1942 to '50	36	Gail Liberty U.S. women's pistol champ, 1961 to '63
12	Walter Case Harness-record 1,077 wins in 1998	37	Stump Merrill Maine catcher, Yankees manager
13	Bob Legendre Bronze in 1924 Olympic pentathlon	38	L.L. Bean Invented waterproof boots in 1912
14	Abby Spector Four Maine amateur golf titles	39	Erik Nedeau Ran 3:59.6 mile for Northeastern
15	Al McCoy Versatile boxer of the 1930s and '40s	40	Danny Bolduc First Maine player to reach NHL
16	John Winkin Led Maine to six College World Series	41	Gary Williamson Southern Maine baseball star
17	Eric Weinrich Defenseman for Maine and in NHL	42	Julie Parisien Two U.S. ski championships in 1991
18	Freddy Parent Shortstop for 1903 champ Red Sox	43	François Bouchard Hoops HS All-America
19	John Bower First U.S. skier to win Holmenkollen	44	Shawn Walsh Coached Maine to two hockey titles
20	John Huard Linebacker for Maine and Broncos	45	Fred Tootell Won 1924 Olympic gold in hammer
21	Dot Petty Twice world candlepin champion	46	Barbara Krause Multisport star at Freeport High
22	John Wassenbergh NAIA basketball All-America	47	Coley Welch World's No. 3 middleweight in 1942
23	Carl Willey Career ERA of 3.76 in eight years	48	Bob Prince Star outfielder for Southern Maine
24	Paul Junior Lightweight boxer was 476-13	49	Mike Thurston Clinched 1969 state hoops title
25	Tony Miner 35-game college hitting streak	50	Charles Milan III 23 candlepin titles

This is the list from the State of Maine produced by *Sports Illustrated Special Edition, December 27, 1999-January 3, 2000*, purporting to be the 50 greatest athletes. The list can and should be condemned for its omissions of Andrew Sockalexis and Louis Sockalexis, arguably two of the state's absolute greatest athletes of all time.

SOCKALEXIS FAMILY CHART

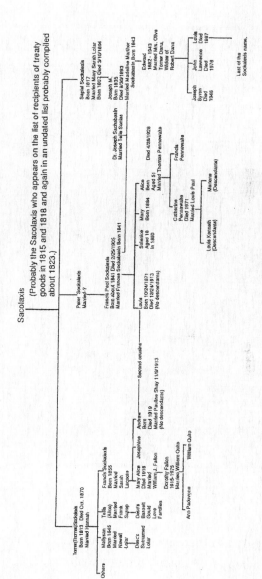

Sacolaxis

(Probably the Sacolaxis who appears on the list of recipients of treaty goods in 1815 and 1818 and again in an undated list probably compiled about 1823.)

Andrew Sockalexis and Louis Sockalexis who both gained fame in the sports world were second cousins. Their grandfathers were brothers. Both athletes had fathers whose first name was Francis, which probably gave rise to the supposition that they weere brothers. The last of the family name Sockalexis died June 16, 1987. This last Louis Sockalexis was second cousin once removed to Andrew, and had relationship through two lines with Louis the ballplayer. The two Louis' were second cousins once removed through the Sockalexis line and first cousins once removed through the Sochobasin line.

Note: Penobscot names   Tomer - Thomas   Peal - Peter   Sapiel - Jean Pierre (John Peter)
Tellis - Alice   Mallysan - Mary Ann

Author Collection: Courtesy of the late Glenn Starbird Jr.

This photo of Andrew Sockalexis, finishing 2nd at the
Boston Marathon in 1912, appeared in the *Boston Post*, on
April 20, 1912.

Boston Post

328,529 | 408,007

MONDAY, JULY 15, 1912 Copyright, 1912, by Post Publishing Co. FOURTEEN PAGES—ONE CENT

RECORD IN TO LIGHT

Distance in 5 Hrs.
4-5 Sec.—Sullivan,
Wise Also Accomplish Swim

SOUTH AFRICAN WINS MARATHON

McArthur Defeats Pick of World's Runners—Gertshaw, Another South African, Is Second, Strobino of America Third—Winner's Time Was 2 Hours 36 Minutes

BIG STRIKE OF 30,000 IS THREATENED

8000 Operatives in New Bedford Will Walk Out Today

NEW BEDFORD, July 14.—The walkout of the 8000 weavers and loom fixers called for tomorrow morning to protest against the new grading system, threatens to result in a general strike of all the 30,000 operatives and the closing down of every one of the 90 cotton mills in the city.

Both the operatives and the mill owners are obdurate and resist any idea of arbitration. The leaders of the workers declare that nothing but the revocation of the grading system and the tearing down of the grading notices will prevent the strike. The owners insist that the system will continue and the notices will remain in place.

I. W. W. URGES STRIKE

Although there has been little talk of a general strike among the majority of the organized operatives who are affiliated...

ANDREW SOCKALEXIS

CROWD WATCH FIGHT FOR LIFE

Ira River, the thousand daughter of Max river of Water street, Quincy...

Sockalexis, Picked as the Winner, Finishes in Fourth Place

POOR JUDGMENT LOST THE RACE FOR AMERICA

7 Americans in First 12—De Mar Was 12th Man

TODAY'S PROGRAMME AT OLYMPIC GAMES

1600-metre relay race, final.
Northwestern cross-country run.
Hop, step and jump.
Decathlon, final events.

FINISH OF LEADERS IN BIG MARATHON

Winner—K. K. McArthur of South Africa. Time—2h. 36m.
Second—C. W. Gertshaw of South Africa. Time—2h. 37m. 56s.
Third—Gaston Strobino of Paterson, N. J. Time—2h. 38m. 42 3-5s.
Fourth—Andrew Sockalexis, Oldtown, Me.
5—J. Duffy, Canada.
6—J. Jacobsson, Sweden.
7—John J. Gallagher, Yale University.
8—Joseph Erxleben, Missouri A. C.

This was the front page of the *Boston Post* on Monday, July 15, 1912, announcing the results of the Olympic marathon and the prominent place of Andrew Sockalexis in that event.

On Saturday, April 19, 1913, the Boston Post offered portraits of several of the favorites to win the 17th annual Boston Marathon that day, including, at far left, Andrew Sockalexis. Note the map of the then 24.5-mile course, starting in Ashland, rather than Hopkinton, and finishing at the BAA Clubhouse on Exeter Street in downtown Boston.

The headline below announces the second straight second-place finish of Andrew Sockalexis, the disappointment-riddled, eyewitness account of his wife-to-be Pauline Shay, and a one-paragraph brief exclaiming "Think Sockalexis Should Have Won."

This headline blared out on Saturday, August 22, 1914, in the *Bangor Daily Commercial* and the account was filled with the events of the day, all held as a fund-raiser to support Andrew Sockalexis and his medical expenses at Hebron Sanatorium where he battled tuberculosis.

Photos: Courtesy of Penobscot Nation and the Abbe Museum

Left, Andrew Sockalexis runs for the camera in a 1912 portrait taken on Indian Island. The photographer was A. F. Orr. At right, again he poses for a camera portrait while running on Indian Island in 1913. He is wearing a running singlet with the U.S. Olympic crest. This portrait was taken by photographer H. Ellison Gray.

Once Andrew Sockalexis (second row, second from left, wearing singlet with "BHS") became a national-caliber runner at the 1911 Boston Marathon, runners from the prestigious Boston-area-based North Dorchester Amateur Athletics (NDAA) club made several railroad trips to Indian Island, in 1912 and 1913, to race against him. The author deeply regrets he could not find a version of the photo where the NDAA runners are identified. The gentleman in running garb, standing at the far left, appears to be the great Clarence DeMar. That's Tom Lilley, also a 1912 Olympic marathon participant, seated on the ground in the very front row, at right. Standing, fourth from the left, is William "Doc" Fallon, and, fifth from the left, is Alice Sockalexis, Andrew's sister. They married in November of 1913. Andrew's headdress-wearing father, Francis Sockalexis, is standing third from the right and that is Andrew's mother, Sarah, standing immediately to his right. The photo was taken in 1912 in front of Andrew's Oak Hill home on Indian Island.

Photo: Author's collection

This portrait of the U.S. athletes arriving in Stockholm for the Olympic Games of 1912, shows Andrew Sockalexis, at far right, and Tom Lilley, standing right next to him.

Photos Courtesy: Penobscot Nation and Abbe Museum

Photographer F. A. Orr took these two portraits of Andrew Sockalexis on Indian Island in 1912, perhaps before he set off for the Olympic Games in Stockholm. The trophies are from his second place finish in the 1912 Boston Marathon and third-place finish at the Brockton (Massachusetts) Marathon in the fall of 1911. At the top, Andrew stands beside his trophies in front of his Oak Hill home on Indian Island. At right, he stands behind them for a closer, more formal portrait, wearing his North Dorchester Amateur Athletics club jersey.

Photo Courtesy: UPI/Corbis

This photo was taken in late July or early August, 1913 at Ebbetts Field in Brooklyn, New York. This is where Andrew Sockalexis, at far right, made his professional racing debut, in a match race, pairing two well-known Native American runners against two accomplished professional runners, Alfred Shrubb of England and Fred Meadows of Canada. Standing immediately to Andrew's right is Tom Longboat, the legendary Canadian Indian runner who won the 1907 Boston Marathon in then record time.

Photo: John Clarke Russ

This tag was available for purchase on Andrew Sockalexis Tag Day, which took place on August 22, 1914, as a day-long fund-raiser to help with Andrew's medical expenses while he battled tuberculosis at the Hebron Sanatarium in Maine. The author purchased the tag on E-bay in 2007, from a vendor who mistakenly believed he was selling an artifact connected Andrew's more famous cousin, Louis Sockalexis, the first American Indian to play Major League baseball. Louis died in December of 1913. Told that he was "misrepresenting" the item, the vendor immediately sold the tag to the author for considerably less than its posted price!

This hatchet was reportedly made by Andrew Sockalexis as a present for his brother-in-law, William "Doc" Fallon, a fellow member of the North Dorchester Amateur Athletics club. The hatchet was given as a present to the author in the late 1990s by Steve Padovano and the late Ann Padovano, who was a granddaughter of Andrew's sister, Alice. Alice Sockalexis married Doc Fallon in the fall of 1913 and the couple lived in Stoughton, Massachusetts.

Photo: John Clarke Russ

Photo: Courtesy of Evie Gillis family

This ornately-carved "war club," designed as a tool to protect the home from unwanted intruders, was reportedly a gift from Andrew Sockalexis to Charles Billings, who worked as a surveyor on the road through Etna, Maine, sometime between 1914 to 1916. Both Sockalexis and Billings were boarders on the Withee family farm (Evie Gillis's mother was Eleanor Withee Mathews), and Sockalexis worked summers on the farm. Billings gave the club to Evie's father, George Mathews, in 1918. Evie Gillis says her mother wrote that her brother Carl, who was 6 or 7 years old at the time, said he had a vivid memory of seeing Sockalexis, "in his blue trunks and moccasins" and that Sockalexis "always ran there (in Etna) in moccasins." The name "Sockalexis" is carved into the handle of the club. Stricken by tuberculosis in 1913, Sockalexis never again ran competitively, and died of the disease in 1919.

Photo: Courtesy of
Penobscot Nation

Photo: Courtesy of
Penobscot Nation

This portrait of Andrew Sockalexis appeared in the now-defunct *Boston Sunday Post*, on August 11, 1912. It accompanied a lengthy article on the marathoner, who had finished 2nd at the Boston Marathon in April and 4th at the Olympic Games in Stockholm in June.

Louis Sockalexis, Andrew's second cousin, was the first American Indian to play Major League baseball and inspired the nickname "Indians," upon his arrival in 1897 when the team was known as the "Spiders." The Cleveland team officially adopted the nickname "Indians" in 1915.

This is the grave site for Andrew Sockalexis, who died on August 26, 1919 and was buried near his home on Indian Island, Maine. On the back side of the grave, in barely legible script, is a notation proclaiming Andrew's stature as a world-class athlete and a member of the United States Olympic team for the Stockholm Games of 1912. The author has established the Sockalexis Fund (see web site at www.sockalexis.info) , on Indian Island, to help raise funds to refurbish this grave.

Photo: Courtesy of Jim Falvo

Celebrating the induction of both Andrew Sockalexis and Louis Sockalexis, Penobscot Nation legends, into the American Indian Athletic Hall of Fame, in a ceremony held in the spring of 2000 in Tulsa, Oklahoma are, from left to right: Steve Padovano, representing his wife, the late Ann Padovano, grand daughter of Alice Sockalexis (Andrew's sister); the author; Penobscot Nation Tribal Elder Butch Phillips; William Quito, grandson of Alice Sockalexis; and Betty Shannon, president of the American Indian Athletic Hall of Fame.

* * *

Notes

Chapter 1

1. *Boston Post*, August 11, 1912
2. *Old Town Enterprise*, November 10, 1913.
3. **Morrow**.
4. **Speck**.
5. Ibid.
6. Ibid.
7. Ibid.
8. Ibid.
9. *Old Town Enterprise*, April 27, 1912.
10. **Ranco**.
11. *Old Town Enterprise*, April 27, 1912.
12. **Ranco**.
13. Ibid.
14. *Boston Post*, August 11, 1912.
15. Ibid
16. Ibid.
17. Ibid.
18. Ibid.
19. Ibid.

20. Ibid.

21. Ibid.

22. Ibid.

23. Ibid.

24. *Boston Post*, April 19, 1914.

25. Ibid.

26. **Becker.**

Chapter 2

1. *Old Town Enterprise*, Nov. 15, 1913.

2. *Boston Post*, April 17, 1911.

3. Ibid.

4. **Nason.**

5. Ibid.

6. **DeMar.**

7. Ibid.

8. *Boston Post*, April 21, 1911.

9. *Bangor Daily Commercial*, Dec. 1, 1911.

10. Ibid.

11. *Bangor Daily News*, Dec. 1, 1911.

12. *Bangor Daily Commercial*, Dec. 1, 1911.

13. *Bangor Daily News*, Dec. 1, 1911.

Chapter 3

1. *Bangor Daily News*, April 13, 1912.

2. *Old Town Enterprise*, April 20, 1912.

3. *Bangor Daily News*, April 15, 1912.

4. *Boston Post*, April 16, 1912.

5. Ibid.

6. Ibid.

7. Ibid.

8. *Bangor Daily News*, April 16, 1912.

9. *Boston Post*, April 18, 1912.

10. *Bangor Daily News*, April 20, 1912.

11. Ibid.

12. Ibid.

13. *Boston Post*, April 20, 1912.

14. Ibid.

15. Ibid.

16. Ibid.

17. *Bangor Daily Commercial*, April 20, 1912.

18. Ibid.

19. Ibid.

20. Ibid.

21. Ibid.

22. **Nason.**

23. Ibid.

24. Ibid.

25. Ibid.

26. *Bangor Daily News*, April 22, 1912.

27. bid.

28. bid.

29. Ibid.

30. Ibid.

31. Ibid.

32. Ibid.

33. Ibid.

34. Ibid.

35. Ibid.

36. Ibid.

37. Ibid.

38. IIbid.

39. Ibid.

40. Ibid.

41. *Old Town Enterprise*, April 20, 1912.

42. Ibid.

43. Ibid.

44. Ibid.

45. Ibid.

Chapter 4

1. **DeMar.**

2. Ibid.

3. *Bangor Daily News*, April 11, 1912.

4. Ibid.

5. Ibid.

6. Ibid.

Chapter 5

1. *Bangor Daily News*, May 4, 1912.

2. *Bangor Daily Commercial*, April 22, 1912.

3. *Bangor Daily Commercial*, April 25, 1912.

4. *Old Town Enterprise*, April 27, 1912.

5. *Bangor Daily News*, April 26, 1912.

6. Ibid.

7. Ibid.

8. Ibid.

9. Ibid.

10. Ibid.

11. *Bangor Daily Commercial*, April 26, 1912.

12. Ibid.

13. Ibid.

14. *Old Town Enterprise*, May 11, 1912.

15. *Old Town Enterprise*, May 25, 1912.

16. *Bangor Daily News*, May 18, 1912.

17. Ibid.

18. *Bangor Daily News*, May 20, 1912.

19. Ibid.

20. *Bangor Daily News*, May 31, 1912.

21. Ibid.

22. Ibid.

23. Ibid.

24. Ibid.

25. Ibid.

26. Ibid.

27. *Bangor Daily News*, June 5, 1912.

28. *Bangor Daily News*, June 7, 1912.

29. Ibid.

30. *Bangor Daily News*, June 8, 1912.

31. Ibid.

32. *Bangor Daily News*, June 11, 1912.

33. *Bangor Daily News*, June 25, 1912.

34. Ibid.

35. Ibid.

36. Ibid.

37. Ibid.

38. Ibid.

39. Ibid.

40. Ibid.

41. *Bangor Daily News*, June 26, 1912.

42. *Bangor Daily News*, June 28, 1912.

Chapter 6

1. *Bangor Daily News*, April 13, 1912.

2. *Bangor Daily News*, July 4, 1912.

3. *Bangor Daily News*, July 6, 1912.

4. *Old Town Enterprise*, July 6, 1912.

5. Ibid.

6. Ibid.

7. *Bangor Daily News*, July 8, 1912.

8. Ibid.

9. *Boston Post*, July 14, 1912.

10. Ibid.

11. Ibid.

12. Ibid.

13. Ibid.

14. Ibid.

15. Ibid.

16. Ibid.

17. Ibid.

18. Ibid.

19. Ibid.

20. Ibid.

21. Ibid.

22. Ibid.

23. Ibid.

24. Ibid.

25. Ibid.

26. Ibid.

27. Ibid.

28. Ibid.

29. Ibid.

30. Ibid.

31. Ibid.

Chapter 7

1. *Boston Post*, July 15, 1912.

2. **DeMar.**

3. *Bangor Daily News*, Aug. 3, 1912.

4. *Boston Post*, July 15, 1912.

5. Ibid.

6. Ibid.

7. Ibid.

8. Ibid.

9. Ibid.

10. Ibid.

11. Ibid.

12. Ibid.

13. **DeMar.**

14. *Boston Post*, July 15, 1912.

15. Ibid.

16. *Bangor Daily Commercial*, July 15, 1912.

17. *Bangor Daily News*, July 15, 1912.

18. Ibid.

19. Ibid.

20. Ibid.

21. Ibid.

22. Ibid.

23. Ibid.

24. Ibid.

25. Ibid.

26. Ibid.

27. Ibid.

28. Ibid.

29. Ibid.

30. Ibid.

31. Ibid.

32. Ibid.

33. Ibid.

34. Ibid.

35. Ibid.

36. Ibid.

37. Ibid.

38. Ibid.

39. Ibid.

40. Ibid.

41. Ibid.

42. Ibid.

43. *Bangor Daily Commercial*, July 15, 1912.

44. Ibid.

45. Ibid.

46. Ibid.

47. Ibid.

48. *Bangor Daily News*, July 15, 1912.

49. *Bangor Daily News*, July 24, 1912.

50. Ibid.

51. Ibid.

52. Ibid.

53. Ibid.

54. Ibid.

55. Ibid.

56. *Bangor Daily News*, July 16, 1912.

57. *Bangor Daily Commercial*, July 16, 1912.

Chapter 8

1. *Bangor Daily News*, July 16, 1912.

2. *Old Town Enterprise*, July 20, 1912.

3. Ibid.

4. Ibid.

5. *Bangor Daily Commercial*, July 15, 1912.

6. Ibid.

7. *Bangor Daily News*, Aug. 3, 1912.

8. *Bangor Daily Commercial*, Aug. 3, 1912.

9. *Old Town Enterprise*, Aug. 10, 1912.

10. *Bangor Daily News*, Aug. 3, 1912.

11. *Bangor Daily Commercial*, Aug. 3, 1912.

12. *Old Town Enterprise*, Aug. 10, 1912.

13. *Bangor Daily News*, Aug. 3, 1912.

14. *Bangor Daily Commercial*, Aug. 3, 1912.

15. *Old Town Enterprise*, Aug.10, 1912.

16. *Bangor Daily News*, Aug. 3, 1912.

17. *Bangor Daily Commercial*, Aug. 3, 1912.

18. *Old Town Enterprise*, Aug. 10, 1912.

19. *Bangor Daily Commercial*, Aug. 3, 1912.

20. *Old Town Enterprise*, Aug. 10, 1912.

21. Ibid.

22. *Bangor Daily News*, Aug. 3, 1912.

23. *Old Town Enterprise*, Aug. 10, 1912.

24. *Bangor Daily News*, Aug. 3, 1912.

25. Ibid.

26. Ibid.

27. **DeMar.**

28. Ibid.

29. *Bangor Daily News*, Aug. 3, 1912.

30. Ibid.

31. Ibid.

32. *Bangor Daily Commercial*, Aug. 3, 1912.

33. Ibid.

34. Ibid.

35. Ibid.

36. Ibid.

37. Ibid.

38. Ibid.

39. Ibid.

40. Ibid.

41. Ibid.

42. Ibid.

43. *Bangor Daily News*, Aug. 3, 1912.

44. *Bangor Daily Commercial*, Aug. 3, 1912.

45. *Old Town Enterprise*, Aug. 10, 1913.

46. Ibid.

47. *Bangor Daily News*, Aug. 3, 1912.

48. *Bangor Daily Commercial*, Aug. 3, 1912.

49. Ibid.

50. *Old Town Enterprise*, Aug. 10, 1912.

Chapter 9

1. *Old Town Enterprise*, Aug. 3, 1912.

2. *Old Town Enterprise*, Aug. 10, 1912.

3. Ibid.

4. *Bangor Daily Commercial*, Aug. 3, 1912.

5. *Bangor Daily Commercial*, Aug. 8, 1912.

6. *Bangor Daily Commercial*, Aug. 12, 1912.

7. Ibid.

8. *Bangor Daily Commercial*, Aug. 15, 1912.

9. *Bangor Daily Commercial*, Aug. 22, 1912.

10. *Bangor Daily Commercial*, Aug. 27, 1912.

11. *Bangor Daily Commercial,* Aug. 28, 1912.

12. *Bangor Daily Commercial,* Aug. 29, 1912.

13. Ibid.

14. Ibid.

15. *Bangor Daily News,* Aug. 29, 1913.

16. Ibid.

17. *Bangor Daily News,* Aug. 30, 1913.

18. *Bangor Daily News,* Sept. 2, 1912.

19. *Bangor Daily Commercial,* Sept. 2, 1912.

20. Ibid.

21. Ibid.

22. Ibid.

23. *Bangor Daily Commercial,* Sept. 14, 1912.

24. Ibid.

25. Ibid.

Chapter 10

1. *Bangor Daily Commercial,* Sept. 17, 1912.

2. *Bangor Daily Commercial,* Sept. 20, 1912.

3. Ibid.

4. Ibid.

5. Ibid.

6. *Bangor Daily News,* Sept. 20, 1912.

7. *Bangor Daily News,* Sept. 21, 1912.

8. *Old Town Enterprise,* Sept. 28, 1912.

9. *Bangor Daily Commercial,* Sept. 21, 1912.

10. *Bangor Daily Commercial,* Sept. 23, 1912.

11. *Bangor Daily News,* Sept. 23, 1912.

12. *Old Town Enterprise*, Sept. 28, 1912.

13. *Bangor Daily News*, Sept. 23, 1912.

14. *Bangor Daily Commercial*, Sept. 23, 1912.

15. *Bangor Daily News*, Sept. 23, 1912.

16. *Old Town Enterprise*, Sept. 28, 1912.

17. *Bangor Daily News*, Sept. 23, 1912.

18. *Bangor Daily Commercial*, Sept. 21, 1912.

19. Ibid.

20. *Bangor Daily News*, Sept. 23, 1912.

21. *Bangor Daily Commercial*, Sept. 21, 1912.

22. *Bangor Daily News*, Sept. 23, 1912.

23. Ibid.

24. Ibid.

25. Ibid.

26. Ibid.

27. Ibid.

28. *Bangor Daily Commercial*, Sept. 21, 1912.

29. Ibid.

30. Ibid.

31. *Bangor Daily Commercial*, Sept. 23, 1912.

32. *Bangor Daily News*, Sept. 23, 1912.

33. *Bangor Daily Commercial*, Sept. 23, 1912.

34. Ibid.

35. *Bangor Daily News*, Sept. 23, 1912.

36. *Bangor Daily Commercial*, Sept. 23, 1912.

37. *Bangor Daily News*, Sept. 23, 1912.

38. *Bangor Daily Commercial*, Sept. 23, 1912.

39. *Bangor Daily News*, Sept. 23, 1912.

40. *Bangor Daily Commercial*, Sept. 23, 1912.

41. *Bangor Daily News*, Sept. 23, 1912.

42. *Bangor Daily Commercial*, Sept. 23, 1912.

43. *Bangor Daily News*, Sept. 23, 1912.

44. *Old Town Enterprise*, Sept. 28, 1912.

45. Ibid.

46. Ibid.

47. Ibid.

48. *Bangor Daily Commercial*, Sept. 23, 1912.

49. *Bangor Daily News*, Sept. 21, 1912.

50. *Bangor Daily Commercial*, Sept. 23, 1912.

51. Ibid.

52. *Bangor Daily Commercial*, Oct. 3, 1912.

53. Ibid.

54. *Bangor Daily Commercial*, Oct. 4, 1912.

55. *Bangor Daily Commercial*, Oct. 7, 1912.

56. *Bangor Daily Commercial*, Nov. 30, 1912.

57. Ibid.

58. *Bangor Daily News*, Dec. 12, 1912.

Chapter 11

1. *Boston Post*, April 18, 1913.

2. Ibid.

3. Ibid.

4. Ibid.

5. *Boston Post*, April 19, 1913.

6. Ibid.

7. Ibid.

8. Ibid.

9. Ibid.

10. Ibid.

11. *Bangor Daily Commercial*, April 19, 1913.

12. *Bangor Daily News*, April 21, 1913.

13. Ibid.

14. Ibid.

15. Ibid.

16. Ibid.

17. Ibid.

18. Ibid.

19. Ibid.

20. Ibid.

21. *Boston Post*, April 21, 1913.

22. *Bangor Daily News*, April 21, 1913.

23. *Boston Post*, April 21, 1913.

24. *Bangor Daily News*, April 21, 1913.

25. *Boston Post*, April 21, 1913.

26. *Bangor Daily News*, April 21, 1913.

27. Ibid.

28. Ibid.

29. Ibid.

30. *Boston Post*, April 21, 1913.

31. *Bangor Daily News*, April 21, 1913.

32. *Boston Post*, April 21, 1913.

33. *Bangor Daily News*, April 21, 1913.

34. Ibid.

35. Ibid.

36. Ibid.

37. *Boston Post*, April 21, 1913.

38. Ibid.
39. Ibid.
40. Ibid.
41. Ibid.
42. Ibid.
43. Ibid.
44. Ibid.
45. Ibid.
46. Ibid.
47. Ibid.
48. Ibid.
49. Ibid.
50. Ibid.
51. Ibid.
52. Ibid.
53. Ibid.
54. Ibid.
55. Ibid.
56. Ibid.
57. Ibid.
58. Ibid.
59. *Bangor Daily Commercial*, April 23, 1913.
60. Ibid.

Chapter 12

1. *Bangor Daily Commercial*, April 23, 1913.
2. *Bangor Daily Commercial*, April 28, 1913.

3. *Bangor Daily News*, May 7, 1913.

4. *Bangor Daily Commercial*, May 7, 1913.

5. *Bangor Daily Commercial*, May 10, 1913.

6. *Bangor Daily Commercial*, May 26, 1913.

7. Ibid.

8. *Bangor Daily Commercial*, May 27, 1913.

9. *Bangor Daily News*, May 28, 1913.

10. *Bangor Daily Commercial*, May 28, 1913.

11. Ibid.

12. Ibid.

13. *Bangor Daily News*, May 29, 1913.

14. Ibid.

15. Ibid.

16. Ibid.

17. *Bangor Daily Commercial*, May 29, 1913.

18. *Bangor Daily News*, May 30, 1913.

19. *Bangor Daily Commercial*, May 30, 1913.

20. Ibid.

21. Ibid.

22. Ibid.

23. *Bangor Daily Commercial*, May 31, 1913.

24. Ibid.

25. Ibid.

26. Ibid.

27. Ibid.

28. Ibid.

29. Ibid.

30. *Bangor Daily Commercial*, June 2, 1913.

Chapter 13

1. *Bangor Daily News,* June 6, 1913.
2. Ibid.
3. *Boston Post,* June 24, 1913.
4. *Boston Post,* July 11, 1913.
5. *Boston Post,* July 14, 1913.
6. Ibid.
7. *Boston Post,* July 17, 1913.
8. *New York Tribune,* July 15, 1913.
9. *Boston Post,* July 13, 1913.
10. *Boston Post,* July 22, 1913.
11. *New York Tribune,* July 26, 1913.
12. *New York Tribune,* July 27, 1913.
13. Ibid.
14. Ibid.
15. Ibid.
16. *New York Tribune,* July 28, 1913.
17. *New York Tribune,* Aug. 3, 1913.
18. Ibid.
19. Ibid.
20. *Boston Post,* Aug. 4, 1913.
21. *Worcester Telegram,* Aug. 4, 1913.
22. Ibid.
23. *New York Tribune,* Aug. 10, 1913.
24. *Worcester Telegam,* Aug. 13, 1913.
25. *Old Town Enterprise,* Aug. 16, 1913.
26. Ibid.

27. *Boston Post*, Aug. 28, 1913.

28. Ibid.

29. *Boston Post*, Aug. 31, 1913.

30. *Boston Post*, Sept. 2, 1913.

31. Eastern Argus, Sept. 27, 1913.

32. *Eastern Argus*, Oct. 1, 1913.

33. *Eastern Argus*, Oct. 4, 1913.

34. *Bangor Daily News*, Oct. 3, 1913.

35. *Eastern Argus*, Oct. 10, 1913.

36. *Eastern Argus*, Oct. 11, 1913.

37. Ibid.

38. Ibid.

39. *Old Town Enterprise*, Sept. 26, 1913.

40. *Old Town Enterprise*, Nov. 15, 1913.

41. Ibid.

42. Ibid.

43. Ibid.

44. Ibid.

45. Ibid.

46. Ibid.

47. Ibid.

48. Ibid.

49. Ibid.

50. Ibid.

51. State of Maine Marriage Certificate

52. *Old Town Enterprise*, Nov. 15, 1913.

53. *Bangor Daily News*, June 3, 1912.

54. Ibid.

55. *Bangor Daily News*, Dec. 29, 1912.

56. *Bangor Daily News*, Dec. 26, 1913.

57. *Bangor Daily News*, Jan. 1, 1914.

Chapter 14

1. *Old Town Enterprise*, April 18, 1914.

2. *Old Town Enterprise*, April 11, 1914.

3. *Bangor Daily News*, April 19, 1914.

4. Ibid.

5. *Old Town Enterprise*, May 9, 1914.

6. *Old Town Enterprise*, July 4, 1914.

7. *Maine Sanatorium News*, July 1914.

8. *Old Town Enterprise*, July 18, 1914.

9. *Old Town Enterprise*, July 25, 1914.

10. *Bangor Daily Commercial*, Aug. 19, 1914.

11. *Bangor Daily Commercial*, Aug. 21, 1914.

12. Ibid.

13. Ibid.

14. *Old Town Enterprise*, Aug. 22, 1914.

15. *Bangor Daily News*, Aug. 22, 1914.

16. Ibid.

17. Ibid.

18. *Bangor Daily Commercial*, Aug. 22, 1914.

19. Ibid.

20. Ibid.

21. Ibid.

22. Ibid.

23. Ibid.

24. Ibid.

25. Ibid.

26. *Bangor Daily Commercial*, Aug. 24, 1914.

27. Ibid.

28. Ibid.

29. Ibid.

30. Ibid.

31. Ibid.

32. *Bangor Daily News*, Aug. 24, 1914.

33. Ibid.

34. Ibid.

35. *Bangor Daily Commercial*, Aug. 26, 1914.

36. Ibid.

37. *Maine Sanatorium News*, August 1914.

38. *Bangor Daily News*, Sept. 12, 1914.

39. Ibid.

40. *Bangor Daily News*, Dec. 12, 1914.

41. Ibid.

Chapter 15

1. *Bangor Daily News*, Aug. 26, 1916.

2. Ibid.

3. Ibid.

4. *Bangor Daily News*, July 14, 1916.

5. **Ranco.**

6. Ibid.

7. Ibid.

7. **DeMar.**

8. Ibid.

9. **Ranco.**

10. Ibid

11. Maine State Records: Sockalexis Divorce Petition, Jan. 4, 1919.

12. Ibid.

13. Maine State Certificate of Death for Andrew Sockalexis, Aug. 26, 1919.

14. *Bangor Daily Commercial*, Aug. 28, 1919.

15. Ibid.

16. *Old Town Enterprise*, Aug. 30, 1919.

17. Ibid.

18. Ibid.

19. *Bangor Daily News*, Aug. 28, 1919.

20. Ibid.

21. **Becker.**

* * *

Bibliography

Becker, Edna, interview with author, Bangor, July, 1988.

DeMar, Clarence, **Marathon: The Clarence DeMar Story** (Tallahassee, Florida: Cedarwinds Publishing, 1992).

Derderian, Tom, **Boston Marathon: The History of the World's Premier Running Event** (Champaign, Illinois: Human Kinetics Publishers, 1994).

Ecker, Tom, **Olympic Facts and Fables** (Cedar Rapids, Iowa: Tafnews Press, 1996).

Falls, Joe, **The Boston Marathon** (New York City: Macmillan, 1977).

Higdon, Hal, **Boston: A Century of Running**, (Emmaus, Pennsylvania: Rodale Press, Inc., 1995).

Maine Sanatorium News, August 1914.

Maine State Records: Certificate of Death for Andrew Sockalexis, Aug. 26, 1919.

Maine State Records: Sockalexis Divorce Petition, Jan. 4, 1919.

Morrow, Mary Frances, letter to author, dated March 7, 2003.

Nason, Jerry, *The Story of the Boston Marathon*, booklet published by the *Boston Globe*, 1966.

Neptune, James, Penobscot Nation Museum director, interview with author, Indian Island, 2003.

Ranco, Michael, phone conversations and personal "interviews," 1986–2006.

Ranco, Michael, "Andrew Sockalexis, Olympic Marathon Runner," pamphlet, 1971.

Sockalexis, Louis Edward, interview with author, Augusta, Maine, April, 1985.

Sockalexis Memorial Arena Grand Opening, supplement to *Bangor Daily News*, November, 1984.

Speck, Frank G., **Penobscot Man** (Orono, Maine: University of Maine, 1998).

Starbird, Glenn, Jr., Penobscot historian, interviews with author, Indian Island, 1987–88.

* * *

Acknowledgements

While I was researching the manuscript that became
my biography of Andrew's cousin, baseball player Louis
Sockalexis, a number of my friends teased me for **not**
researching "the Sockalexis who was a runner." A dedicated
runner myself, I knew about Andrew and began allotting
him research time once I entered into the writing phase of
what became my first book, **Baseball's First Indian, Louis
Sockalexis: Penobscot Legend, Cleveland Indian** (Tide-
mark Press: Windsor, Connecticut, July 2003).

Today, I owe a number of my friends in the Maine running
community a debt of gratitude for all their enthusiastic
encouragement in support of my working on and completing
this publishing "marathon." In particular, they include:
Dr. Peter Millard and Emily Wesson, David and Katherine
Wilson, Newell Lewey, Judson Esty-Kendall, Robin Emery,
Steve and Anne Norton, Joan Merriam, Danny Paul, Kim
Moody, Marc Violette, Maria Girouard, Abra Iwanko and
Peter Lodge, Anna Perna and Earl Black, Laura Zegel, Louisa
Dunlap, Denny Morrill, Loren Ritchie, Larry Allen, Carol

Weeks, OJ Logue, Scott Dorrity (AKA "Spud Landers"), and the late Fred Merriam...to name just a few.

I've been fortunate enough to make the acquaintance and, in a couple of instances, become friends with some of the best American runners of my generation, and I want to acknowledge the lifetime of inspiration I have taken from the stories of Roberta "Bobbi" Gibb, Billy Mills, Joan Benoit Samuelson, Bruce Bickford, Ralph Thomas, and Bill Rodgers.

Principal thanks, for the actual creation of this book, goes to long-time friend Richard B. "Dixie" Tourangeau of Boston for his invaluable help in researching several events and dates I requested of him, using the resources he found at the Boston Public Library and the Lamont Library at Harvard.

I received important computer assistance from long-time friend Dr. Peter Millard and also Michael Rice (no relation) and Patricia Barry of the IT Department at the University of Maine at Orono.

I'm particularly indebted to the support and encouragement I received from the following Penobscot Nation representatives: the late S. Glenn Starbird, Jr., Penobscot historian; Angelo Quito and the late Ann Padovano, direct bloodline descendents of Andrew Sockalexis, plus Ann's husband Steve; Penobscot State of Maine House of Representatives Rep Donna Loring; Penobscot Tribal Elder Butch Phillips; former Penobscot Tribal Governor Barry Dana; James Neptune, Penobscot Nation Museum director; Carol Binette, Penobscot Nation census office; the late Edna Becker and the late Louis Edward Sockalexis, direct bloodline descendents of Andrew Sockalexis.

Thanks, as well, to the helpful staff at the University of Maine's Fogler Library and to Charlie Campo, *Bangor Daily News* librarian.

Thanks, too, to Stella Ekholm for her help in locating some additional information for the book, late in the researching game.

A very special "Thank You" (to include hugs and kisses!) goes to my significant other, Susan Gibson, who matched me step-for-step in proofreading the entire manuscript for final publication, catching some nasty errors and making some invaluable editing notes.

Also, heartfelt thanks go to Mike Swenson, an outstanding high school runner, who helped immeasurably in the editing of the final manuscript. The author, of course, takes responsibility for any and all errors that remain.

On a personal note, I'm grateful for the loving support of: my daughter, Meisha; my dad, Al Rice of Scottsdale, Arizona and his second wife, Phyllis Doner-Rice; my "brother," supportive high school pal Mike Swenson of Orono; my former father-in-law, Arnold Leavitt of Auburn; my brilliant godson, Joseph Faucher; and...especially, the woman who brings the sweetest music to my life, Susan Gibson.

In memoriam: Mom, Ruthe Rice, and Little Brother, Gary Rice, plus inspirational friend, Fred Merriam, and inspirational heroes, Ginny DelVecchio and Terry Fox.

* * *

About the author

Born in Brookline, Mass., Ed Rice grew up in Bangor, Maine and graduated from Bangor High School in 1966. He holds a B.A. from Northeastern University and an M.Ed. from the University of Southern Maine.

Formerly a reporter for several daily newspapers, Rice has served as the editor of the *Weekly Journal* in Brewer, Maine and the *Winchester Town Crier*

Photo: John Clarke Russ

in Winchester, Mass. He has been a theater critic and arts commentator for the *Portland Press Herald, Maine Sunday Telegram, Maine Times* and Maine Public Broadcasting System's "*Maine Things Considered*" on radio.

A community college English and communications teacher in the Bangor, Maine area, Rice has taught journalism and communication studies at the University of Maine at

Orono and Doane College in Crete, Nebraska. He has also taught high school English and coached cross country.

In February of 2000 he wrote the biographical profile of Louis Sockalexis which annually appears in the *Cleveland Indians Media Guide* and on the team's web site pages. Rice also spearheaded the nomination drive that led to the induction of both Louis and Andrew Sockalexis into the national American Indian Athletic Hall of Fame in Lawrence, Kansas in April of 2000. His nomination, as well, led to the induction of Andrew Sockalexis, second cousin of Louis, into the Maine Running Hall of Fame in 1990.

An avid long distance runner who has run and completed 27 marathons (including 8 Boston Marathons), Rice created Bangor's popular Terry Fox 5-K Run in 1982 and continued to direct the charity event for over 20 years, a tribute run which has now raised over $100,000 for regional cancer research, including breast cancer research at Eastern Maine Medical Center in Bangor. In 1997 he ran across the State of Massachusetts (162 miles in 7 days) in support of a friend, the late Ginny DelVecchio who was dying of ALS, or Lou Gehrig's disease, and a research fund he co-created at Mass General Hospital to find a cure for this insidious disease.

Rice published his first book, **Baseball's First Indian, Louis Sockalexis: Penobscot Legend, Cleveland Indian**, in 2003, with Tide-mark Press of Windsor, Connecticut.

In December of 2005, The Angel Fund published a book edited by Rice entitled **If They Could Only Hear Me,** a collection of 30 personal essays (including one by Rice) that describe the many ways people have taken up the fight against ALS. All proceeds from the sale of the book benefit The Angel Fund and its support of the ALS research wing at Massachusetts General Hospital in Boston. Co-founded by Rice, The Angel Fund raises money for research to find a cure for ALS.

A resident of Orono, Maine, Rice also lives in St. Andrews by the Sea, New Brunswick, with musician Susan Gibson and an always regal-in-appearance cat named Pre. Rice has a web site at www.sockalexis.info.